"This fine book will be of inter Christians — not just intellectual growth, but true growth in godliness. Christopher Cone's biblical, original, practical, and well illustrated approach to transformative learning provides step by step instructions in studying and communicating the Scriptures."

–Thomas L. Constable, Th.D
Senior Professor Emeritus in Bible Exposition
Dallas Theological Seminary

"From the example of Jesus Himself as well as the writers of the Scriptures, authentic teaching of God's Word simultaneously targets the heart and the mind of the hearer. Dr. Cone's book is a needed reminder to those who stand behind the pulpit or lectern, and an encouragement to the ones sitting in the pew that the teaching of the Word is the great privilege and command to all believers. For the believer, this book can be of great value in developing skills to be an able communicator of God's Word."

–Paul Benware, Th.D
Bible Professor, Theologian, Author

"In this book Cone provides a well conceived, highly organized path by which Bible students, Bible teachers and pastors may improve their ability to effectively communicate God's word, no matter their level of experience or understanding. There is something here for everyone."

–Patrick Belvill, Th.D
President, Tyndale Theological Seminary
Pastor, Tyndale Bible Church

"There are books on exegesis. And there are books on exposition. But rarely do you see a book that puts the two together. Dr. Cone has done just that with both insight and comprehensiveness. Best of all, he illustrates each principle with case studies to show the learner exactly how to practice his principles. His work is a valuable tool for anyone who wants to bring the timeless truths out of God's Word to a generation crying out for some meaning and direction in a world that seems to be spinning out of control."

–Dave Anderson, Ph.D
President, Grace School of Theology

"Dr. Cone, throughout his ministry, has championed the vital necessity of rightly dividing and rightly delivering the Scriptures. He challenges all believers as voices of truth to uphold the processes of transmission that begin with careful preparation in life and study, and that close with accurate delivery to the audience of God's choosing – be it a congregation, a classroom, or in an individual encounter."

–Henry A. Vosburgh
Pastor, Heritage Bible Church
Exec. Director, Midwest Church Extension

"Dr. Cone addresses one of the most crucial issues facing the church today: the need for expository preaching and teaching. *Integrating Exegesis and Exposition* lays out clear steps for arriving at sound exegetical conclusions and then follows up with how these conclusions can be effectively communicated to today's audiences. This book is a must read for all pastors and other Bible communicators."

–George Gunn, M.Div, D.D
Shasta Bible College and Graduate School

"*Integrating Exegesis and Exposition* reflects the heart of a pastor who deeply cares for the growth of God's sheep, and the mind of a first-rate academic exposing the fatal flaws of the prevailing mediocre pattern of modern Bible exposition. However, the value of this work is not simply in pointing out the problem, but in Dr. Cone's process for correcting our missteps. This work should be required reading for pastoral students and every person in our pews."

–Steve Spurlin, Ph.D
Pastor, Cornerstone Bible Church

"Dr. Cone's fantastic book is firmly rooted in the truth that the Bible transforms those who are equipped by it. The wisdom outlined here will help the reader become an effective communicator, one who lets God's word equip the saints, so that they will be able to teach others also. This book will not only bless its readers, but will equally bless those who will be taught by them."

–Grant Hawley
Director, Bold Grace Ministries

"The living Word of God is transformative and life-changing. Any believer teaching or preaching the Bible needs to realize both the privileges and responsibilities of handling that Word. As Cone writes, "Biblical communication is not to be undertaken lightly or without purpose." With *Integrating Exegesis and Exposition*, Cone succeeds in demonstrating how exegesis governed by sound hermeneutics is the true basis of passionate, loving, and efficient biblical exposition."

–Gilles Despins, Th.D
Professor of Bible and Exegesis
École Théologique ProFAC

"When our understanding of the Bible has been spoon-fed to us, laced with presuppositions, and marketed to our faulty preferences, why do we wonder when we possess a lackluster, if not befuddled, view of Scripture? Here, Christopher Cone asserts that we start anew – not with a new and novel method of interpretation, but with a timeless hermeneutic that works according to patterns demonstrated in the Bible itself. The Bible contains its own built-in hermeneutic and governs its own presuppositions and worldview. It is a beacon that stands on its own. Those seeking the truth – no matter how unpalatable or painful – will stand to benefit greatly from the steps outlined. *Integrating Exegesis and Exposition* is a great tool that will help us accomplish that."

–Arnfield Cudal, MBA, Ph.D
Editor, HARK Publications

CHRISTOPHER CONE

INTEGRATING EXEGESIS AND EXPOSITION

BIBLICAL COMMUNICATION FOR TRANSFORMATIVE LEARNING

INTEGRATING EXEGESIS AND EXPOSITION:
BIBLICAL COMMUNICATION FOR TRANSFORMATIVE LEARNING

©2015 Christopher Cone

Published by Exegetica Publishing
Ft. Worth, TX

ISBN10 – 097659305X

ISBN13 – 978-0-9765930-5-8

All rights reserved. No part of this publication may be reproduced, stored in a retrieval system, or transmitted in any form or by any means – electronic, mechanical, photocopy, recording, or any other – except for brief quotation in printed reviews, without the prior permission of the publisher.

All Scripture quotations, except those noted otherwise are from the New American Standard Bible, ©1960,1962,1963,1968,1971,1972,1973,1975, 1977, and 1995 by the Lockman Foundation.

This volume is dedicated to those who have encouraged the renewing of my mind, who have served to model in word and deed a persevering faithfulness in the study, practice, and sharing of God's word.

TABLE OF CONTENTS

SECTION I: AN INTEGRATIVE APPROACH FOR TRANSFORMATION AND REPLICATION 1

1. The Transformative Objective of Biblical Communication 3
2. Integrating Exegesis and Exposition: Preaching and Teaching for Spiritual Independence 13
3. Brothers We Are Not Chefs 27
4. Distinctives of This Approach 33
5. Teaching for Independence 37
6. A Necessary Ingredient of Biblical Literacy 41
7. The Expositor's Challenge 43

SECTION II: OVERVIEW OF THE EXEGETICAL PROCESS 47

8. The Nine Steps: Preliminary Considerations 49
9. The Nine Steps: (1) Verify Text and Translation 53
10. The Nine Steps: (2) Understand Background and Context 59
11. The Nine Steps: (3) Identify Structure 69
12. The Nine Steps: (4) Identify Grammatical and Syntactical Keys 85
13. The Nine Steps: (5) Identify Lexical Keys 89
14. The Nine Steps: (6) Identify Biblical Context 93
15. The Nine Steps: (7) Identify Theological Context 97
    Case Study: Logical Errors of Affirming a Disjunct in John 10 105
16. The Nine Steps: (8) Secondary Verification 109
17. The Nine Steps: (9) Development of Exposition 113
18. The Hermeneutic and Exegetical Implications of Descriptive and Prescriptive 119
19. Biblical Wordplay Doesn't Obfuscate Meaning 125
20. Diversity, Biblical Interpretation, Sunrise Over the Atlantic 129

SECTION II: OVERVIEW OF THE EXPOSITIONAL PROCESS 133

21. The Prerequisites of Passion and Love 135
22. The Biblical Difference Between Preaching and Teaching.....................141
23. Seven Informal and Formal Methods for Preaching and Teaching:
(1) Informal Preaching 153
    Case Study: Contending for the Faith Without Being Contentious 155
24. Seven Informal and Formal Methods for Preaching and Teaching:
(2) Formal Preaching 159
    Case Study: Jonathan Edwards, "Sinners in the Hands of
    an Angry God" 166
    Case Study: When Faith Goes to College, What Comes Home?............. 184
25. Seven Informal and Formal Methods for Preaching and Teaching:
(3) Informal Teaching 195
    Case Study: A Formal Discipleship Outline for
    Informal or Formal Discipleship Pedagogy 197
26. Seven Informal and Formal Methods for Preaching and Teaching:
(4) Formal Teaching: The Synthetic Preview... 203
    Case Study: Overview of the Book of Amos... 207
27. Seven Informal and Formal Methods for Preaching and Teaching:
(5) Formal Teaching: The Exegetical Journey 221
    Case Study: An Exegetical Analysis of Matthew 18:15-20:
    The Purpose and Nature of Correction in the Church 228
28. Seven Informal and Formal Methods for Preaching and Teaching:
(6) Formal Teaching: The Analytical Summary... 245
    Case Study: The Doctrine of God in The Book of Romans.....................248
29. Seven Informal and Formal Methods for Preaching and Teaching:
(7) Formal Teaching: Teaching Topically 263
    Case Study: New Years Resolutions for Every Day
    (A New Years' Walk Through Psalm 90) 266
    Case Study: Coniah's Judgment: Did the Grinch Steal Christmas? 268
    Case Study: Memorials Demand Action 270
    Case Study: Comfort in the Midst of Tragedy 272

30. Three Styles for Preaching and Teaching: Extemporaneous, Note Aided, and Read Presentation 275
31. Biblical Rationale for Dynamics in Preaching and Teaching 279
32. Technology and Biblical Communication 291
33. What are the Essentials? 295
34. "I Have Many More Things to Say to You, But You Cannot Bear Them Now" 301
Bibliography 305

SECTION I

AN INTEGRATIVE APPROACH

1
The Transformative Objective of Biblical Communication

After exploring the depths of God's remarkable mercies, Paul exhorts believers to *"be transformed* by the renewing of the mind" (Rom 12:2). Romans 1-11 teaches its readers about God's mercies, as a testament to His glory and as a motivator for proper response. Part of the expected response to that taught content of God's mercies (along with presenting one's body a living and holy sacrifice) is to *be transformed* (present passive imperative, *metamorphousthe*). God doesn't tell us to do what He has already done or what He will do for us, so the fact that *be transformed* is an imperative is very significant. At the same time, the imperative is passive – it is not our job to do the transforming, but rather it is our responsibility to allow that process to take place. In order to submit to that process, we need to understand what it means.

There are two contemporary and thought provoking lexical definitions for the word *transformative*:[1] (1) to change into another

---

[1] The term *transformative* in this work does not refer to the transformative learning pedagogy of Jack Mezirow, though the interlocutor will find some similarities (and marked dissimilarities) between my usage and his. Rather, the term is simply employed here in its lexical sense in order to qualify the expected outcomes of Biblical study, practice, and communication. For a consideration of some of the theological implications of Mezirow's transformative pedagogy, see Gino

substance, and (2) to change in condition, nature, or character.² First, when an unbeliever becomes a believer we can say that such a person has changed into another substance, having transitioned from deadness to life (Eph 2:1-5). By virtue of the mercy of God, old things have passed away, and what remains is a new creature (2 Cor 5:17), even if temporarily housed in an earthly and corruptible tent (1 Cor 15:42-49). The change from unbelief to belief comes from hearing, and hearing by the word of Christ (Rom 10:17). This fits the first definition of *transformative* very well. Second, we observe that as a believer progresses from spiritual infancy to spiritual maturity, that believer is certainly encountering a change in condition and character (perhaps suggesting a change *in nature* during this growth process is too strong, since the change in nature takes place at the moment of conversion). This fits well enough the second definition given for *transformative*. So whether for unbeliever or believer, the process of receiving Biblical communication is to be truly transformative.

Because it is the word of God that equips (2 Tim 3:16-17), because our only offensive weapon against the world-forces (thus, against being conformed to the world) is the sword of the Spirit (Eph 6:12, 17), and because being filled with His Spirit entails being filled with and controlled by His word (Eph 5:17-18), it is evident that the renewing of the mind prescribed by Paul in Romans 12:2 is synonymous with allowing God's word to dwell richly within us (Col 3:16). The gospel (specifically, the revealed word of God regarding salvation) is God's ability to transform the unbeliever into a believer (Rom 1:16), and by the word of God the believer is equipped for every good work (2 Tim 3:17). Further, the word of God provides the certainty of Christlikeness and glorification (Rom

---

Pasquariello, "The Way In and the Way On: A Qualitative Study of the Catalysts and Outcomes of Transformative Learning," Ed.D Diss., Asuza Pacific University, 2009.
² "Transformative" in Dictionary.com, viewed at
http://dictionary.reference.com/browse/transformative.

8:28-30). Thus from beginning to end, the transformative learning process is centered on God's word, exclusively and comprehensively.

Because of the centrality of God's word for both unbeliever and believer, Biblical communication is not to be undertaken lightly or without purpose. We must look to God's word to discover prescribed methods, content, and expected outcomes, in order to be faithful stewards of what God has freely given (1 Cor 2:12), and diligent workers handling accurately the word of truth (2 Tim 2:15).

Biblical Goals for Teaching: Equipping and Replication

> Let the word of Christ richly dwell within you, with all wisdom teaching and admonishing one another with psalms and hymns and spiritual songs, singing with thankfulness in your hearts to God. Whatever you do in word or deed, do all in the name of the Lord Jesus, giving thanks through Him to God the Father (Col 3:16-17).[3]

These verses encourage believers, exhorting them to be teaching and admonishing one another. Now, there is specific methodology considered in this context (psalms, singing, thankfulness, etc.), but notice the general principle that believers are to be teaching one another. Teaching is not just a pastoral responsibility. We find in Romans 12:6-7 there is a gift of teaching not specifically tied to pastoral ministry. In Titus 2:3 we discover that older women are to be teaching younger women. *Believers teach one another.* Exegesis is not the exclusive property of the pastor, and

---

[3] All English Scripture quotations, besides those translated by this writer, and unless otherwise noted are from the *New American Standard Bible: 1995 Update* (LaHabra, CA: The Lockman Foundation, 1995). Hereafter referred to as the NASB. All Greek Scripture quotations are from Barbara Aland, Kurt Aland, Matthew Black et al., *The Greek New Testament*, 4th ed., 50 (Federal Republic of Germany: United Bible Societies, 1993).

neither is exposition. Pastoral ministry demands teaching, but teaching is not simply the property of pastors. Every believer is responsible for every bit of Scripture, and every believer is responsible to teach other believers. Here is something to consider: it is not only those who are pastoring that need to spend time in the Biblical languages and in God's word. We all have those responsibilities. If we want to know God, we need to be in His word.

Consider Ephesians 4:11-13. In this passage we learn of apostles and prophets. We learn of evangelists, pastors and teachers. Ephesians 2:20 refers to the church being "built on the foundation of the apostles and prophets, Christ Jesus Himself being the corner *stone*." Christ is the cornerstone. Apostles and prophets are the foundation and in Ephesians 4:11 we then have apostles, prophets, evangelists, and then pastors and teachers.

In verse 11, the *kai* connects *poimenas* and *didaskalous*, and so reads "pastors and teachers." The idea is that these shepherds are also teachers. Not all teachers are pastors but all pastors are teachers – by role, by definition. Verse 12 tells us that the purpose is *pros – unto* the equipping of the saints for the work of service. The end, in this narrow context, is the equipping of saints. But notice that the pastors and teachers aren't doing the equipping, neither are the apostles and prophets or evangelists. The equipping is accomplished by the word of God, as evident from several contexts (e.g., Rom 12:1-2, Col 3:16, 2 Tim 3:16-17).

For those of us who are pastors, and for those of us who may be pursuing pastoral ministry, we have to consider the wrongheadedness of the concept that somehow we are the ones equipping. If we have that great arrogance to think that it is we who are doing the equipping, then that arrogant presupposition will negatively affect every aspect of our ministry. But if we understand that it is God's word that does the equipping, and we understand that pastors and teachers have been given to the church in order to *facilitate* this equipping, we can be cognizant of the great responsibility that we have in these roles to do our part to make sure this equipping actually takes place. It has been said that we can lead a horse to water but we can't make it drink. A wise man added that while we can't make it drink, we can salt the horses oats. Our job is not the equipping, but we have a responsibility to facilitate important aspects of the process of equipping. And if it is the word of God that does the equipping, then we have a grave responsibility to make sure His word is handled accurately.

The basic goal of Biblical exposition is the equipping of believers for the work of service. According to Ephesians 2:10, these works are those that God created beforehand that we should walk in them. Whatever these works may be, we are to be equipped by His word to do them. Ephesians 4:12 adds, "to the building up of the body of Christ" or "unto the building up of the body of Christ." The consequence here is that there is to be spiritual maturity not just of the individual, but of the whole body. Individuals aren't seen in isolation but they are seen as members of the body of Christ.

To help facilitate this body-wide growth, pastors and teachers have a dual role – but also, by the way, a plural role. Here is another challenge to some popular thinking. This passage uses the plural of pastors and teachers, and in every instance in the New Testament where pastors, elders, and overseers are cited in practice, the references are plural. (1 Timothy 3:1 may appear to be an exception, but it is describing an individual who desires to be an overseer. It is not prescribing or recommend that there be only one.) In every instance where there is pastoring in practice, overseeing in practice, elders in practice, there is always a plurality. We see that exemplified in Acts 20:17 and 28. Consequently, not only do we have a problem when we think that pastors and teachers are the ones equipping the saints, but also when we disregard the importance of plurality, and in practice the pastor/teacher becomes the one singular person "equipping" the church. This spiritual guru model is surprisingly prominent, and yet it often seems to create the *least* encouraging environment for actually training up people to spiritual maturity. As we consider the processes of exegesis and exposition, we need to consider that Biblically prescribed methodology is a necessity if we expect to see the desired outcome achieved.

Paul describes in further detail to Timothy the outcome of Biblical training: "but the goal of our instruction is love from a pure heart and a good conscience and a sincere faith" (1 Tim 1:5). This seems simple enough. *Goal* is *telos*, and can also be rendered as *end* or *completion*. The three characteristics of that love is that it derives from a pure heart, a good conscious and a sincere faith. In other words, the instruction is a means to an end, which is the right kind of love. God's word is not the end in itself, but is rather a means to an end. We have to remember, especially as students in an academic setting, there is a tendency to fall in love with a particular pursuit or study. It's easy to look at the Bible and say, "That's my life's pursuit. I'm a Bible student." To an extent that's good, but if we're studying the Bible as the end in itself, we have missed the purpose of God's communication. Paul explains that there is a purpose for the instruction and the communication. It is designed to have a result and an impact. We are not just trying to communicate to people these truths so that they will have more knowledge. We need to understand these truths first, so that we will have love from a pure heart, a good conscious and a sincere faith. In other words, if sound doctrine isn't accompanied by love, then it isn't complete. If doctrine isn't accompanied by love, then it isn't *sound* doctrine. If we aren't demonstrating love, then our exposition will not be complete.

Consider 2 Timothy 2:2: "And the things you have heard me say in the presence of many witnesses entrust to believing (or faithful) men." What had Timothy heard from Paul? It was the word of God, the teachings and the traditions that Paul had handed down which He received from Christ. He says, "You have heard these in the presence of many witnesses." This was not something that was spoken in private or in quiet. He exhorts, "These things entrust to believing or faithful men, reliable men." Notably, whether Paul intends *believing* or *faithful* in the sense of reliable, either way Paul is telling Timothy to be discriminate about whom he is teaching. The reason is evident in that last phrase: "who will be able to teach others also." The goal is that these people will develop into the next generation of those entrusting God's word to others. This is an important process of replication.

We don't find the word *disciple* (*mathetes*) used anywhere in the New Testament outside of the Gospels and Acts. So one might question the significance of discipleship in the church today. The term *disciple* simply means *follower*. In 2 Timothy 2:2, what is Paul telling Timothy to do? Make followers – and not just followers, but rather followers who will be able to make other followers. Not followers of Timothy or Paul, but rather but followers of what is taught – followers of the message who will be able to teach the message. Paul makes an important distinction here that it's not about the *messenger* it's about the *message* being communicated and replicated in the hearts of other people. That is a vital concept.

If we are teaching and we don't have in view these Biblical goals, then what in the world are we doing? Are we teaching because it's a career, or a job, or something we simply enjoy doing? Are we teaching because of pride – because it makes us feel elevated that other people are listening to us, and are being impressed with our knowledge? There are many problematic reasons for which we might be attracted to teaching, but the Biblical ones are simple: for the equipping of saints, and for replication – all for His glory.

Consider 2 Timothy 3:14-17. "You, however, continue in the things you have learned and become convinced of, knowing from whom you have learned them, and that from childhood you have known the sacred writings which are able to give you the wisdom that leads to salvation through faith which is in Christ Jesus. All Scripture is inspired by God and profitable for teaching, for reproof, for correction, for training in righteousness; so that the man of God may be adequate, equipped for every good work." One of the words I really appreciate in this context is translated here as *continue*. Continue in the things you have learned. The Greek word is *mene*, which is *abide* or *dwell, remain*.

Timothy had a tremendous amount of knowledge. In 2 Timothy 2:15 he's told to be diligent to handle the word accurately even though he had all this knowledge, but now in Chapter 3 he's being told to *remain, to abide*. This is the same word Jesus used when he exhorts His disciples in John 15 to "abide in Me and I in you." There is a familiarity that comes with abiding. For example, if we are married, living with a wife or husband, we become familiar with them. We know them. We understand them and we live with them in consideration. We are *with* them. This is the idea that Paul is communicating to Timothy – abide, dwell with. The same thing is communicated in John 15: *be with Christ*. If we're not walking with Him, how can we expect to honor Him? How can we expect to bear fruit as He describes in John 15? It's about abiding. We need to personally abide, and not just teach the subject material and then set it aside.

These Sacred Writings, described in verse 15, are able to give wisdom leading to salvation through faith. The idea is that if they are powerful for leading to salvation through faith in Christ Jesus, then they are sufficient for our equipping, as verse 17 describes. In Verse 17, we are told the purpose for Scripture. Verse 16 asserts that Scripture is God-breathed, it is useful and profitable, and then verse 17 explains the purpose: it is *in order that* the man of God may be adequate, equipped for every good work. Remember Ephesians 2:10 – these works have been created that we should walk in them. Recall Ephesians 4:11-12, which describes saints being equipped for the work of service. Notice the centrality of the word of God as the subject matter of the teaching, and the sufficiency of that word for adequacy and equipping. Consequently, if we are Bible teachers, and we are not teaching people with a view to their equipping, then we miss the point.

Consider one more example. You go to a restaurant you really like. You go there because maybe they make something that is just fantastic that you can't duplicate at any other restaurant or at home. So anytime you want that, what do you have to do? You have to go to that particular place and buy that meal. In other words, you are totally dependent on the restaurant for that particular meal or that particular food because you can't duplicate it. The restaurant is not in the business of trying to teach you how to cook, because what happens if they teach you to prepare that dish, or if they publish the recipe? Well, you duplicate it. You don't return to the restaurant, and the restaurant loses your money. Sadly, we see the same thing happening in churches, often unintentionally, but the outcome is the same nonetheless. We guard our trade secrets. If I teach you how to do what I do, then you won't need me anymore. Perhaps you won't even come back. You'll grow to independence, and instead I might prefer you to be a paying customer. It's a horrible addiction that we've got. This is what develops when church leadership stunts the growth of the people they are commissioned to help. So, I would suggest, instead of presenting ourselves as chefs who are preparing tremendous meals for people to partake, we need to look at ourselves as if we are teaching people how to cook. We're trying to teach people how to sustain themselves. Instead of making dependents, we need to be making disciples. The old adage of not giving a person a fish but instead teaching them how to fish, is a fitting emphasis here.

We can probably think of many other examples. How many times have we seen someone who has been in a church for thirty, forty, or fifty years and yet they couldn't explain or teach a passage if their life depended on it. We have a big responsibility, and it is not too late for us to meet that responsibility. God has left us here for a time. While He has given us breath, let's use it as He designed. And while we are at it, we should understand that we are going against the current, and that there will be obstacles.

2

Integrating Exegesis And Exposition: Biblical Communication For Spiritual Growth And Independence[4]

Introduction

To assess the implications of literal grammatical-historical hermeneutics (LGH) for the handling of the Bible it is helpful to consider three related stages of application. The first stage establishes warrant for preferring LGH to other historical and contemporary interpretive methods. This stage considers the epistemological basis for such a preference, and arrives at a prescriptive if/then conclusion from descriptive premises. The second stage explicates a particular method for applying the principles of LGH in the exegetical process. This stage quantifies LGH, parsing exegetical steps to insure LGH adherence. This second stage is, simply put, the exegetical method as governed and required by LGH.

Whereas the first stage justifies LGH, and the second stage

---

[4] Presented to The Council on Dispensational Hermeneutics, October 3, 2012 as "Integrating Exegesis and Exposition: Preaching and Teaching for Spiritual Independence."

applies LGH in exegesis, the third stage provides certain important ground rules for *praxis* and an *expositional approach* that are equally as governed by LGH as are the stages of justification and exegesis. In other words, if we understand LGH to be preferred and even prescribed, then we do well to consider the implications of that preference and prescription for *all textual considerations*, not just interpretive ones. If LGH is to govern our exegesis, then we are inconsistent if we do not allow the same to govern our praxis and exposition. This present discussion considers the first two stages (epistemological justification and exegetical method) with a view to understanding their implications for the third stage (praxis[5] and exposition), and for arriving at a model to integrate the second and third stages.

First-Stage Logic of LGH: Justification

Preference of LGH over other historical and contemporary interpretive methods rests on a simple, logical flow of ideas that can be formalized as follows:

P1: There exists an uncreated God who created.[6]

P2: Both language[7] and humanity[8] originated from God.

P3: God communicated[9] with humanity using language.[10]

P4: God's use of language confirms language to be a suitable

---

[5] The term is used here to describe theory of practice, meaning the grounding or basis of practice.
[6] Gen 1:1, Jn 1:3, Rom 1:20, Col 1:16.
[7] Gen 1:3.
[8] Gen 1:26-27.
[9] Gen 2:16-17.
[10] By language is meant the method of spoken communication involving the structured use of words.

vehicle for God's revelation.[11]

P5: The earliest recipients of God's communication understood it to have meaning, and ascertained that meaning based on a normative use of language.[12]

P6: The earliest and definitive model of interpretation was one in which God's words were taken at face value, were understood to follow basic rules of grammar, and were understood within a historical and contextual frame of reference.[13]

P7: Of historical and contemporary hermeneutic methods, LGH uniquely represents this early and definitive model.[14]

C: If Biblical interpreters are to understand the intended meaning of God's communication in the manner of the earliest recipients, then LGH must be employed.[15]

This argument, with its Biblical underpinnings, shows our LGH preference to be multidisciplinary in its implications. For example, from a Biblical perspective epistemology is neither rationalist nor empiricist. Instead, certainty is grounded in a specific perspective of God through revelation.[16] Despite the efficacy of natural revelation for rendering all without excuse,[17] necessary knowledge of the Divine is exclusively ascertainable through special revelation.[18]

---

[11] Ex 3:14, 17:14, 34:1.
[12] Gen 3:1-5, 9-13.
[13] Ex 19:8, 24:3-7.
[14] Gen 6:13-22.
[15] Prov 30:5, Deut 8:3, Mt 4:4.
[16] Job 28:28, Prov 1:7, 9:10.
[17] Rom 1:20.
[18] Ps 34:11, cf. Prov 1:2 and 1:7.

Likewise, historical linguistics is not merely a study of the evolution of language as having no traceable beginning point. Rather from a Biblical perspective there is a beginning point[19] followed soon after by a transitional event[20] that together serve as explanatory devices governing linguistic disciplines. Anthropology, if discerned Biblically, considers humanity to be broken with no intrinsic ability for repair.[21]

By contrast, non-Biblical anthropology generally views humanity to be on an upward trajectory, independent of divine aid. A Biblical psychology regards there to be a non-corporeal aspect of humanity, and emphasizes human responsibility for one's thoughts and actions.[22] This is not so in secular psychology, which considers the soul to be no more than mind, and human thought and action to be no more than a series of physiological causes and effects.

These are just a few examples of the broad influence of Biblical hermeneutics. Further, these examples show LGH a device effecting much more than just a few strategic prophetic passages. Rather, it is a comprehensive tool for understanding humanity, history, the world, and God Himself. If we take the Biblical data seriously as the product of a creative God who communicated with His creation through the use of language, then we have no alternative to LGH as *the* interpretive device, lest we sacrifice meaning itself in favor of the meaningless and arbitrary.

Second-Stage Logic of LGH: Exegesis

An exegetical method that is governed by LGH includes a series of steps, all of which are necessary for ascertaining the meaning of any given passage. These steps represent a sort of *sine qua non* for doing exegesis.

---

[19] Gen 1:3, 2:16.
[20] Gen 11:1, 7-9.
[21] Gen 6:5, 8:21, Rom 3:10-20, Eph 2:1-10.
[22] Gen 2:15-17, 3:17, Ps 139:23-24, Rom 1:20.

Step 1: Verify the text and translation.
Step 2: Understand background and context.
Step 3: Identify structure.
Step 4: Identify grammatical and syntactical keys.
Step 5: Identify lexical keys.
Step 6: Identify Biblical context.
Step 7: Identify theological context.

Step 1: Verify the Text and Translation

If we recognize that God communicated at specific times using particular languages, then we must realize (1) the implications of our being generations removed from the original manuscripts, and (2) how much is lost when we translate from those languages. This first exegetical step considers especially lower criticism, examining the text in the original language to determine the scope and limits of the passage, and to verify the text itself.

For example, P66 records John 3:13 as ending with the phrase, ὁ υἱὸς τοῦ ἀνθρώπου,[23] while the same passage in Stephen's TR, ends with ο υιος του ανθρωπου ο ων εν τω ουρανω.[24] Though this variant is seemingly not doctrinally significant, the latter reading would constitute at least a confusing representation of Christ (as being concurrently in heaven and on earth). Absent this step of verifying the text itself along with the veracity of the translation, we *can't even begin* the exegetical process, being unable to determine something so basic as *what the text actually says*. Biblical exegesis demands at least a basic understanding of lower criticism and the Biblical languages.

---

[23] Consistent with Sinaiticus and Vaticanus, neither of which include the phrase *who is in heaven*.
[24] Consistent with Jerome's Vulgate, which includes the phrase *qui est in caelo*.

Step 2: Understand Background and Context

The normative use of language requires a consideration of the text *in context*, and in light of key background information. Considerations in this step include higher criticism, authorship, timing, audience and culture, literary genre, and occasion, to name a few aspects. For example, it is increasingly popular to recognize the Gospels as *Graeco-Roman bios*, a literary form that allows for non-literal meanings of otherwise literal language. Michael Licona illustrates this in his explanation of Matthew 27:52-53:

> Given the presence of phenomenological language used in a symbolic manner in both Jewish and Roman literature related to a major event such as the death of an emperor or the end of a reigning king or even a kingdom, the presence of ambiguity in the relevant text of Ignatius, and that so very little can be known about Thallus's comment on the darkness...it seems to me that an understanding of the language of Matthew 27:52-53 as 'special effects' with eschatological Jewish texts and thought in mind is most plausible.[25]

If we conclude that the resurrections described in Matthew 27:52-53 are special effects, then on what textual authority can we argue that the resurrection of Christ was not also special effects? Were the Gospels divinely inspired historical accounts, or were the writers simply skilled in the historical fiction paradigm of the day? What is understood of background and context profoundly influences the remaining exegetical steps.

---

[25] Michael Licona, *The Resurrection of Jesus: A New Historiographical Approach* (Downers Grove, IL: IVP, 2010), 552.

Step 3: Identify Structure

Internal clues to the structure of Biblical books are both readily available and necessarily discerned for understanding the theses and supporting material of each book. Genesis uses the word תּוֹלְדֹת (*toledoth,* meaning *generations*) to divide the book.[26]

John 20:30-31 describes σημεῖα as the building blocks of his Gospel. Acts 1:8 provides the geographical and chronological outline of the book. Revelation 1:19 introduces the three sections of that prophecy. As is evident in these examples, the normative use of language places tremendous weight on rhetorical structure for ascertaining meaning.

Step 4: Identify Grammatical and Syntactical Keys

Grammar and syntax consider normative principles for relationships of words to each other. Grammar is the framework of rules, while syntax is descriptive of usage. Both are important, in historical context, for discerning meaning. Acts 2:38 provides an important example of the importance of understanding word-relationships: "Peter *said* to them, "Repent, and each of you be baptized in the name of Jesus Christ for the forgiveness of your sins; and you will receive the gift of the Holy Spirit."

Peter's imperative seems, in English, to require water baptism in order to receive forgiveness and the gift of the Holy Spirit. However, the imperative μετανοήσατε, the second pronoun ὑμῶν (the sins *of you*), and the verb λήμψεσθε are all second person plural, while the imperative βαπτισθήτω is in the third person singular. In light of the syntactical relationships of these words and phrases, the passage could be read, "Repent for the forgiveness of your sins and you will receive the gift of the Holy Spirit, and let each of you be baptized in the name of Jesus Christ." Relationships of words, and rules governing those relationships are often dispositive for understanding the meaning of phrases and

---

[26] Gen 2:4, 5:1, 6:9, 10:1, 11:10, 11:27, 25:12, 25:19, 36:1, 36:9, 37:1.

passages.

Step 5: Identify Lexical Keys

Words are the fundamental building blocks of language. Consequently, for ascertaining meaning the normative use of language demands that words be understood. Before examining a word in its Biblical or theological context, the interpreter should first understand the lexical meaning and etymology of the word. The importance of this principle is evident in Daniel 9:24, as the KJV, NASB, and ESV all translate the first phrase of the verse as *seventy weeks*.

If the Hebrew שָׁבֻעִים (*shabe'yim*) has a lexical meaning best translated as *weeks*, then to conclude that the word *weeks* is referencing a period of seven years requires non-literal interpretation and an abandonment of LGH. To conclude thus requires a departure from the normative use of language. However, שָׁבֻעִים is literally translated *sevens*,[27] as is the corresponding ἑβδομάδες (*hebdomades*) in the LXX. In this case the translations are misleading in regards to the simple definition and earliest Biblical usage of this word.

Step 6: Identify Biblical Context

Recognizing Biblical context is one of the most critical steps in the exegetical process, and is rightly understood to be an elementary aspect of the normative use of language. Whether the applicable context is immediate (adjacent to the passage), near (within the book), or broad (related context but from a different Biblical book), the meaning of a given passage is not discernible with certainty until related contexts are acknowledged and understood. For example, 2 Chronicles 7:14 records a promise for God's healing of His people's land. If considered separate from its immediate

---

[27] E.g., Gen 5:7.

context, this appears a universal principle. However, 7:15 qualifies that promise as response to prayers offered *from Solomon's temple*.

In Job 34:35-37, it appears that Elihu incorrectly indicts Job of sin. However, 34:34 clarifies that Elihu is representing the views of Job's other friends. Context is the difference between Elihu being completely wrong, and being completely accurate.

Step 7: Identify Theological Context

Though Biblical context is more central to discerning meaning, theological context is also important. For example, in John 14:1-3, the doctrine of the rapture seems lexically and perhaps even syntactically absent. However, when read in conjunction with other passages,[28] it is evident that the rapture is theologically in view. Further, understanding the theological relationship of works, faith, and justification in Romans 4 helps to resolve a potentially sticky discussion of that same relationship in James 2.

Understanding theological context is important for discerning meaning. However, reading theological conclusions into the text as a hermeneutic device is incompatible with LGH. If an interpretation is derived from a theological conclusion, rather than a textual analysis that considers theological context, that interpretation is invalid in the sense of being improperly earned.

Verification and Implications

After the seventh step, secondary verification is a helpful exercise for confirming adherence to LGH throughout the exegetical process, and involves considering secondary, extra-Biblical data (commentaries, teachers, and other resources). Consulting secondary sources cannot be considered part of the exegetical process, *per se*, but their utilization can help the interpreter ensure that no steps have been missed. Such interpretive humility is

---

[28] Especially 1 Thes 4, 2 Thes 2, and 1 Cor 15.

important. Still the interpreter must be courageous enough to allow the Biblical text to speak for itself, even if the secondary sources disagree with the exegetical results. In short, secondary verification is not an exercise in extra-Biblical proof-texting, instead, it is a process for checking adherence to the hermeneutic and to the process itself.

Each of these seven steps together (along with secondary verification) and in succession represent a reasonable application of LGH that is consistent with the seven aforementioned premises for justifying the preference of LGH. If the trajectory of the argument has successfully guided us from Point A (justification) to Point B (application in exegesis), then we must be open to the implications of that trajectory for arriving at Point C (praxis and exposition).

Third-Stage Logic of LGH: Praxis and Exposition

Beyond justifying LGH and applying it in the exegetical process, LGH also governs praxis and exposition. In respect to believers *doing* the word, the Bible has much to say. Scripture is univocal in asserting its sufficiency not just for learning and/or teaching, but also for personal appropriation in thought, speech, and action. A truly Biblical praxis demands proper application of LGH in the exegetical process and, in fact, cannot stand without it. Likewise, the proper application of LGH in the exegetical process leaves the interpreter unable to escape the many Biblical prescriptions – for the unbeliever, to respond in faith, and for the believer, to walk in faith.

How can one fulfill James's prescription for believers to Γίνεσθε δὲ ποιηταὶ λόγου (become workers of the word) if *the word* has not been correctly understood?[29] Paul exhorts believers to engage in correct thinking and action on the basis of the mercies of God.[30] Such conduct is the logical (λογικὴν) service of believers.

---

[29] Jam 1:22.
[30] Rom 12:1.

Paul's comments here are significant, as he encourages believers to employ *logic* or *reason* in understanding the basis for their motivation. For Paul to exhort in that manner absent the expectation that his readers would actually understand what was revealed about the mercies of God in Romans 1-11 would be strange, to say the least. It is evident that the same principles required to understand God's mercy are required for walking in it. In order to walk in a manner worthy of the believer's calling, the believer must ascertain the correct meaning of that calling.[31]

Correct exegesis is prerequisite to correct praxis. Further, correct praxis without correct exposition is oxymoronic. LGH is necessary for exegesis, for praxis, and consequently for exposition. While praxis is inextricably dependent on LGH, it is evident that exposition is simply one of many facets of practice. Believers are universally exhorted to teach others,[32] even if not all believers are said to have the gift of teaching,[33] and not all believers will serve as pastor-teachers.[34]

Regardless of one's role in the body of Christ, all share the same responsibility for knowing all of God's word.[35] With respect to accountability for Biblical knowledge and duty in sharing it with others, the Scripture draws no clergy/laity distinction. All believers are to let the word of Christ dwell richly in them.[36] All believers are to be equipped for every good work.[37] Arguably, all believers are to follow the apostles in their responsibility to make disciples – a process which includes *teaching*.[38]

---

[31] Eph 4:1.
[32] Col 3:16.
[33] Rom 12:7.
[34] Eph 4:11-12, 1 Tim 3:1-7, Jam 3:1.
[35] Heb 5:12.
[36] Col 3:16.
[37] 2 Tim 3:17.
[38] Mt 28:19-20.

Purpose, Content, and Mechanics of Biblical Teaching

The purpose of Biblical teaching is described succinctly in two particular contexts. Ephesians 4:11-12 describes pastoral teaching as being purposed for or unto (πρὸς) the equipping or adequacy (τὸν καταρτισμὸν) of the saints. Importantly we must realize that *pastoral teaching does not equip saints*. Nor does any other human ministry. Rather, these ministries are purposed *for* the equipping of saints. Second Timothy 3:16-17 describes the content of Biblical teaching as *all Scripture* (πᾶσα γραφὴ), and characterizes it as that which is beneficial (ὠφέλιμος) for the qualification (ἄρτιος) and adequacy or equipping (ἐξηρτισμένος, same root used in Eph 4:12) of the man of God. Consequently, if the purpose of Biblical teaching is for saints to be equipped *by the word of God* (rather than by the teacher), then it is incumbent upon Biblical teachers to ensure that they are handling God's word in the most responsible manner possible, with the ultimate goal always in view.

The mechanics of Biblical teaching is not a matter of preference. That too, like exegesis and all other aspects of praxis, is subject to LGH. Paul illustrates the mechanics of Biblical teaching in 2 Timothy 2:2, when he says, "entrust these to faithful men who will be able to teach others also." The process is one of *entrusting these things* (ταῦτα παράθου) – *the word of God*. The goal of teaching is elsewhere defined as adequacy or equipping of saints, but in this passage, Paul offers a tangible method for measuring the effectiveness of Bible teaching. Are those learners who are entrusted to our care developing a capability to teach others? Are we giving them the tools to do so, or are we simply telling them what actions to avoid and which ones to prefer? Are we trying to simplify things because they couldn't possibly understand if we just taught *the Text*? Are we teaching them that when they need answers they should open their Bibles...and call on us? These scenarios have no place in Paul's model of Biblical teaching.

God revealed Himself using language. That he revealed

Himself in such a way has tremendous implications for teaching. God expected that His audience would be sufficiently skilled in the principles of the languages He used so that they could understand His meaning. We all need to understand *how to understand God's word*. We all need to know how to handle variants, translations, background, rhetorical structure, grammar, syntax, vocabulary, and context. If we as pastors or other Bible teachers are simply spouting Biblical data without showing learners *how to discover and understand that data for themselves*, then we are failing in our stewardship. We are making dependents rather than disciples, hearers rather than doers, and warriors who have no idea how to wield a sword.

Conclusion

Biblical learners, whether during Ezra's time[39] or Paul's, understood the basics of LGH and the exegetical process, even if not always intentionally, because those principles involved the simple, natural, everyday use of the languages God employed. Even those that were too young to understand, were taught at home by their fathers so that they could understand.[40]

Because in our time most of those we teach are unfamiliar with those languages, we face a unique dilemma that, seemingly, neither Ezra nor Paul faced. But how we respond to that challenge will go a long way in determining the quality of our teaching ministries. We can keep the exegetical process to ourselves. In so doing, we are inconsistent insofar as we argue that LGH is warranted, that we must use it to derive our Biblical interpretations, and that it governs our praxis, but that it has no place in exposition.

If we would be consistent, we must recognize that our exposition is also governed by LGH. In so doing, we ought to integrate our exegesis with our exposition – meaning that *we ought*

---

[39] Ezra 8.
[40] Deut 6:6-9.

simply to teach the text as it is written and show our work. We ought to be forthright about how we derive conclusions. We ought to be transparent about why we interpret passages as we do. We ought to immerse learners in the principles of the Biblical languages, teaching them grammar, syntax, and vocabulary wherever possible. We ought to handle the Text word by word, phrase by phrase, line by line, book by book – all the while modeling the exegetical process. *Doing, while being observed* is a critical component of the teaching process. That principle was modeled by God when he prescribed to Israel that fathers should behave in such a way that their sons and grandsons would fear the Lord and be obedient.[41]

Can our children and grandchildren in the faith observe how we handle His word, follow our example, grow to maturity, and so teach others? If so, we will have successfully integrated exegesis and exposition and taken LGH to its logical conclusion.

---

[41] Deut 6:1-2.

3
Brothers, We Are Not Chefs: On the Role of Biblical Languages in Understanding, Applying, and Teaching the Bible[42]

The essential premise of the previous section is that if the Biblical languages are necessary for exegesis, then they are also necessary for application and teaching. This premise has profound implications, and invites certain basic questions, addressed here.

Question
Does the assertion of the necessity of Biblical languages imply that the only folks truly qualified to interpret the Bible are those skilled in Greek and Hebrew exegesis?

Answer
Yes and no. On the one hand, we can't really do exegesis of the Bible without being aware of the actual text in the original language. On the other hand, I don't argue for *technical proficiency*,

---
[42] Adapted from Christopher Cone, "Brothers We Are Not Chefs," Submitted to The Council on Dispensational Hermeneutics, October 7, 2012.

but rather for *technical awareness*. One doesn't need to be an expert to have the basic skills needed for interpreting the Bible. One does need to be aware that behind the English text are Hebrew, Aramaic, and Greek texts that are often more precise than their English translations. Being aware of that, and considering that throughout the exegetical process is very important. With the many tools available today (electronic and otherwise) the languages are not inaccessible.

Question
Isn't this arguing for elitism – that only those with elite skill can handle the word well?

Answer
No. In fact, I am arguing against elitism. Those with awareness of the languages and of how to find the information needed can indeed handle the word well. I am arguing that Bible teachers should make a concerted effort, as an intrinsic and necessary part of their teaching, to provide those tools to learners.

Question
The problem with this is that not every teacher or pastor has the time, funds, or aptitude for Greek and Hebrew, at the level to be truly proficient.

Answer
Proficiency can sometimes be the enemy of awareness, just as great can sometimes be the enemy of good. As Biblical educators, we make a key mistake when we tell people that if they can't fully commit to the languages, they shouldn't engage them at all. A wise man once told me, "if it is worth doing, it is worth doing…poorly." Better to attempt at a basic level than not to attempt at all. Even someone with very basic skills in the languages has a huge

advantage in understanding the Bible over someone who doesn't (as long as they don't handle the language irresponsibly). And after all, to establish proficiency in any particular area requires a lifetime of study.

Question
Can one be a good teacher or pastor and not be proficient in Greek or Hebrew?

Answer
Not be proficient? Yes. Not be aware? No. As long as the interpreter is aware of the languages and has the ability to find the information (whether by one's own use of basic tools or consulting the research of others), that interpreter has an opportunity to handle the Bible well.

Question
Can one be proficient in Greek or Hebrew and not be a good teacher or pastor?

Answer
Absolutely. Skill in languages is no guarantee of good Biblical interpretation. One can abuse the languages and can also have an inconsistent hermeneutic method. Just as a very good reader will not always be a very good student or teacher, there are many factors that play into quality learning and teaching.

Question
Only 25% of people will have any aptitude for languages. So how can we place such a burden on the other 75%?

Answer

I think the premise here is destructive: '*most people can't learn languages.*' That premise is simply and completely untrue. Everyone has a capacity for languages – almost everyone knows at least the basics of at least one language. If we are willing to be diligent and patient, and help people understand components of Biblical language in the same ways they learned their native tongues, then there is very good opportunity for them to grasp the basics they need for interpreting the Bible.

Again, proficiency is not necessarily the aim, but rather simply awareness and the ability for a person to find the needed data themselves. For example, when our children ask us questions, do we always give them a direct answer, or do we sometimes send them to a web search, dictionary, concordance, or other tool? Why do we do that? Because we want to guide them into developing the skills on their own. Spiritual parenting is no different.

Question

Doesn't this put at a disadvantage people in other cultures where illiteracy is higher, since the Biblical languages are not accessible to them?

Answer

Not at all, because, again, the premise isn't accurate. Even among the most illiterate in any culture, there is still the ability to grasp the basics of language. Just about everybody has enough capacity for language to speak and understand at least their native tongue. As for me, I didn't really learn the nuts and bolts of English until I began to study Greek. At that point I began to value the structure and components of language, because I realized that God had chosen to communicate through language. If I wanted to understand what He had said, I needed to appreciate and grasp some basic elements of language. This is the same in any culture. As

Bible teachers our goal is to facilitate the equipping of believers for maturity – for spiritual independence, so that they can understand, obey, and teach the Scriptures for themselves. Sometimes that means along the way we will have to teach people to read, to listen, to question, to analyze, etc.

Question
Isn't this assertion of the necessity of the Biblical languages idealistic and impossible to implement?

Answer
First of all, it doesn't matter. We are not responsible for results, but rather for obedience and effort. Just because something is difficult our responsibility is not diminished. Pragmatism is often the enemy of obedience. Second, no, the necessity of Biblical languages is neither purely idealistic nor impossible to implement. If we approach things as a parent teaching a child, we understand there is a progression from immaturity to maturity, and dependence to independence. As parents we don't look at how far our infant has to go to become a mature adult, shrug our shoulders and neglect the process because the road seems too long and arduous. No, instead, we take it one day at a time. One moment at a time, diligently laboring, and we thank the Lord along the way for such a precious opportunity.

Question
A chef doesn't bring people into his dirty kitchens and make them eat amongst the greasy pots and pans, instead, he prepares an excellent meal that is both wholesome and aesthetically pleasing, right?

Answer

Once again, the premise is problematic. So problematic, in fact, that this is the core issue: *we are not chefs*! Ours is not to spoon-feed people beyond infancy (yes, there is a time for spoon-feeding), rather ours is to help them develop the skills to be mature adults in Christ – to be able to feed themselves and others. *Our job is to bring people into the kitchen and show them how to use those pots and pans to prepare their own meals.*

Notice the progression in believers growth, from infancy to the expectation of maturity: Infancy: "I gave you milk to drink, not solid food; for you were not yet able to receive it (1 Cor 3:2)." "Like newborn babies, long for the pure milk of the word, so that by it you may grow in respect to salvation (1 Pet 2:2)." Expectation of maturity: "For though by this time you ought to be teachers, you have need again for someone to teach you the elementary principles of the oracles of God, and you have come to need milk and not solid food. For everyone who partakes only of milk is not accustomed to the word of righteousness, for he is an infant (Heb 5:12-13)."

> Therefore leaving the elementary teachings about the Christ, let us press on to maturity...(Heb 6:1).

Believers are not to remain in infancy, but are expected to grow to maturity. As Bible teachers we cannot teach in such a way that our students are not developing spiritually. And they cannot develop spiritually without an increasing ability to feed themselves. Just as an infant begins its life with total dependence on its parents, and is gradually weaned and taught to care for itself, so it is with spiritual children as well. *Brothers, we are not chefs. We are disciplers, mentors and parents.*

4
Distinctives of This Approach

This work assumes the reader has some previous experience in Biblical languages, and presents a basic review of exegetical principles and introduces a process whereby one can progress from the technical aspects necessary for the study and application of a passage, to critical elements of planning, preparation and delivery of the passage in preaching and teaching settings.

There are two distinctive aspects of this approach. First of all, (1) it focuses not only on the teacher's responsibility to teach the content of the passage, but also on the responsibility to teach *how* to study the content, in order that listeners may learn to feed themselves, in keeping with the principle of developing disciples and not dependants; consequently, the expositional process is characterized by the presence of and transparency in handling exegetical elements, and (2) this approach emphasizes the responsibility of the communicator to keep the focus on God and His message rather than on the personality and merits of the messenger. Consequently, rhetorical aspects are given secondary consideration.

Now, both of these aspects are controversial issues. First of all, there is a pretty attractive and typical model of church leadership that sets the pastor up as a CEO, and he is perceived as the spiritual guru who is overseeing the flock. When the congregation has concerns and need counseling, they go to him. When they need spiritual feeding, they go to him. He is the one expected to have knowledge, and no one else really has or needs it. This isn't a Biblical model, and it isn't particularly healthy, but it is all too common in churches. While many of this book's readers will be pastors or pastors in training, it is my hope that it will find a broader reading *among all who simply want to know Him better and who recognize the central role of the Bible in that pursuit.* Consequently, this work is not designed to promote the spiritual guru model, but rather it is designed to challenge every believer to a deeper more accurate study of His word.

In keeping with that, the focus we will have is on training up people to be spiritually independent, much like parenting. We don't train up our children so that when they grow up they can't function without us – *we are trying to make disciples, not dependents*. In spite of this focus, it is remarkable how uncommon it is to train up people so that they can grow to spiritual independence and maturity. Teaching for spiritual maturity is not as prominent in churches as we might hope, in part due to a prevailing seminary culture that often seems to foster the spiritual guru model. This book represents an attempt to counter that culture.

There is a second controversial aspect of this approach. Homiletics, rhetorical aspects, and basic public speaking abilities are important for communication in general. Nobody wants to listen to someone that is nervously jangling keys in their pockets, or constantly saying "umm" or "you know," or picking their nose while they're teaching. There are some common-sense things that we learn to avoid through accountability, as we gain some experience in public speaking and learn to communicate in a considerate way. However, communicating the Bible is much less about the theatrics of public speaking than it is about actually communicating *the Bible*. This work addresses homiletic issues but places far greater emphasis on reproduction – teaching for spiritual independence and spiritual reproduction, and in so doing, centralizes the message rather than the messenger.

Four Major Objectives

There are four major objectives that are central here. First, we need to gain further skill in handling accurately the word with regard to personal study, with a view to a closer, more obedient walk with the Lord. This is vital. I ask students why they come to seminary and often hear in response, "I want to be a pastor," "I'm going to study to pastor," or "I want to teach." We need to be cautious not to miss the order of priority. We need to understand the word so that we can *personally* grow. We need to have a view toward personal growth through our study and through our exegesis and exposition as opposed to simply considering how we can communicate to someone else for their growth and benefit.

Second, we need to have a method for selecting content to teach and handling that content, from the first point of observation to the final point of message delivery. In other words, we are going to work from the very beginning process of opening the Bible and trying to then determine what and how to teach. How do we select a passage? How do we handle that passage? How do we live that passage? And how do we actually communicate the passage with someone else? We need to be fairly comprehensive, and even technical at times. We need to have more ambition than simply relying on big-idea approaches; and three-point sermonizing won't get us where we need to go. A more comprehensive method is needed than those two models provide, because though they are excellent methods for teaching *about* the text, they simply aren't designed as methods for teaching *the text*.

Third, we need to have an understanding of the dependence of exposition on the exegetical process and how to employ exegetical principles in exposition. We can't have one without the other. To try to communicate truth without having first earned the right through exegeting Scripture is highly problematic. We want to understand the relationship of the two processes, how they connect, at what point they intersect, and also the differences between the two.

Finally, we need to gain a more acute awareness of the urgency, stewardship and responsibilities involved in teaching the word of God, with a view toward satisfying God's standards for Biblical teaching. Consider 2 Timothy 2:15 – Paul's exhortation to Timothy that he study to show himself approved, a workman handling accurately the word of truth. In thinking about that passage, I'm struck by the fact that Timothy was, at that point in his life, very well trained in the Scripture. He was raised from his childhood knowing the Scriptures. He had tremendous advantages over his peers in that respect. Still, that Paul would tell him to be diligent is a testament to the importance of this kind of study. Like Timothy, we need to understand the weight of these issues. We want to fulfill what God's design is for understanding the Word, for handling it accurately, and ultimately, for teaching it. So while we are attentive to the process of teaching and presenting to someone else, we must not miss the aspect of our own responsibility and our own personal growth in that process.

5
Teaching for Independence

Every week in America, tens of thousands of pastors give messages to millions of people. And then they do it again the next week. And the next. And the next. The cycle repeats as it has year after year after year. But why? How many of these pastors are actually aware of what they are supposed to be achieving? What is, in fact, the goal of pastoral teaching in the church?

Ephesians 4:11-12 describes various roles and gifts given to the church, including the pastor (*poimen*, shepherd) and teacher (*didaskalos*). Note from the passage that the pastor and teacher are not two separate roles – the pastor is also a teacher. While there are teachers in the church who are not pastors (e.g., every believer, see Col. 3:16), there is no Biblical model of pastors who are not teachers.

So, pastors are supposed to teach. But *what* and *why*? In order to understand the *what*, we first have to consider the *why*. Ephesians 4:12 makes the *why* very clear: for the equipping of saints, to the building up of the body of Christ. Notice that the teaching itself doesn't equip the saints, but rather it is intended *for* (or *to*) the equipping of saints. Pastoral teaching is for the equipping of saints, but it isn't the equipping of saints. In other words, the goal of pastoral teaching is so that saints are equipped, but the saints are actually equipped by something other than pastoral teaching (Heb 13:20-21).

Paul explains in 2 Timothy 3:16-17 that *all of God's word* is the vehicle for the equipping of saints (same root, *artizo*, is used in Eph 4:12, 2 Tim 3:17, and also Heb 13:21). God's word is profitable for teaching, for reproof, for correction, for training in righteousness in order that the follower of God may be equipped or made adequate for every good work.

If the reason for pastoral teaching is the equipping of saints, and the vehicle God provided for the equipping of saints is His word, then *what* should pastors be teaching? Very simply, pastors should be teaching His word. Anything else is a waste of time and resources.

I will never forget once walking into a "Bible church" in the Chicago area. The pastor had been trained at a highly regarded local Bible institute, and we expected him to teach the word. The introduction to his message went something like this (verbatim, as I recall it): "Next week we will get back into the word of God, but this week, I wanted to share some of my own thoughts that I have had this week." During his opening prayer, we snuck out quietly and never returned. Is there anything wrong with sharing personal thoughts? Of course not, but there is a time and a place for everything. Pastors don't have the freedom to choose their teaching material. It is the word of God, and nothing but the word of God. If a pastor is not attentive to the *why* and the *what*, he is in grave danger of falling into the trap that is, I believe, the greatest affliction to churches: *teaching for dependence*. Or, phrased differently, if pastors are not focused on teaching Biblically, then they are most probably developing a cult of personality that is enslaving their listeners rather than freeing them for growth and maturity.

In 2 Timothy 2:2 Paul tells Timothy to "entrust these things (the teachings of Paul) to faithful men who will be able to teach others also." The goal in this context is replication – that those who are taught be able to teach others. If we simply sermonize, we are hiding the exegetical process from our listeners. We are not showing them how to study and learn the Bible for themselves. We are telling them how to think, speak, and act, *without showing them how to discover those things for themselves*. We are feeding people for a day and teaching them that they can't fish – that they have to come hear us every week if they should get hungry. This is the equivalent of parents trying to keep their children dependent on them for their entire lives. We would consider that child abuse. So what do we consider it when we do that same thing in a spiritual sense?

Instead, pastors, when we stand before the folks He has entrusted to our care, let us teach the word. Let us teach in such a way that our listeners will develop an understanding of how to handle the word – so that they grow to be independent of us, and so that they will develop the ability to teach others the word of God. Let's stop all the rhetoric and simply do what we are told to do – teach His word. *Teach for independence, not dependence.*

6
A Necessary Ingredient for Biblical Literacy

Knowing God's word is a central responsibility and privilege for Christians. It is by His word that we get to know Him, and it is His word that equips us (2 Tim 3:16-17; Eph 4:12). His word protects us (Eph 6;11-17), guides us (Ps 119:11, 105), sustains us (Mt 4:4), and transforms and renews us (Rom 12:2; Eph 4:23). We are to let His word dwell richly in us (Col 3:16).

While all this requires that we learn His word, it isn't enough just to hear it or to be able even to recite it. Additionally, we need to be doers of His word. If we are simply taking it in without *doing* it, then we are deceiving ourselves into thinking we are Biblically literate when we aren't (Jam 1:22-23).

Biblical literacy is not just an intellectual awareness of what the Bible says. Notice the missing word in these passages:

> The goal of our instruction is _____ (1 Tim 1:5).

> If I have…all knowledge…but do not have _____…I am nothing (1 Cor 13:2).

> Knowledge makes arrogant, but _____ edifies (1 Cor 8:1).

> Everyone who _____(s) is born of God and knows God (1 Jn 4:7).

If the purpose of our instruction is *love*, then we haven't put that instruction to proper use until we are demonstrating love. If we have knowledge without love, we are of no use. If we have knowledge without love, we will be more prone to arrogance than to building others up. And as John explains, it doesn't make sense that we would claim to know God and not exhibit love toward those He has made.

I was recently on a teaching assignment, sitting at a hotel enjoying a continental breakfast. At the table nearby were seven pastors (I assume, based on their conversation) who were in town attending a conference. They were discussing, among other things, how to make their Sunday mornings as effective as possible. They discussed a number of strategies, all of which made some degree of sense, but sadly the conversation never came around to the centrality of the teaching of God's word, and the simple exhortation that we *do what it says*. This is emblematic of a pervasive problem not only in our churches but in our lives: *we want the results, but we aren't using the right formula.*

Spiritual maturity requires a high degree of Biblical literacy. And Biblical literacy requires that *knowledge bears fruit*. There are no gimmicks that will facilitate that. There are no shortcuts. The formula is given in two contexts: "he who abides in Me and I in Him, he bears much fruit, for apart from Me you can do nothing" (Jn 15:5), and "walk by the Spirit and you will not carry out the deeds of the flesh" (Gal 5:16). Walking with Him ensures that we will be in the right place, doing the right thing, with the right enablement. If our Bible study doesn't result in a closer walk with Him, then we are doing it wrong.

7
The Expositor's Challenge

One of the most prevalent and substantive obstacles to the spiritual growth of the church is the failure of leadership to teach people for spiritual independence or spiritual maturity. It is all too common for pastors to create dependants rather than disciples. The most charismatic and engaging leaders can be successful at developing a following that mimics growth (and in fact does create numerical growth), but the disciples made in this model are disciples of that dominant leader, not disciples of Christ through His word. Consider the following exhortation to "preachers:"

> A distinctive characteristic purpose of expository preaching... [is] its instructional function. An explanation of the details in a given text imparts information that is *otherwise unavailable to the average untrained parishioner* and provides him with a foundation for Christian growth and service.[43] (emphasis mine)

What's being said here is very significant: in practice there is often another mediator between God and man, and it's not just the

---

[43] John F. MacArthur Jr., *MacArthur Pastor's Library on Preaching* (Nashville, TN: Thomas Nelson Publishers, 2005), 107.

man Christ Jesus – it's the expositor. In this model, the expositor is uniquely trained, and what the expositor is presenting "is otherwise unavailable to the average untrained parishioner." Certainly those things can be true, but the question is how to fix the problem of the "untrained parishioner." The simple solution is to *train* the parishioner. Unfortunately the prevailing model for exposition is to try to simplify things to the point that the listener doesn't *need* to be trained. Instead, he or she can simply rely on the expertise and knowledge of the expositor, without paying any real attention to developing personal skill in handling the word of God. Further, the description of this style of exposition, as providing the parishioner with a foundation for Christian growth and service, is an admittance that the things which are foundational for Christian growth and service are important, but that they can only be provided by the expositor, and even then only by a process of simplification. Far better to simply train the listeners to be able to discern those foundational issues for themselves.

Obviously, we need to start simply – just as in parenting, we wouldn't demand that a toddler do algebra – but we need to promote growth by the prescribed Biblical method: believers' allowing the word of Christ to dwell richly in them (Col 3:16). The expositor should have as a significant goal the process of training people to drink the milk of the word (1 Cor 3:2; Heb 5:12-13; 1 Pet 2:2), then to digest the solid food of the word (1 Cor 3:2), and finally to be knowledgeable enough to be doers of the word (Jam 1:22), and to be able to teach the word when afforded the opportunity (2 Tim 2:2). This process requires much more depth than the simplification necessary to provide foundational truths to the untrained parishioner. Incidentally, Paul refutes the simplification model as the pattern for ongoing growth. He rebukes the Corinthians for their fleshliness that resembled infancy (1 Cor 3:1-3), lamenting their failure to grow, and indicating that their need for milk was a problem that needed to be remedied by their becoming spiritual (1

Cor 2:14-16). The simplification model was for infants and for the fleshly. It was not the norm for the church as a broader whole. The writer of Hebrews adds a stern exhortation that his readers leave the elementary (basic) teachings of Christ and press on to maturity. That doesn't mean they should forget or neglect the elementary teachings, but rather that they should master them and then move on in spiritual growth. Now this is not easy for anybody, of course, and it is the central challenge faced by the expositor. Consider this exhortation:

> A previously issued warning is worth repeating here: A transition from exegesis to Bible exposition is mandatory. Pulpiteers who are fluent enough to expound the technical data of exegesis and still hold the attention of an average congregation have been and are extremely rare.[44]

Very true – sad, but true. But again, how do we address the problem? By succumbing to it? By not aspiring to be exceptional expositors, and instead accepting the typical mediocrity? The solution prescribed in the popular model is as follows:

> The information gleaned from exegesis must be put into a format that fits the understanding of the person in the pew and is applicable to his or her situation.[45]

Now clearly, when we're teaching we have to understand something about teaching. Teaching is not about a person giving information to someone else. That's talking. Teaching includes learning. For there to be a teaching process there must be a learning process, which means if someone is just communicating their data and the other person isn't getting it, then there's not

---
[44] Ibid., 113.
[45] Ibid.

communication, there's just talking. So this particular prescription is correct in that respect. Biblical exposition isn't just about talking. If we began discussing principles of trigonometry with a five-year-old, it's likely that the average five-year old will not able to understand the more advanced concepts. But the problem with the mathematical analogy is that we are not teaching trigonometry to five-year olds. We're teaching God's word to people who are supposed to be new creations in Christ who are commanded to let the word of Christ richly dwell in them. Ironically, Colossians 3:16 exhorts believers to teach one another. How can they do that if they remain "untrained parishioners?"

So the question is how to help an untrained parishioner become a trained parishioner. Paul tells us in passages like Romans 12:1-2 (transformation by the renewing of the mind) and Ephesians 4:11-12 (the teaching of God's word for the equipping of saints). It isn't the pastor's job to equip saints. The pastor's job is to teach the word so that the saints will be equipped. It is the word that does the equipping (2 Tim 3:16-17), and the meaning of Scripture must not be lost in the transition from the exegetical process to the expositional one.

SECTION II

OVERVIEW OF
THE EXEGETICAL PROCESS

SECTION II: OVERVIEW OF THE EXEGETICAL PROCESS

8

Nine Steps for Biblical Exegesis and Exposition: Preliminary Considerations

Bible study is not the exclusive possession of pastors or career theologians. All believers are called to know God – in fact, Jesus explains that knowing God is the very core of eternal life (Jn 17:3). Consequently, if we want to live well, we need to allow His word to dwell richly in us (Col 3:16) and handle it accurately (2 Tim 2:15). We are all accountable for what we do with God's word, and we should all be diligent to understand it. In addition to helping us know God better, it equips us with all we need to accomplish all He intends for us (2 Tim 3:16-17).

The method described here is introduced in *Prolegomena on Biblical Hermeneutics and Method* (Tyndale Seminary Press, 2012). Admittedly, this isn't the only way to exegete the Bible; some might reorder the steps or combine some of them, but the basic elements are generally considered to be important components of the exegetical process. This particular approach is a straightforward, organized method that will help Bible students ensure they aren't missing important aspects of inquiry.

Before delving into the method, we need to consider three

vital prefatory concepts. First: prayer. Notice that prayer isn't listed as a step in the process. That is for the very simple reason that we are to pray without ceasing (1 Thes 5:17). If we say a nice prayer before Bible study, that is all well and good, but we must remember that the process of Bible study should be a part of our communion with God. For believers there should be no distinction between academic and devotional study of the Bible. We should always be in the text for the purpose of knowing Him better and spending time with Him. So we should be in prayer throughout the entire process of exegesis and exposition – not just when we begin and end.

Second, we need to remember that we are not studying to teach someone else. We are studying for our own growth in Him, and to deepen our relationship with Him. Too often we take in information with the purpose of giving it to others, and we forget to first apply it to ourselves. Ezra provides us a beautiful example: he sought to learn the Law of the Lord, to practice it, and to teach it (Ezra 7:10). He got the order right: learn, do, and then if God provides opportunity – teach.

Finally, we need to understand that the Bible itself gives us the method of interpreting the Bible, so we don't need to be puzzled about how to interpret the text. For example, when God told Adam about the fruit of the tree of the knowledge of good and evil (Gen 2:15), it took a deception from Satan to muddy the meaning (Gen 3:1ff). Later, God held Adam and Eve accountable for literally violating His literal command (Gen 3:11ff). When God told Noah to build a boat (Gen 6:14), Noah didn't consider there to be some deep spiritual meaning – he built a boat (Gen 6:22)! When God told Abraham to go (Gen 12:1), Abraham went (Gen 12:4). Like Adam, Noah, and Abraham, we need to take God's words at face value. This is what the literal, grammatical-historical interpretive method is all about: *literal*, in that it takes the text naturally; *grammatical*, in that it recognizes the importance of following the grammatical rules of the original language; and *historical*, in that it recognizes the importance of the times and the historical contexts in which the words were originally written.

Once we understand the importance of Bible study, the role of prayer and personal application, and the centrality of interpretive method, we can embark on the exegetical journey. The nine steps for Biblical exegesis and exposition are:

(1) Verify Text and Translation
(2) Understand Background and Context
(3) Identify Structure
(4) Identify Grammatical and Syntactical Keys
(5) Identify Lexical Keys
(6) Identify Biblical Context
(7) Identify Theological Context
(8) Secondary Verification
(9) Development of Exposition

Note that the first seven steps are actually exegesis (drawing from the text itself). We need to be sure we are avoiding eisegesis (reading ideas into the text) throughout these steps. Step eight is an assessment of our exegetical work, and step nine puts the passage to further use (hopefully, we are already putting the passage to proper use throughout the entire process of studying it).

9
Nine Steps for Biblical Exegesis and Exposition: (1) Verify Text and Translation

There are three components to this first step: verify the boundaries of the text, verify the best reading of the text, and write a brief passage overview. Keep in mind that at every step some understanding of the original languages is a necessity, because the Bible was originally written in Hebrew, Aramaic, and Greek. The exegete doesn't have to be an expert in Biblical languages, but one should be able to read at least a little bit and have a working knowledge of available tools and how to use them, because true exegesis can't be done in a secondary language. There are many inexpensive (and even free) Bible software options that can help make the study and application of Biblical languages accessible, so there is little excuse for not interacting at least to some extent with the languages.

First, verify the boundaries of the passage. Recognize that the passage is a propositional unit and a complete thought. Understand where that thought begins and ends. Dividing a passage unnaturally can cause tremendous misunderstanding. For example, compare the ending of Matthew 16 with Mark 9:1-2. Keep in mind that chapter and verse divisions were not part of the original text but were added much later. Sometimes they are helpful, other times not.

Next, verify the best reading of the text. There are many manuscripts in the original languages, and consequently there are frequent variants in the text. Usually the differences are not of great significance, but sometimes they can be. A series of external and internal evidences can be helpful for recognizing the best reading. External considerations include age of manuscripts and geographical distance between agreeing manuscripts. Internal considerations include consistency in style, length of reading (shorter preferred over longer) and difficulty of reading (difficult preferred over simpler).

The Majority Text of the New Testament (or Byzantine), is a comparison of extant manuscripts, deriving from them the most numerically prominent readings. Consequently, the Majority Text favors more recent manuscripts, since they are more numerous. Hodges and Farstad's Greek New Testament[46] is based upon the Majority Text.

The Textus Receptus, or Received Text (upon which the KJV is based) is primarily derived from editions related to Erasmus' 1516 edition of the Greek New Testament. Being rooted in a few later manuscripts, the Textus Receptus largely resembles the Majority Text, though there are some one thousand differences between the Textus Receptus and Majority Text.

The Critical Text refers to the method employed by editions such as Westcott-Hort[47] and Nestle-Aland,[48] and which prefers earlier manuscripts to the later and more numerous. The Westcott-

---

[46] Zane Hodges and Arthur Farstad, *The Greek New Testament According to the Majority Text*, 2nd *Edition* (Nashville, TN: Thomas Nelson, 1985).
[47] B.F Westcott and F.J.A Hort, *Westcott–Hort Greek New Testament With Dictionary* (Peabody, MA: Hendrickson, 2007).
[48] Institute for New Testament Textual Research, *Novum Testamentum Graece: Nestle–Aland* (Stuttgart: German Bible Society, 2012).

Hort Critical Text differs from the Received Text in some thirty-six hundred instances, while Nestle-Aland differs some thirty-three hundred times.

The following are instances of agreements between the Majority and Received Texts that differ from the Critical Texts:

>Matthew 5:44, 6:13, 17:21, 18:11, 20:16, 20:22,23, 23:14, 24:36
>Mark 6:11, 7:8,16, 9:43-46, 9:49, 10:24, 11:26, 14:19, 15:28, 16:9-20
>Luke 1:28, 9:55-56, 11:2-4, 11:11, 22:43-44, 23:17, 23:34
>John 1:18, 5:3-4, 6:69, 7:53-8:11, 59
>Acts 2:30, 13:42, 15:42, 18:21, 23:9, 24:6-8, 28:29
>Romans 8:1, 10:15, 11:6, 14:6, 16:24
>1 Corinthians 6:20, 9:20, 14:38
>Galatians 3:1
>Ephesians 5:30
>Philippians 3:16
>1 Timothy 6:5
>Hebrews 10:34
>1 Peter 2:2
>1 Peter 4:14
>2 Peter 1:21
>1 John 3:1
>1 John 4:3
>1 John 5:13
>Jude 22-23, 25
>Revelation 22:14

In many of these instances, the Majority and Received Texts have words, phrases, verses, or in some cases large sections that are not in the Critical Texts.

The Hebrew Bible relies primarily on the Masoretic Text, the earliest of which is dated around the tenth century. The Masoretes showed remarkable skill and care in reproducing the text, and while there are some variants, they are relatively few and insignificant. Critical editions of the Hebrew Bible, such as *Biblia Hebraica Stuttgartensia*[49] include critical apparatus' that also consider ancient translations and versions, including the Dead Sea Scrolls, Samaritan Pentateuch, Aramaic Targums, Septuagint, Syriac Peshitta, and Vulgate.

The exegete should compare the various manuscripts to determine the best reading, and in doing so will quickly discover the underlying premises behind the two competing traditions. The external and internal evidences are interpreted differently by the majority and critical schools. This author prefers the critical method and interpretation of evidences, not because of the notable personalities involved, but because only the critical method allows the interlocutor to examine all the variants. Neither the Majority nor Received Texts offer such transparency (though Hodges-Farstad does attempt a critical approach to the Majority tradition).

In the Critical approach, external evidences include:

(1) That which is supported by earliest external sources is generally authentic.
(2) Age, location, and character, rather than number of manuscripts is more determinate of authenticity.
(3) When there is broadly evidenced conflict, special attention should be placed on agreement between manuscripts originally separated by the greatest distances.
(4) Great care and attention to detail must be used in following these evidences.

Likewise, internal evidences considered in the Critical approach include:

---

[49] Karl Elliger and Wilhelm Rudolph, *Biblia Hebraica Stuttgartensia* (Stuttgart: German Bible Society, 1997).

(1) The reading which is congruent with a writer's style, nature, and context is to be preferred over that which lacks these evidences.
(2) Shorter reading is preferred over the longer.
(3) The difficult reading is preferred over the simpler.
(4) The reading from which other readings most likely developed is to be preferred (e.g., 1 Thes 2:7 *nepioi* vs. *epioi*).[50]

After completing these two steps, write a brief overview of the passage including four components:

(1) Identify and summarize the variants discovered in the text,
(2) Briefly summarize the passage,
(3) Summarize your current understanding of the theological impact of the passage, and
(4) Identify your own doctrinal presuppositions in approaching the passage.

Thinking through each of these aspects will help the reader handle the passage with accuracy and open mindedness.

---

[50] Adapted from Milton Terry, *Biblical Hermeneutics* (Eugene, OR: Wipf and Stock, 1997), 132-133.

10

Nine Steps for Biblical Exegesis and Exposition: (2) Understand Background and Context

Once we have established the boundaries of the passage we are studying, and are confident that we have the best reading, we can march ahead in our exegesis. In the second step, we seek to understand the background and context of the passage.

First, we need to identify and explain the significance of literary form and genre. We should not apply different hermeneutic approaches for different genres – we need to be consistent in our methodology, but recognizing the type of literature will help us in a number of these steps.

There are four basic literary forms used in the Bible: narrative, poetry, prophecy, and epistle. Narrative in the Bible has two functions: primary and complementary. *Primary historical narrative* advances the chronology of Biblical history, including Genesis, Exodus, Numbers, Joshua, Judges, 1 and 2 Samuel, 1 and 2 Kings, Ezra, Nehemiah, The Gospels, and Acts. *Complementary Historical Narrative* complements as contemporaries of the primary historical narratives. This category includes Job, Leviticus, Deuteronomy, Ruth, 1 and 2 Chronicles, and Esther. *Poetry and Praise* includes Psalms, Proverbs, Ecclesiastes, Song of Solomon, and Lamentations.

Prophecy is often interspersed with historical narrative and poetry, this form presents, usually, God's revelation of judgment and restoration. Prophetic books include Isaiah, Jeremiah, Ezekiel, Daniel (although not included in the Nebi'im section of the Hebrew Old Testament, its form is prophetic and complementary historical), the twelve Minor Prophets, and the New Testament book of Revelation. *Epistles* – or letters include the Pauline and general epistles (Hebrews, James, 1 and 2 Peter, 1, 2, and 3 John, and Jude).

Genres like near east myth, Greco-Roman bios, and apocalyptic are not employed by Biblical literature. While some argue that Genesis is Near-East myth, Genesis claims to be and is attested to be historical narrative. While some perceive the Gospels as Greco-Roman bios, the Gospels themselves claim to be historical narratives representing actual events. While some argue that Daniel and Revelation are apocalyptic, these two books have internal claims to and external attestation of historical narrative and prophecy. Once we understand the literary genre, we can have some insight into the building blocks of the book, and of the passage we are handling.

Next, to continue our pursuit of the background and context, we need to research key questions regarding the background of the book – questions like (1) Who wrote this book? (2) To whom is the book addressed? (3) Where was it written? (4) When was it written? (5) What was the occasion of the writing? (6) What was the purpose for the writing? (7) What were the circumstances of the author when he wrote? (8) What were the circumstances of those to whom he wrote? (9) What glimpses does the book give into the life and character of the author? (10) What are the leading ideas of the book? (11) What is the central truth of the book? (12) What are the characteristics of the book? These are a few important questions we try to answer from the text itself. If we can't find answers in the text (or nearby texts), then for now we accept our limitations and press on to other questions.

From our pursuit of background and context, we should summarize our findings, highlighting the following elements: historical, social, geographical, authorship, date, and literary form. Finally, we should explain how these findings are significant to the interpretation of the passage.

Case Study: What Kind of Literature is Genesis 1?

The Bible contains four basic genres of literature: historical narrative, poetry, prophetic, and epistolary. The genre classification of Genesis 1 is very important for our understanding of the overall message of Scripture, because the chapter deals with so many foundational details, including the character of God, the nature of creation, and the backdrop for how we understand sin and redemption.

For example, in Genesis 1:26-28 God is recorded as having a very important conversation with Himself. If this conversation literally happened, then the passage is an early and potent evidence for the concept of the triunity of the Godhead. On the other hand, if the conversation can be dismissed as figurative language – as anthropomorphism, for example – then perhaps we would not conclude that the conversation actually happened, but that it was instead simply a poetic expression.

Clearly Genesis 1 is neither prophetic nor epistolary, as it makes no statements regarding the future beyond its immediate context, nor is it addressed to any particular recipients. So the genre question regarding Genesis 1 is between historical narrative and Hebrew poetry. That Genesis 1 is Hebrew poetry is a fairly common view, but not necessarily because of the literary characteristics of the chapter, but rather because of the quality of the propositions made – huge statements, for sure. But does this chapter contain enough actual poetic characteristics to be considered poetry, or is it more obviously historical narrative?

Hebrew poetry is discernible by a number of literary devices

– especially parallelism (the repetition of one thing in two or more different ways). Parallelism is evident in passages like Psalm 119:105: "Your word is a lamp to my feet and a light to my path" (NASB). What is particularly striking about Hebrew poetic parallelism is that it usually occurs within close proximities – in other words, within narrow, rather than broad contexts.

Genesis 1 lacks these parallelisms. There are certainly propositions connected by the Hebrew *vav*, which often functions as the English conjunction *and*. But in each of these cases in Genesis 1, the propositions following the conjunctions are not poetic restatements of the earlier propositions, but rather communicate resulting conditions of the earlier propositions. To illustrate, let's examine each *vav* conjunction in the first 5 verses, represented by the English and in the list below.

> 1:1 heavens *and* the earth – two different entities, no restatement.
>
> 1:2 and the earth was – prefixes the noun, followed by a verb, no restatement.
> 1:2 formless *and* void – without form and empty, two distinct characteristics, no restatement.
> 1:2 and darkness was over the surface of the waters – not a restatement, having nothing to do with the previous descriptions, but adding detail.
> 1:2 and the Spirit of God was moving over the surface of the waters. – unless we are to understand that the darkness and the Spirit of God are synonymous, then there is no parallelism here either.
>
> 1:3 and God said – again, followed by a new verb, no restatement.
> 1:3 and there was light – followed by distinct verb, a result

of the former statement, not a restatement of it.

1:4 and God saw – new verb describing God's action.
1:4 and God separated – verb distinct from that of the previous proposition (separating is not a restatement of seeing).

1:5 and God called the light day
1:5 and the darkness He called night
1:5 and there was evening
1:5 and there was morning – in none of the four instances of the vav in verse 5 is there restatement of a previous proposition.

These samples show no particular correspondence to Hebrew poetry at all.

It is also helpful to note an important grammatical principle of Biblical Hebrew: a literary device called the vav consecutive: when the first verb is in the perfect tense and subsequent verbs are imperfect, the vavs are consecutive, and denote a continuous narrative in the past. (Incidentally, in prophetic literature, there is continuous narrative referring to the future, which is indicated by the first verb in the imperfect, and subsequent verbs in the narrative in the perfect.)

Let's take a quick look at the verbs in these same five verses:

1:1 (bara, created) – perfect

1:2 (hayetah, it was) – perfect
1:2 (merakepet, was hovering) – piel intensive

1:3 (wayyomer, and He said) – imperfect
1:3 (yehiy, let there be) – imperfect
1:3 (yehiy, and there was) – imperfect

1:4 (yereh, and saw) – imperfect
1:4 (wayabedel, and caused to be divided) – hiphil imperfect

1:5 (wayiqerah, and called) – imperfect
1:5 (qarah, called) – perfect
1:5 (wayehiy, and it was) – imperfect
1:5 (wayehiy, and it was) – imperfect

Verse 1 makes a statement, that God created the heavens and the earth. Verse 2 introduces an explicative narrative, with vav consecutives up to the middle of verse 5. The perfect verb in verse 5 is followed by vav consecutives with the time stamp (it was evening and it was morning one day). Simply put, the series and placement of vav consecutives and time stamps makes this a series of historical narratives. In short there are several overwhelming evidences that Genesis 1 is historical narrative and not poetic:

- Genesis 1 does not contain the parallelism that is characteristic of Hebrew poetry.
- Genesis 1 does contain repeated instances of the vav consecutive, indicating continuous narrative of the past.
- Further, Genesis 1 does also contain sequential time stamps (evening and morning, one day-second, etc.)

The text of Genesis 1, taken at face value, should be recognized as historical narrative and not poetic. This is very significant for our understanding of the things discussed in Genesis 1. God's character is as described. The heavens and earth were created as described. What follows in Genesis is grounded on the platform of historicity, so what we understand from the Biblical record about humanity, sin, and salvation is reliable and based on historical truth.

Case Study: Is the Book of Revelation Apocalyptic Literature?

It may seem odd to suggest that the book entitled *Apocalupsis* does not belong to the genre of literature commonly referred to as apocalyptic, nonetheless that is my suggestion here. The term employed in the title of the book denotes a revelation or disclosure.[51] While this particular *revealing* or *disclosing* describes a broad swathe of eschatological events, it is not its own literary genre.

Apocalyptic as a genre is described as "characteristically pseudonymous; it takes narrative form, employs esoteric language, expresses a pessimistic view of the present, and treats the final events as imminent."[52] Henry Barclay Swete (Cambridge), even while arguing that Revelation is apocalyptic literature, admits that the book differs from that genre, in that the book of Revelation (1) is not pseudepigraphic, (2) it engages a specific audience [i.e., seven churches], (3) has a significant church focus, rather than a purely Israel nation-centered focus, and (4) includes notes of insight and foresight that are more indicative of inspiration than is found in earlier extra-biblical apocalyptic literature.[53]

Despite these differences between Revelation and extra-biblical apocalyptic literature, Swete considered the gift of revelation to be not entirely the same as the gift of prophecy, and thus revelation stood distinct as a particular manifestation of the spirit,[54] "in which the spirit of the prophet seemed to be carried up

---

[51] Walter Bauer, William Arndt, and F. Wilbur Gingrich, *A Greek English Lexicon of the New Testament and Other Early Christian Literature* (Chicago, IL: University of Chicago Press, 1957), 114.
[52] Robert Lerner, "apocalyptic language" at Brittanica.com, viewed at http://www.britannica.com/EBchecked/topic/29733/apocalyptic-literature.
[53] Henry Barclay Swete, *The Apocalypse of John, Third Edition* (London: MacMillan and Co., 1911), xxviii-xxx.
[54] Ibid., xxiii.

into a higher sphere, endowed for the time with new powers of vision, and enabled to hear words which could not be reproduced in the terms of human thought, or could be reproduced only through the medium of symbolic imagery."[55]

The irony of Swete's commentary here is that in footnote he appeals to 1 Corinthians 12:4, a passage in which Paul describes words heard in the third heaven which man is not permitted to speak. However, in Revelation, John is given a direct commission to record all of what he sees. Further, in 1:3 and 22:18 there are blessings and warnings for those who hear the words written in the prophecy, and we read seven times in chapters 2-3 and once again in 13:7 the repeated refrain, "he who has an ear, let him hear…" In the first seven instances, the content is expressly, "what the Spirit says to the churches."

As for the gift of revelation as a unique manifestation of the Spirit, no such gift is evident in Revelation (or anywhere else in the NT, for that matter). Swete appeals to Ephesians 1:17 as in instance of the "gift of spiritual vision,"[56] and while the passage indeed uses the noun (ἀποκαλύψεως), it is in the context of a request made on behalf of all believers (or at least all believers in Ephesus at the time). In short, Paul is not requesting that believers be granted a mystical gift (in the sense Swete employs the term – as an ability), but that believers be granted a spirit of wisdom and revelation in the knowledge of Christ. This deeper, more mature understanding of Christ seems Paul's common expectation for all believers, not some mystical enlightenment for only an elite few.

While the unsurprising dissimilarities between Revelation and extra-biblical apocalyptic literature are convincing enough to this writer that Revelation should not be considered a part of the apocalyptic genre, the internal genre-identification is dispositive. Revelation 1:3 and 22:7, 10, 18, and 19 all refer to the writing as

---

[55] Ibid.
[56] Ibid., xxii.

prophecy. The final reference in 22:19 is *to the book of this the prophecy* (τοῦ βιβλίου τῆς προφητείας ταύτης). It is evident that the use of the term revelation or unveiling (Ἀποκάλυψις) in 1:1 is not a genre-technical term, but is rather an explanation of the content of the prophecy: the revealing of Jesus Christ.

The genre placement of the book has significant hermeneutic implications – in fact, the interpretation of the book is predetermined by the genre classification. If the book fits in the apocalyptic genre, then we shouldn't expect it to be understood literally at all. An apocalyptic genre placement would support the preterist interpretation (a non-literal view that the events were fulfilled during the first century), the historicist or continuist interpretation (a non-literal approach that views the book as describing events in the church between the apostolic age and the second coming of Christ), the idealist interpretation (a non-literal view that the book doesn't predict actual events at all, but rather symbolizes the epic struggle between good and evil), and the eclectic interpretation (a hybrid approach, popularized by George Ladd, this view combines the preterist and futurist interpretation).

On the other hand, only the futurist model (a literal interpretation in which the events described in the book, beyond chapters 2-3, are still yet in the future) is supported by the simple genre classification of the book as prophecy. The futuristic interpretive model is the only one of the five models that stems from the literal grammatical-historical hermeneutic, and is initially derived from the simple past-present-future commission of John in Revelation 1:19: "Therefore, write the things which you have seen, and the things which are, and the things which will take place after these things."

It should come as no surprise that those who prefer a non-literal interpretation of the book would also gravitate toward the apocalyptic classification, but it is surprising how many futurist interpreters likewise follow their non-literal colleagues in the apocalyptic classification. The simplest and most obvious approach is to call the book what it calls itself: *prophecy* – a prophecy regarding the unveiling of Christ, and which is largely about "the things which will take place after these things."

11

Nine Steps for Biblical Exegesis and Exposition: (3) Identify Structural Keys

After verifying the text and translation of the passage we are considering, and after examining the background and context, we need to identify the structural keys – or building blocks – of the book so that we can recognize shifts in thought or argument, and developments in the narrative. In some books, structural keys are easy to identify, while in others the structural keys take a bit more effort to discover. We start with reading the entire book a few times:

> (1) The first reading is to grasp the overall message. In this introductory reading we observe some key words and themes. While not ignoring detail, this is a flyover to gain perspective on the whole picture.

> (2) The second time through the book, we read it to discern the major thoughts and divisions, to perceive the more specific themes and dialogic divisions of the text.

> (3) In the third reading we begin to give further attention to

individual contexts and begin to identify difficult or challenging passages.

(4) After we have read the book a few times, we can outline the book based on identified internal divisions that we have identified.

(5) Continuing to read, we can develop an understanding of the introductory material and setting, at this point only from internal clues (as opposed to relying on secondary source data), and as we continue reading to verify what we have observed thus far, and then we have some foundational background to begin the formal work of outlining and analyzing the text.

Incidentally, it has been said that before one should ever teach a passage, they should have read it at least twenty-five times, and while that statement sounds hyperbolic, it isn't far from the truth. The point is simply that we need to spend time reading God's word, if we expect to have any understanding of it.

To illustrate the handling of structural keys, we can consider some Biblical books. Genesis is divided in two different ways. First, by the Hebrew *toledoth* (translated as "the generations of" or "the account" as in Gen 5:1, 6:9, 10:1, etc.):

Outline of Genesis Based on *toledoth*:

1:1-2:3 Introduction: Creation (no *toledoth*)
2:4-4:26 *toledoth* of the Heavens and Earth
5:1-6:8 *toledoth* of Adam
6:9-9:29 *toledoth* of Noah
10:1-11:9 *toledoth* of Shem, Ham, and Japheth
11:10-26 *toledoth* of Shem

11:27-25:11 *toledoth* of Terah
25:12-18 *toledoth* of Ishmael
25:19-35:29 *toledoth* of Isaac
36:1-37:1 *toledoth* of Esau[57]
37:2-50:26 *toledoth* of Jacob

A secondary approach to outlining Genesis is by named key events and persons. Genesis develops God's working in history through a particular lineage, as reflected in the outline below (which follows the narrative shifts from key person to key person, rather than the *toledoth* divisions).

Outline of Genesis Based on Key Events and Persons:

1-2 Creation
3 The Fall
4 Abel, Cain, and Seth
5-10 Noah, the Flood, and the Noahic Covenant
11 The Tower of Babel
12-25:11 Abraham
25:12-27:46 Isaac
28-36 Jacob
37-50 God Preserves Israel Through Joseph

In Habakkuk, the structural keys are the shifts in the dialogue, as evidenced by the pronouns used. Habakkuk asks God two questions, God answers them, and then Habakkuk offers a prayer of praise and trust. The pronouns in 1:1-4 are *I*, referencing Habakkuk, and *You*, referencing the Lord. The pronouns shift in 1:5-11, as in verse 5 the *I* refers to the one doing something

---

[57] The term *toledoth* is also used in 36:9, as a continuation from 36:1. The term isn't used in the first division (1:1-2:3), so there are eleven distinct sections, and ten instances of *toledoth*, though the term is not used in every division.

incredible (including raising up the Chaldeans, something in which Habakkuk had no part), and the *you* addresses the incredulous observer – Habakkuk, in this case.

We observe another shift in 1:12, as the *You* speaks of God, while the *my* indicates an individual who is addressing God, and representing *we*, those who will not die because of God's activity. The next transition is not found in 2:1, but rather in 2:2b, as the *I* of 2:1 is the same as in 1:12. In 2:2b, the Lord (identified in the third person) addresses His listener (*me*, 2:2a), and the pronouns remain consistent until the next transition in 3:1 which introduces a new literary component (a prayer), and which is followed by a shift in pronouns (Habakkuk refers to himself in the first person and to the Lord in the second person). Notice especially how the chapter and verse division strangely displaces the transition in 2:2, illustrating a degree of limitation in the chapter and verse system we employ.

Outline of Habakkuk Based on Dialogic Structural Keys:

1:1-4 Habakkuk's First Question:
    Why is Wickedness Not Judged?
1:5-11 God's Answer:
    Judgment is Coming (Chaldeans)
1:12-2:1 Habakkuk's Second Question:
    Why Use the Wicked to Judge?
2:2-20 God's Answer:
    The Five Woes
3 Habakkuk's Prayer:
    Rejoicing in God's Sovereignty

Chiasm is a literary structure in which the pattern resembles half of the Greek letter *chi* (x), and in which the center of the chiasm is the emphatic point rather than the introductory or concluding matter, as in more narrative literary structure. In Jeremiah's

Lamentations, for example, chapters 1 and 5 are similar to each other, and chapters 2 and 4 bear similarity to one another, but chapter 3 stands alone as the central focus of the book, revealing a chiastic structure. Notice 3:18-26 and the tremendous emphasis there.

Lamentations has another set of structural keys besides chiasm: chapters 1-4 are written in acrostic form, and chapter 5 is not. So in that way, chapter 5 is set apart. Lamentations has two layers of emphasis (not two layers of meaning): (1) the narrative climax of chapter 5, which is Jeremiah's prayer for mercy, as set apart by the non-acrostic structure, and (2) the chiastic emphasis of 3:18-26.

Chiastic Outline of Lamentations:

    A. Chapter 1– Weeping For Judgment on Israel
        B. Chapter 2 – Judgment: Thorough, Deserved
            C. Chapter 3 – Hope in God
        B2. Chapter 4 – Judgment: Detailed
    A2. Chapter 5 – Praying for Mercy on Israel

John's Gospel also possesses readily apparent structural keys. John identifies his purpose for writing in John 20:30-31 – so that his readers would be believing in Christ, and have life. The primary device John appeals to is recorded *signs* (*semaion,* used seventeen times in John) that point to the Person and work of Christ, and in so doing form the skeletal system of John's Gospel. Notice, for example, the connection between John 20:30, John 2:11, and each of the other occurrences of *semaion* in John's Gospel:

2:11	This **beginning of His signs** Jesus did in Cana of Galilee, and manifested His glory, and His disciples believed in Him.	Ταύτην ἐποίησεν ἀρχὴν τῶν **σημείων** ὁ Ἰησοῦς ἐν Κανὰ τῆς Γαλιλαίας καὶ ἐφανέρωσεν τὴν δόξαν αὐτοῦ, καὶ ἐπίστευσαν εἰς αὐτὸν οἱ μαθηταὶ αὐτοῦ.
2:18	The Jews then said to Him, "What **sign** do You show us as your authority for doing these things?"	Ἀπεκρίθησαν οὖν οἱ Ἰουδαῖοι καὶ εἶπαν αὐτῷ τί **σημεῖον** δεικνύεις ἡμῖν ὅτι ταῦτα ποιεῖς;
2:23	Now when He was in Jerusalem at the Passover, during the feast, many believed in His name, observing His **signs** which He was doing.	Ὡς δὲ ἦν ἐν τοῖς Ἱεροσολύμοις ἐν τῷ πάσχα ἐν τῇ ἑορτῇ, πολλοὶ ἐπίστευσαν εἰς τὸ ὄνομα αὐτοῦ θεωροῦντες αὐτοῦ τὰ **σημεῖα** ἃ ἐποίει∑
3:2	this man came to Jesus by night and said to Him, "Rabbi, we know that You have come from God *as* a teacher; for no one can do these **signs** that You do unless God is with him."	οὗτος ἦλθεν πρὸς αὐτὸν νυκτὸς καὶ εἶπεν αὐτῷ ῥαββί, οἴδαμεν ὅτι ἀπὸ θεοῦ ἐλήλυθας διδάσκαλος οὐδεὶς γὰρ δύναται ταῦτα τὰ **σημεῖα** ποιεῖν ἃ σὺ ποιεῖς, ἐὰν μὴ ᾖ ὁ θεὸς μετ' αὐτοῦ.
4:48	So Jesus said to him, "Unless you *people* see **signs** and wonders, you *simply* will not believe."	εἶπεν οὖν ὁ Ἰησοῦς πρὸς αὐτόν ἐὰν μὴ **σημεῖα** καὶ τέρατα ἴδητε, οὐ μὴ πιστεύσητε.
4:54	This is again **a second sign** that Jesus performed when He had come out of Judea into Galilee.	Τοῦτο [δὲ] πάλιν δεύτερον **σημεῖον** ἐποίησεν ὁ Ἰησοῦς ἐλθὼν ἐκ τῆς Ἰουδαίας εἰς τὴν Γαλιλαίαν.
6:2	A large crowd followed Him, because they saw the **signs** which He was performing (see chapter 5) on those who were sick.	ἠκολούθει δὲ αὐτῷ ὄχλος πολύς, ὅτι ἐθεώρουν τὰ **σημεῖα** ἃ ἐποίει ἐπὶ τῶν ἀσθενούντων.
6:14	Therefore when the people saw the **sign** which He had performed, they said, "This is truly the Prophet who is to come into the world."	Οἱ οὖν ἄνθρωποι ἰδόντες ὃ ἐποίησεν **σημεῖον** ἔλεγον ὅτι οὗτός ἐστιν ἀληθῶς ὁ προφήτης ὁ ἐρχόμενος εἰς τὸν κόσμον.
6:26	Jesus answered them and said, "Truly, truly, I say to you, you seek Me, not because you saw **signs**, but because you ate of the loaves and were filled.	Ἀπεκρίθη αὐτοῖς ὁ Ἰησοῦς καὶ εἶπεν ἀμὴν ἀμὴν λέγω ὑμῖν, ζητεῖτέ με οὐχ ὅτι εἴδετε **σημεῖα**, ἀλλ' ὅτι ἐφάγετε ἐκ τῶν ἄρτων καὶ ἐχορτάσθητε.

SECTION II: OVERVIEW OF THE EXEGETICAL PROCESS 75

6:30 So they said to Him, "What then do You do for a **sign**, so that we may see, and believe You? What work do You perform?

Εἶπον οὖν αὐτῷ τί οὖν ποιεῖς σὺ **σημεῖον**, ἵνα ἴδωμεν καὶ πιστεύσωμέν σοι; τί ἐργάζῃ;

7:31 But many of the crowd believed in Him; and they were saying, "When the Christ comes, He will not perform more **signs** than those which this man has, will He?"

Ἐκ τοῦ ὄχλου δὲ πολλοὶ ἐπίστευσαν εἰς αὐτὸν καὶ ἔλεγον ὁ χριστὸς ὅταν ἔλθῃ μὴ πλείονα **σημεῖα** ποιήσει ὧν οὗτος ἐποίησεν;

9:16 Therefore some of the Pharisees were saying, "This man is not from God, because He does not keep the Sabbath." But others were saying, "How can a man who is a sinner perform such **signs?**" And there was a division among them.

ἔλεγον οὖν ἐκ τῶν Φαρισαίων τινές οὐκ ἔστιν οὗτος παρὰ θεοῦ ὁ ἄνθρωπος, ὅτι τὸ σάββατον οὐ τηρεῖ. ἄλλοι [δὲ] ἔλεγονΣ πῶς δύναται ἄνθρωπος ἁμαρτωλὸς τοιαῦτα **σημεῖα** ποιεῖν; καὶ σχίσμα ἦν ἐν αὐτοῖς.

10:41 Many came to Him and were saying, "While John performed no **sign**, yet everything John said about this man was true."

καὶ πολλοὶ ἦλθον πρὸς αὐτὸν καὶ ἔλεγον ὅτι Ἰωάννης μὲν **σημεῖον** ἐποίησεν οὐδέν, πάντα δὲ ὅσα εἶπεν Ἰωάννης περὶ τούτου ἀληθῆ ἦν.

11:47 Therefore the chief priests and the Pharisees convened a council, and were saying, "What are we doing? For this man is performing many **signs**.

Συνήγαγον οὖν οἱ ἀρχιερεῖς καὶ οἱ Φαρισαῖοι συνέδριον καὶ ἔλεγον τί ποιοῦμεν ὅτι οὗτος ὁ ἄνθρωπος πολλὰ ποιεῖ **σημεῖα**;

12:18 For this reason also the people went and met Him, because they heard that He had performed this **sign**.

διὰ τοῦτο [καὶ] ὑπήντησεν αὐτῷ ὁ ὄχλος, ὅτι ἤκουσαν τοῦτο αὐτὸν πεποιηκέναι τὸ **σημεῖον**.

12:37 But though He had performed so many signs before them, *yet* they were not believing in Him.

Τοσαῦτα δὲ αὐτοῦ σημεῖα πεποιηκότος ἔμπροσθεν αὐτῶν οὐκ ἐπίστευον εἰς αὐτόν,

20:30 Therefore many other **signs** Jesus also performed in the presence of the disciples, which are not written in this book;

Πολλὰ μὲν οὖν καὶ ἄλλα **σημεῖα** ἐποίησεν ὁ Ἰησοῦς ἐνώπιον τῶν μαθητῶν [αὐτοῦ], ἃ οὐκ ἔστιν γεγραμμένα ἐν τῷ βιβλίῳ τούτῳ

Outline of John's Gospel Based on Chronological *semaion:*

1-12 Presentation of the God-man
    1:1-34 The Word and His Witness
    1:35-51 His Disciples
    2:1-12 His First Sign: Water Into Wine
    2:13-25 His Zeal: Cleansing the Temple
    3:1-21 His Teaching: Second Birth, Nicodemus
    3:22-36 His Witness: John's Teaching
    4:1-45 His Compassion: The Woman at the Well
    4:46-54 His Second Sign: Healing the Official's Son
    5 His Third Sign: Sabbath Healing, Explanation
    6 His Fourth and Fifth Signs (Feeding 5k, Walking on Water) and Explanation (Bread of Life)
    7:1-52 His Authority: Teaching at the Feast of Booths
    7:53-8:11 His Mercy: Woman Caught in Adultery
    8:12-8:59 His Presentation and Rejection
    9-10 His Sixth Sign: Healing the Man Born Blind and Explanation
    11:1-46 His Seventh Sign: Lazarus Raised and Explanation
    11:47-57 His Opponents: Chief Priests and Pharisees
    12 His Hour Begun: Anointing, Triumphal Entry, and Death Foretold

13-17 Explanation by the God-man
    13-14 His Disciples Prepared: His Example, Betrayal Foretold, Holy Spirit Promised
    15 His Instruction: Parable of the Vine, Command to Love, Hatred by the World
    16 His Warnings: Hatred by the World, Holy Spirit Promised, His Program
    17 His Prayer

18-21 Verification of the God-man
    18 His Betrayal, Arrest, and Trial
    19 His Crucifixion and Burial
    20-21 His Resurrection and Appearances

The narrative and geographical divisions of Acts 1:8 provide an outline of the book. Acts can also be outlined based on prominent characters (i.e., Peter and Paul):

The Book of Acts Outlined Based on Geography and Prominent Persons:

1:1-8:3 Jerusalem
            1:1-12:23 Ministry of Peter
    1 Commission and Preparation of the Disciples
    2 Pentecost: Coming of the Holy Spirit, Peter's Explanation, Birth of the Church
    3 Peter's Miracle (Lame Beggar Healed) and Explanation
    4:1-31 Peter and John Arrested and Released
    4:32-5:11 Purifying the Church: Ananias and Sapphira
    5:12-42 Peter and Apostles Arrested and Released
    6:1-7 Leadership in the Church: Seven Men Chosen
    6:8-8:3 Stephen's Ministry, Arrest, Defense, Murder

8:4-9:43 Judea and Samaria
    8:4-25 Philip, Peter and John in Samaria
    8:26-40 Philip and the Ethiopian Eunuch
    9:1-31 Saul's Conversion and Early Ministry
    9:32-43 Peter in Joppa: Raising of Tabitha

10:1-28:31 Outermost Parts of the Earth

78 INTEGRATING EXEGESIS AND EXPOSITION

> 10:1-11:18 Salvation and the Holy Spirit to the Gentiles: Peter and Cornelius
> 11:19-30 The Church at Antioch: First Called Christians
> 12:1-23 Arrrest and Release of Peter and Death of Herod
> *12:24-28:31 Ministry of Paul*
> 12:24-14:28 First Missionary Journey: Paul, Barnabus, and John Mark
> 15:1-35 Council of Jerusalem and James' Leadership
> 15:36-18:22 Second Missionary Journey: Paul and Silas
> 18:23-21:26 Third Missionary Journey
> 21:27-40 Paul Arrested
> 22:1-23:11 Paul's Defense Before the Jews and the Sanhedrin
> 23:12-35 Paul Protected: Plot Uncovered
> 24 Paul's Defense Before Felix
> 25:1-12 Paul's Defense Before Festus: Appeal to Caesar
> 25:13-26:32 Paul's Defense Before Agrippa
> 27-28 Paul Journeys to Rome

James repeatedly employs the phrase *my brethren* to emphasize or advance arguments in his letter. In 3:10-12 he uses the phrase repeatedly for emphasis within one pericope He also occasionally adds the adjective *beloved* to the phrase for emphasis (1:16, 19, 2:5). Here are the fifteen occurrences of *brethren* in James:

1:2	Consider it all joy, my **brethren**, when you encounter various trials,	Πᾶσαν χαρὰν ἡγήσασθε, **ἀδελφοί** μου, ὅταν πειρασμοῖς περιπέσητε ποικίλοις,
1:16	Do not be deceived, my beloved **brethren**.	Μὴ πλανᾶσθε, **ἀδελφοί** μου ἀγαπητοί.
1:19	*This* you know, my beloved **brethren**. But everyone must be quick to hear, slow to speak *and* slow to anger;	Ἴστε, **ἀδελφοί** μου ἀγαπητοίΣ ἔστω δὲ πᾶς ἄνθρωπος ταχὺς εἰς τὸ ἀκοῦσαι, βραδὺς εἰς τὸ λαλῆσαι, βραδὺς εἰς ὀργήνΣ

SECTION II: OVERVIEW OF THE EXEGETICAL PROCESS 79

2:1	My **brethren**, do not hold your faith in our glorious Lord Jesus Christ with *an attitude of* personal favoritism.	Ἀδελφοί μου, μὴ ἐν προσωπολημψίαις ἔχετε τὴν πίστιν τοῦ κυρίου ἡμῶν Ἰησοῦ Χριστοῦ τῆς δόξης.
2:5	Listen, my beloved **brethren**: did not God choose the poor of this world *to be* rich in faith and heirs of the kingdom which He promised to those who love Him?	Ἀκούσατε, **ἀδελφοί** μου ἀγαπητοί⸱ οὐχ ὁ θεὸς ἐξελέξατο τοὺς πτωχοὺς τῷ κόσμῳ πλουσίους ἐν πίστει καὶ κληρονόμους τῆς βασιλείας ἧς ἐπηγγείλατο τοῖς ἀγαπῶσιν αὐτόν;
2:14	What use is it, my **brethren**, if someone says he has faith but he has no works? Can that faith save him?	Τί τὸ ὄφελος, **ἀδελφοί** μου, ἐὰν πίστιν λέγῃ τις ἔχειν ἔργα δὲ μὴ ἔχῃ; μὴ δύναται ἡ πίστις σῶσαι αὐτόν;
3:1	Let not many *of you* become teachers, my **brethren**, knowing that as such we will incur a stricter judgment.	Μὴ πολλοὶ διδάσκαλοι γίνεσθε, **ἀδελφοί** μου, εἰδότες ὅτι μεῖζον κρίμα λημψόμεθα.
3:10	from the same mouth come *both* blessing and cursing. My **brethren**, these things ought not to be this way.	ἐκ τοῦ αὐτοῦ στόματος ἐξέρχεται εὐλογία καὶ κατάρα. οὐ χρή, **ἀδελφοί** μου, ταῦτα οὕτως γίνεσθαι.
3:12	Can a fig tree, my **brethren**, produce olives, or a vine produce figs? Nor *can* salt water produce fresh.	μὴ δύναται, **ἀδελφοί** μου, συκῆ ἐλαίας ποιῆσαι ἢ ἄμπελος σῦκα; οὔτε ἁλυκὸν γλυκὺ ποιῆσαι ὕδωρ.
4:11	Do not speak against one another, **brethren**. He who speaks against a brother or judges his brother, speaks against the law and judges the law; but if you judge the law, you are not a doer of the law but a judge *of it*.	Μὴ καταλαλεῖτε ἀλλήλων, **ἀδελφοί**. ὁ καταλαλῶν ἀδελφοῦ ἢ κρίνων τὸν ἀδελφὸν αὐτοῦ καταλαλεῖ νόμου καὶ κρίνει νόμον⸱ εἰ δὲ νόμον κρίνεις, οὐκ εἶ ποιητὴς νόμου ἀλλὰ κριτής.
5:7	Therefore be patient, **brethren**, until the coming of the Lord. The farmer waits for the precious produce of the soil, being patient about it, until it gets the early and late rains.	Μακροθυμήσατε οὖν, **ἀδελφοί**, ἕως τῆς παρουσίας τοῦ κυρίου. ἰδοὺ ὁ γεωργὸς ἐκδέχεται τὸν τίμιον καρπὸν τῆς γῆς μακροθυμῶν ἐπ' αὐτῷ ἕως λάβῃ πρόϊμον καὶ ὄψιμον.

5:9	Do not complain, **brethren**, against one another, so that you yourselves may not be judged; behold, the Judge is standing right at the door.	μὴ στενάζετε, **ἀδελφοί**, κατ' ἀλλήλων ἵνα μὴ κριθῆτεΣ ἰδοὺ ὁ κριτὴς πρὸ τῶν θυρῶν ἕστηκεν.
5:10	As an example, **brethren**, of suffering and patience, take the prophets who spoke in the name of the Lord.	ὑπόδειγμα λάβετε, **ἀδελφοί**, τῆς κακοπαθίας καὶ τῆς μακροθυμίας τοὺς προφήτας οἳ ἐλάλησαν ἐν τῷ ὀνόματι κυρίου.
5:12	But above all, my **brethren**, do not swear, either by heaven or by earth or with any other oath; but your yes is to be yes, and your no, no, so that you may not fall under judgment.	Πρὸ πάντων δέ, **ἀδελφοί** μου, μὴ ὀμνύετε μήτε τὸν οὐρανὸν μήτε τὴν γῆν μήτε ἄλλον τινὰ ὅρκονΣ ἤτω δὲ ὑμῶν τὸ ναὶ ναὶ καὶ τὸ οὒ οὔ, ἵνα μὴ ὑπὸ κρίσιν πέσητε.
5:19	My **brethren**, if any among you strays from the truth and one turns him back,	**Ἀδελφοί** μου, ἐάν τις ἐν ὑμῖν πλανηθῇ ἀπὸ τῆς ἀληθείας καὶ ἐπιστρέψῃ τις αὐτόν,

Topical Outline of James Considering "My Brethren" Keys:

1:1 Greeting

1:2-20 Church Age Conduct in Trials
        1:2-4 Joy and Purpose in Trials
        1:5-8 Wisdom in Trials
        1:9-11 High Position in Trials
        1:12 Perseverance and Prize of Trials
        1:13-20 Trials of Temptation and Sin

1:21-5:19 Church Age Conduct in Action
        1:21-27 Be a Doer of the Word
        2:1-13 Be Impartial
        2:14-26 Be Faithful: Demonstrate Works
        3:1-12 Be Pure of Tongue
        3:13-18 Be Wise

4:1-12 Sources of Dissension
4:13-17 Condemnation of the Proud
5:1-6 Condemnation of the (Unfaithful) Wealthy
5:7-11 Be Patient
5:12 Do Not Swear
5:13-18 Empathy and Prayer
5:19 Restoring Sinners

Revelation 1:19 provides a chronological key to the divisions of the prophetic book, considering past (the things which you have seen), present (the things which are), and future (the things which will take place after these things). Chapter 1 corresponds to the past tense, 2-3 with the present, and 4-22 with the future. Here is a more detailed outline based on these chronological structural keys:

Outline of Revelation From Chronological Keys of 1:19:

1 Things You Have Seen: The Commission of John

2-3 Things Which Are (Seven Letters)
    2:1-7 To Ephesus
    2:8-11 To Smyrna
    2:12-17 To Pergamum
    2:18-29 To Thyatira
    3:1-6 To Sardis
    3:7-13 To Philadelphia
    3:14-22 To Laodicea

4-22 Things Which Shall Take Place After These Things
    4 The Twenty-Four Elders and the Four Beasts
    5-11 The Book and the Lamb: Seven Seals
        5 The Lamb Worthy to Open the Book
        6:1-2 First Seal: Conquering

6:3-4 Second Seal: War
6:5-6 Third Seal: Famine
6:7-8 Fourth Seal: Death
6:9-11 Fifth Seal: Martyrs Cry for Vengeance
6:12-17 Sixth Seal: Earthquake/Catastrophe
7 The Remnant
8-11 Seventh Seal (Seven Trumpets)
    8:1-7 First Trumpet: Scorched Earth
    8:8-9 Second Trumpet: Scorched Sea
    8:10-11 Third Trumpet: Wormwood
    8:12-13 Fourth Trumpet: Darkness
    9:1-12 Fifth Trumpet: The Abyss
    9:13-11:14 Sixth Trumpet: Army/Book/Witness
    11:15-19 Seventh Trumpet: Kingdom Approaches
12:1-5 Pre-Tribulation
    12:1-2 The Woman (Israel)
    12:3-4 The Dragon (Satan)
    12:5 The Male Child (Messiah)
12:6-16 Early Tribulation
    12:6 The Woman Protected
    12:7-16 Michael Wars With the Dragon
12:17-14:20 Latter Tribulation
    12:17 The Dragon Enraged
    13:1-10 The Beast From the Sea
    13:11-18 The Beast From the Earth
    14:1-5 The Lamb and the 144,000
    14:6-12 The Three Angels
        14:6-7 Proclaiming the Gospel
        14:8 Destruction of Babylon
        14:9-12 Destruction to Beast Followers
    14:13 Blessing

            14:14-20 Reaping
    15-19 Tribulation's Conclusion
            15-19:4 The Seven Angels (Seven Bowls)
                    15 Their Commission
                    16:1-2 First Angel: Malignant Sores
                    16:3 Second Angel: Polluted Sea
                    16:4-7 Third Angel: Polluted Waters
                    16:8-9 Fourth Angel: Scorching Sun
                    16:10-11 Fifth Angel: Darkness, Pain
                    16:12-16 Sixth Angel: Assembling at Armageddon
                    16:17-19:4 Seventh Angel: Judgment of Babylon
            19:5-10 Marriage of the Lamb
            19:11-16 The Second Coming
            19:17-21 Armageddon
    20:1-6 The Millennial Kingdom
    20:7-10 Satan's Last Stand
    20:11-15 Final Judgment: The Great White Throne
    21-22 Eternity
            21:1-8 New Heaven and New Earth
            21:9-22:5 New Jerusalem
            22:6-21 Conclusion

These are just a few examples that illustrate the importance of (and approach to) recognizing *the natural divisions in the book*. Whether the structural keys are immediately recognizable or more challenging to find, we should always be careful in our observation not to miss these important guideposts. Once we have identified the structural keys, we are then equipped to outline the book, identifying major and minor divisions. Once we outline the book, we can begin to see the importance of the structure in the communication of the purposes of the book – which is a vital component for understanding the individual passages and how they contribute to that overall purpose.

12

Nine Steps for Biblical Exegesis and Exposition: (4) Identify Grammatical and Syntactical Keys

After (1) identifying the best reading and translation, (2) recognizing the background and context, and (3) identifying the structural keys of the book the passage is in, we need to (4) identify the grammatical and syntactical keys in the passage.

First, we need to be able to distinguish between grammar and syntax, because they are not the same. Grammar refers to the rules for how words relate to one another, and syntax refers to the actual usage. In other words, grammar is the theory and syntax is the practice. Grammar is the set of rules Paul would have understood and followed when he wrote his epistles, and syntax is the end product.

Also, we need to understand the importance of studying the relationships of words before studying the words themselves. The fifth step for Biblical exegesis is to identify lexical keys, yet we consider grammar and syntax first. Why? Very simply because the context in which a word is used – including its relationship to other words – is vitally important to understanding the intended meaning of the particular word chosen. Without first understanding the structures used for connecting the words, we may be inaccurate in trying to ascertain the intended meaning of the individual word.

Further, we need to identify the grammatical and syntactical keys themselves. We can start by identifying historical/cultural references, figurative language, rhetorical devices, quotations, key sentence structure, clauses, etc. Consider, for example, that Revelation 12 is a narrative describing some important signs. What is sometimes understood to be figurative language in this context is actually not figurative at all, but rather is a literal description of a figure, i.e., a sign.

Notice the consistent *grace and peace* greetings of Paul appearing at the beginning of each of his letters. The only exceptions are found in his letters to Timothy and Titus. The greetings are culturally significant, grace appealing to the gentile mind and peace appealing to the Jewish mind. What then is the significance of Paul's alteration of the greeting?

Next, we should note rhetorical devices employed in the text. Dialogical method is used by Paul in Romans 9:14, 19, 22, 30, and 32. Question and answer adds to the clarity of the passage and demonstrates the use of logical reasoning in Paul's argument, but also indicates the limitations of human logic (9:19-20). Parenesis (encouragement) is found in Romans 12:1-15:13; 1 Thessalonians, etc. Other devices include judicial, deliberative, epideictic (demonstrative, persuasive), etc. Jesus uses figurative language (metaphor) in John 11:11 in describing Lazarus' death. The same metaphor is also applied in Psalm 17:15 and 1 Thessalonians 4:14.

Number of persons is an important key to be aware of. Whether a verb is pertaining to the first, second, or third person, can sometimes make a tremendous difference in a passage. Acts 2:38 includes an important imperative regarding repentance and baptism that seems, in the English translation, to indicate that repentance and baptism are both necessary for forgiveness.

However, the imperative *repent* is second person plural while *be baptized* is third person singular (let him or her – each one – be baptized), and the pronoun (your sins) is also second person. This grammatical key, not seen clearly in the English, is critical to understanding the verse.

Word order is important – especially in Hebrew and Greek. Unlike English, in which word order is often dictated by the parts of speech chosen, in Hebrew and Greek there is much more freedom with regard to word order, so it is significant that a Biblical writer places one word before another. In the creation account of Genesis 1, each day is described as consisting of evening and morning. The order (evening first) is significant. How does this relate to Jewish culture? How impactful is this syntactical repetition in defining the scope of an individual day (i.e., 24 hours)? Does this phrasing lend credence to a literal six-day creation? How can there be evening and morning before the sun is created?

Progress in the text is important. Notice the phrasing of Psalm 1:1. There is a progression from action to inaction (walk, stand, sit). How is this significant in describing the blessed man?

Word endings are important. What is the *rock* in Matthew 16:18? What is the grammatical significance of the distinction between the two word endings: *petros* is a piece of rock or a stone, *petra* is a large rock or boulder. Note the contributions of 1 Peter 2:8, Romans 9:33, and 1 Corinthians 10:4 to the word usage.

As part of recognizing grammatical and syntactical keys in the passage, it is helpful to isolate distinct parts of speech (nouns, adjectives, participles, pronouns, articles, infinitives, prepositions, conjunctions, etc.), then to diagram sentences in the original language to visually identify distinctions and their significance.[58]

---

[58] A helpful line diagramming primer is provided in Thomas Schreiner, *Interpreting the Pauline Epistles* (Grand Rapids, MI: Baker Academic, 2011), 69-97, also in John Grassmick, *Principles and Practice of Greek Exegesis*, 2nd Edition (Dallas, TX: Dallas Theological Seminary, 1976), and in Lee Kantenwein, *Diagrammatical Analysis* (Winona Lake, IN: BMH Books, 1991).

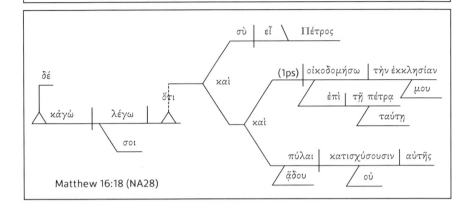

Finally, briefly summarize the importance of grammatical and syntactical keys in the passage. This helps in synthesizing the data, and prepares the exegete for the next step. For a more thorough consideration of critical grammatical and syntactical considerations, there are some beneficial resources such as the intermediate Wallace's *Greek Grammar Beyond the Basics*,[59] as well as Waltke's and Connor's helpful *An Introduction to Biblical Hebrew Syntax*[60]). While ordinarily in the first seven steps of the exegetical process I discourage the use of external sources (in order for the exegete to look at the passage as objectively as possible), at this stage a good grammar or intro to syntax is needed. For most, these tools will provide aid without adding a level of peripheral information so as to hinder the objectivity of the process.

---

[59] Daniel Wallace, *Greek Grammar Beyond the Basics: An Exegetical Syntax of the New Testament* (Grand Rapids, MI: Zondervan, 1997).
[60] Bruce Waltke and M. O'Connor, *An Introduction to Biblical Hebrew Syntax* (Warsaw, IN: Eisenbrauns, 1980).

13
Nine Steps for Biblical Exegesis and Exposition: (5) Identify Lexical Keys

After we have recognized and understood the relationships of words to each other, we need to examine the words themselves. The context of the word is the greatest definer, but lexical meaning is important. At this point a lexicon is a necessity. The standard authority on New Testament Greek is Bauer, Arndt, Gingrich, and Danker (often referred to by the acronym BAG or BAGD),[61] though there are others that are helpful, including Mounce[62] and Louw Nida.[63] For Hebrew, Koehler and Baumgartner's HALOT,[64] Brown, Driver, and Briggs,[65] and Gesenius[66] are helpful resources.

These tools are helpful for understanding etymology and

---

[61] Walter Bauer, William Arndt, and F. Wilbur Gingrich, *A Greek English Lexicon of the New Testament and Other Early Christian Literature* (Chicago, IL: University of Chicago Press, 1957).
[62] William Mounce, *The Analytical Lexicon to the Greek New Testament* (Grand Rapids, MI: Zondervan, 1993).
[63] J.P. Louw and Eugene Albert Nida, *Greek–English Lexicon of the New Testament: Based on Semantic Domains*, 2 Vols. (Swinden, UK: United Bible Societies, 1999).
[64] Ludwig Koehler and W. Baumgartner, *The Hebrew and Aramaic Lexicon of the Old Testament*, 2 Vols. (Boston, MA: Brill, 2002).
[65] Francis Brown, S.R. Driver and Charles Briggs, *The Brown–Driver–Briggs Hebrew and English Lexicon* (Peabody, MA: Hendrickson, 1994).
[66] H.W.F Gesenius, *Gesenius' Hebrew and Chaldee Lexicon to the Old Testament* (Grand Rapids, MI: Baker Book, 1979).

usage, and can especially help the researcher discern when usage is a greater factor than etymology in definition. For example, in English, the word icebox is a compound word that retains the independent elements of the original words – and icebox is literally a box that holds ice. On the other hand, a butterfly has very little to do with butter that flies. The same principle can be seen in the Biblical languages. We still need to understand etymology, but we should not assume too much of its influence on definition.

It also should be noted at this point that what we are after is as much objectivity regarding the definition of the word as possible. We do not want to read theology into the words (so be cautious when using a theological dictionary). Instead we need to recognize the usage of the time in which the word was written, and how the context contributes to that usage.

Once we are armed with some appropriate tools, we can begin to identify key words in the text. What words appear frequently? What words are emphasized by their place in the sentence? What words represent pivots in the thought or emphasis? In reality, every word is a key word, but we need to understand what each word means in that context, and which words the writer is emphasizing.

So first, we identify key words by emphasis, then we need to do word studies to be certain we are handling the words properly. A word study involves several steps: (1) identify, define (grammar and etymology), and parse (morphology) the word with aid of a lexicon, (2) examine usage of the word in other contexts (a concordance is particularly helpful here), and (3) summarize key concepts arising from key words. Here are a few Biblical examples where word studies can be helpful:

- Identify a significant connection between Exodus 3:14 and John 8:24, 28, 58.
- What is the key difference between Exodus 7:13, 22,

8:19, 9:7, 35 and 8:15, 32, 9:34?
- How many times is the phrase *under the sun* used in the book of Ecclesiastes, and why is it significant to the theme of the book?
- Note *yom* in the Old Testament, quantified by context, sometimes as 24-hour period (i.e., Gen. 1), sometimes including a longer period (such as the Day of the Lord [Joel, etc.]).
- What is meant by the term *weeks* as translated (NASB) in Dan. 9:24-27?
- What words for love are used in the dialogue recorded in John 21:15-17? Are they significant, and if so, why?
- What are some important words in John 1:1-18, Romans 5:1-11, Galatians 3:16-22, and Ephesians 1:1-14? How are they used? What is their significance?
- Note the NIV rendering of 1 Corinthians 5:5, *sinful nature* as a translation of the Greek *sarx*, what would be a better rendering?
- How is the meaning of *Savior* pivotal in 1 Timothy 4:10?
- What unique word is repeated six times in Revelation 19:1-6? What does it mean? How is the word connected to Psalm 111:1, 112:1, and 113:1, etc.?

Word studies are a vital way to engage the text, and will usually help us to understand the passage better – *unless* we fail to properly consider how influential the context is in defining the term. If we divorce a word from its context, then word studies can actually be destructive. Unfortunately, it is common for a teacher to rip a word out of context and spend much time talking about that word, instead of explaining how the word contributes to the context. In other words, a word is a vehicle, not a destination. A word is a means to an end. The writer used the word(s) for a reason. Our job as interpreters is to understand *what the writer said by using the words he chose.*

Perhaps the most important thing we can say about a word in a passage is that the word is not the most important thing in the passage. The individual words are vital, and we must understand them in a literal grammatical-historical way. In so doing, we can uphold that all-important principle: *context, context, context.*

14

Nine Steps for Biblical Exegesis and Exposition: (6) Identify Biblical Context

After completing the detailed grammatical, syntactical and lexical analysis, we need to step back and refocus to the bird's eye perspective and do some synthesizing. First, we need to identify the overall theme of the book, but by completing the first steps in the exegetical process, the theme of the chosen book should by now be apparent. If we have done our work well to this point, the remaining steps are easy.

Once we grasp the overall theme of the book, we need to summarize the immediate context surrounding the passage. Note how important it is to recognize the immediate context in relation to the following passages:

- Genesis 49:10 (for context, see 49:1) – the immediate context demonstrates the significance of the statement regarding Judah. What literary kind of statement was it?
- Exodus 20 – The Ten Commandments. Should this passage apply to the church today? Why or why not? How does the immediate context clarify the issue?
- 2 Chronicles 7:14-15 – This passage has often been

applied by the church to the church. Is this appropriate? What does the immediate context say about the intended audience? What kinds of consequences are promised? What is the significance?
- Job 34:37 – Does Elihu indict Job for sinning?
- Psalm 58:6 – How is this an appropriate prayer?
- Isaiah 6:8 – This sounds like a very bold response by Isaiah. How do the preceding events alter that perception of this passage?
- Ezekiel 40-48 – What time period does the context suggest?
- Matthew 13 – Why is Christ speaking in parables. What is the significance?
- Mathew 16:27-28 – Contextually, to what event is Christ referring? (Note the chapter division of Mk. 9, how it fits the context better than the chapter division between Mt. 16-17).
- Acts 2:4 – How does the immediate context define *to speak with other tongues*? See 2:11.
- Galatians 3:28-29 – How does the immediate context define and limit the elimination of all distinctions?
- Ephesians 3:3 – How is *the mystery* defined contextually?
- Hebrews 6:4-6 – Who is being described, believer or unbeliever?

In these, and any other passages, we need to understand the immediate context. What directly precedes our chosen passage, and what immediately follows it? How does the immediate context contribute to and define our chosen passage, and what impact do those contextual factors have on the passage's contribution to the book?

Because context is the single greatest factor in defining words and helping us understand intended meaning, we cannot give too much attention to Biblical context. In discovering that context, we do need to exercise caution that we are focusing on the textual, rather than theological context (that is another step entirely). If we introduce theological concepts before thoroughly considering Biblical context, we can lose our objectivity here. So, we ask simple question, and try to answer them *textually*. What is the overall theme of the book? What immediately precedes and follows our chosen passage, and how does that context impact the passage? And how does our chosen passage contribute to the overall theme of the book?

Finally, we can examine more distant contexts. Does the writer have other Biblical writings that have related contexts that we should consider that can help us understand our chosen passage. Remember, we need to look at (1) the big picture, (2) then near contexts, and (3) then far contexts, in that order.

15
Nine Steps for Biblical Exegesis and Exposition: (7) Identify Theological Context

In Step #6, we considered Biblical context, examining contexts on the basis of immediate and near textual proximity. In Step #7, our concern is theological context – a contextual consideration of theologically (topically) similar passages. The goal here is not to introduce extra-Biblical theological constructs; rather, we are simply trying to recognize the inherent theological components and implications of the passage we are studying.

First, we identify theological principles in the passage we are considering; second, we recognize the connection between those principles and the rest of the book; third, we compare with far reaching (but theologically similar) contexts to verify the theological principles; finally, we summarize our findings regarding the theological themes and principles based on context.

(1) Identify Theological Principles in the Passage

Recognize that generally larger contexts must be observed in order to identify theological principles, although sometimes, key individual words can provide significant theological framework (i.e., justification, redemption, propitiation, predestination, etc.).

For example, what theological principles of the church (*ekklesia*) are presented in Matthew 16:13-20? Who is building the church? What is the scope of the church? Note the importance of a sufficient lexical and grammatical study here, as "upon this rock" has been understood in several different ways: (1) the rock is Peter – a foundational understanding for the development of apostolic succession, (2) the rock is the earth – an argument for the earthly scope of the church and a cog in the defense of replacement theology, (3) the rock is the confession that Peter made – detaching this phrase from key prophetic significance, and (4) the rock is Christ (the view that properly considers each of the necessary exegetical elements).

Note Peter's explanation in 1 Peter 2:4-10 appealing to Isaiah 8:14, etc. If the previous steps (grammatical, syntactical, lexical, contextual, etc.) are not given sufficient attention, the theological principles in a passage can be significantly misunderstood, leading to wide ranging and inaccurate conclusions.

In Romans 3:21-31, what is the theological significance of righteousness? In Ephesians 1:1-14, what is meant by predestination? How does the principle of predestination impact the passage? In James 2:14-26, what is the theological relationship between faith and works?

(2) Connect the Principles to the Overall Context of the Book

What significant theological principle arises from Romans 5:12, 17-19? How does it support the argument of the epistle? In Galatians 3:15-29, what was the purpose for the Law? How does this relate to the theological theme of the epistle?

(3) Compare With Far Reaching Contexts to Verify Theological Principles

In James 3:1-12, regarding the theology of the tongue, compare

Ephesians 4:15, 29-30, 5:4, Colossians 3:5-10, 4:5-6, and also Proverbs 6:17, 10:20 and 31, 12:18-19, 15:2 and 4, 17:4, 18:21, 21:6 and 23; 25:15 and 23, 26:28, and 28:23. What theological principle is clarified by a comparison of John 14:1-3, 1 Corinthians 15:50-58, and 1 Thessalonians 4:13-18 with the outline of the book of Revelation? What key theological principle is outlined in Ephesians 2-3, and how does a comparison of Jeremiah 31, Romans 9-11, 2 Corinthians 3, Galatians 3 and 6:16, 1 John 2:25, and Revelation 19:11-14, 20:1-6 clarify the issue?

(4) Summarize Theological Themes and Principles Based on Context

At this point we are simply recording our findings. With the completion of this step, technically we have completed the purely exegetical portion of our study. The first seven steps are all exegetical – drawing out directly the meaning of the text. The final two stages are actually *not exegetical*, but have to do with external verification and then application. But before we move on toward Step #8, let's take a moment and look at one extended example.

In John 14:1-3, Jesus describes His plans for Himself and His disciples. He says,

> Do not let your heart be troubled; believe in God, believe also in Me. In My Father's house are many dwelling places; if it were not so, I would have told you; for I go to prepare a place for you. If I go and prepare a place for you, I will come again and receive you to Myself, that where I am, *there* you may be also.

Let's trace what Jesus is saying, particularly in vv. 2-3:

> I go to prepare a place for you,
> I will come again,

And receive you to Myself,
Where I am, you may be also.

Notice the verbs:

I *go,*
I will *come* again,
I will *receive* you,
you will be where I am.

Now let's reproduce these verbs graphically:

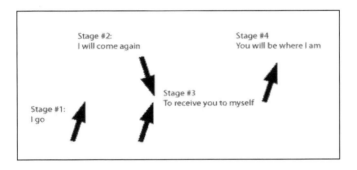

First, He ascends. Next, He descends, but with purpose of receiving them to himself (thus, they ascend). Now, let's look at some other similar passages and see what we can learn. 1 Thessalonians 4:16-17 seems to be describing a similar series of events:

> For the Lord Himself will descend from heaven with a shout, with the voice of *the* archangel and with the trumpet of God, and the dead in Christ will rise first. Then we who are alive and remain will be caught up together with them in the clouds to meet the Lord in the air, and so we shall always be with the Lord.

First, He descends. The dead in Christ rise. Those alive are caught up with them in the clouds to meet Him. We are always with Him. Let's look at this graphically as well:

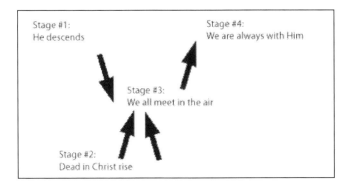

Notice the similarities. Both passages describe Jesus returning, not to the earth, but in the air for the purpose of receiving His own to Himself, to take them back with Him to where He is. 1 Corinthians 15:51-53 adds helpful information about stage #2 in the 1 Thessalonians passage (resurrection of the dead). Because of similarities in content we can recognize these three as parallel passages, and by comparing their theological content we can begin to develop an understanding of the Biblical event we call the rapture, and by a similar comparative process, we can distinguish this event from the events described in Matthew 24 and Revelation 19, thus helping us understand that what Jesus describes in John 14:1-3 is not the same event as His second coming in Revelation 19. That, of course, has tremendous implications for how we understand the future. Further, these distinctions help us to recognize the importance of accurately handling the theological context of passages.

The Eleven Categories of Theology

In assessing the theological context of a passage it is helpful to keep in mind the eleven basic categories of theology. Deriving from two Greek words, *theos* (God) and *logos* (word or discourse), the term theology simply refers to *the study of or discourse about God.* For students of the Bible, theology is the product of Bible study. In other words, it is not something we should read into the Bible or even use as a grid for understanding the Bible. Instead, we should come to the Bible objectively, letting it say what it says. The resulting body of knowledge, derived solely from the text, we could call a *Biblical theology.*

A next and helpful step (after studying the Bible in context) is to systematize the teachings of the Bible, or to categorize them, so that we can understand all of what the Bible teaches on a particular topic. Systematization can help us to avoid making big assumptions about narrow contexts. The product of systematizing Biblical theology into categories is often referred to as *systematic theology,* and there are eleven basic categories of systematic theology representative of a truly *Biblical* theology. We need to understand the Biblical teaching on these eleven topics (even if their titles are artificial):

(1) Bibliology
From the Greek *biblios*, bibliology is the study of the *book*, or more specifically, the study of the Bible. This topic deals with issues of definition, authority, and interpretive method. It is vital to have a solid bibliology, because if we don't approach the Bible properly, then we have no real authority to speak on any of the other areas of systematic theology. 2 Timothy 3:16-17 and 2 Peter 1:20-21 are good passages to study related to bibliology.

(2) Theology Proper
The term *proper* is used in the sense of a proper noun, so theology proper refers to the study of the person of God. This study considers the person, and attributes and character of God.

Oftentimes, this study will include discussion of the Father, Son, and Holy Spirit, though Son and Spirit are often considered as separate studies altogether. Issues like the holiness of God, and the doctrine of the trinity are considered in Theology Proper. Job 38-41, Isaiah 6, 40, and 48, and Revelation 4 are great passages for learning about theology proper.

(3) Christology
From the Greek *christos*, Christology is the study of the person and work of Jesus Christ. The study focuses on his roles as God and man, and as prophet, priest, and king, and introduces His work on the cross. Isaiah 53, and 61:1-2, Luke 4:18-19, John 1:1-18, Colossians 1:15-20, Philippians 2:1-11, the book of Hebrews and Revelation are a few definitive passages regarding Christology.

(4) Pneumatology
From the Greek *pneuma*, meaning *spirit*, Pneumatology is the study of the Holy Spirit. Pneumatology discusses the person and work of the Holy Spirit, especially in respect to His work in revealing Scripture (2 Peter 1:20-21), how He seals believers, guaranteeing their eternal life (Ephesians 1:13-14), how He brings people into the body of Christ (1 Corinthians 12:13), and how He helps believers to grow and bear fruit (Ephesians 5:17-18 and Galatians 5).

(5) Angelology
From the Greek *angellos*, we get our English word angel. Angelology is the study of angels, and includes demonology (study of demons) and satanology (study of Satan). Satan, for example, is discussed at length in passages like Genesis 3, Job 1, Ezekiel 28:11-19, Ephesians 6:13-17, 1 Peter 5:8, and Revelation 20.

(6) Anthropology
Anthropos in the Greek is translated *man*. Anthropology is the study

of humanity. This study considers humanity's creation and initial condition (Genesis 1-2), fall and condemnation (Genesis 3, Romans 5), and ultimate need for God's grace (Romans 3, and Ephesians 2).

(7) Hamartialogy

The Greek word for *sin* is *hamartia*. Hamartialogy is the study of sin. Of special emphasis in this study is how sin began (Ezekiel 28, Genesis 3), and its universal effects on humanity (Genesis 2:17, Romans 1:18-21, 3:23 and 6:23).

(8) Soteriology

From the Greek word *soteria*, meaning *deliverance* or *salvation*, soteriology is the study of salvation. Thankfully, God provided a solution to the problems discussed in hamartialogy. Salvation is and always has been by grace through faith in Him (Genesis 15:6, Habakkuk 2:4, and Ephesians 2:8-9), and results in a new position for believers (2 Corinthians 5:17, and Ephesians 1), provides the opportunity for a new walk (Romans 12:1-2, Ephesians 4:1-3), and a new ultimate destiny (John 3:16, 17:3, 1 Peter 1:3-5).

(9) Israelology[67]

This topic of theology is an important one, because God created and chose Israel for a special purpose (Genesis 18:19), made promises to the nation (Genesis 22:16-17, and Jeremiah 31:31-34), and has a future for Israel (Jeremiah 33:21-22, and Romans 9-11), and will be glorified through Israel (Jeremiah 14:21, and Romans 11:25-36).

(10) Ecclesiology

This is the study of the *ekklesia*, or the assembly – the church. Ecclesiology considers the beginning of the church (Matthew 16:17-

---

[67] Arnold Fruchtenbaum brought awareness to the study of Israel as a necessary topic in theology. See Arnold Fruchtenbaum, *Israelology: The Missing Link in Systematic Theology* (Tustin, CA: Ariel Press, 1994).

18, and Acts 2), its makeup (Ephesians 2:13-22), its relationship to Christ (Ephesians 5:21-33), its blessings (Ephesians 1:3), and its future (John 14:1-3, 1 Thessalonians 4:13-17, and Revelation 19:11-14).

(11) Eschatology

From the Greek term *eschatos*, meaning *last things*, eschatology is the study of last things. Its focus is on still yet unfulfilled prophecy to Israel (Jeremiah 31, and Daniel 9), to the nations and to unbelievers (Revelation 4-19, 20:11-15), to the church (John 14:1-3, and 1 Thessalonians 4:13-17), regarding Christ and His kingdom (2 Samuel 7, and Revelation 20-22), Satan and judgment (Revelation 20:10), and the renewing of all things (Revelation 21-22).

When reading the Bible, it is helpful to think about which of these categories are being discussed. In doing so, the observant Bible student will begin to realize how interrelated are the books and teachings of the Bible – they are cohesive and connected. What we understand in one area will necessarily influence (or even dictate) what we understand in another area. So it is vitally important that we be aware of the various issues discussed in the Bible, and to be aware of their relationships.

Case Study: Logical Errors of Affirming a Disjunct in John 10

The formal structure of a fallacious argument affirming a disjunct looks like this:

> A or B,
> A,
> Therefore not B.

This is not a valid form of argument, yet it is a commonly utilized fallacy. Let's look at two examples often inferred from John

10. John 10:11 reads, "I am the good shepherd; the good shepherd lays down His life for the sheep." The passage can be formalized with an inferred disjunct as follows:

(A) The good shepherd lays down His life for the sheep

(or B) The good shepherd lays down his life for those who are not sheep

(A) The good shepherd lays down His life for the sheep

Therefore, not (B) The good shepherd lays down his life for those who are not sheep

This is a fallacious argument that attempts to validate limited atonement, but John 10:11 makes no statement about who He didn't die for, only about who He did die for. In other words, we can make no positive assertion form John 10:11 that Christ didn't die for someone because that someone is not one of His sheep. Passages like 1 John 2:2 and 1 Timothy 4:10 shed more light on this issue, but John 10:11 is not a proof text for limited atonement. John 10:17 reads, "For this reason the Father loves Me, because I lay down My life so that I may take it again."

The passage can also be formalized with an inferred disjunct as follows:

(A) For this reason the Father loves Me,

(or B) For other reasons the Father loves Me

(A) For this reason the Father loves Me,

Therefore, not (B)

For other reasons the Father loves Me In this passage, Jesus is not identifying all the reasons why the Father loves Him, He is only identifying one, but that is not indicative that there is only one (of course there may be only one, but this passage isn't asserting that). Consequently, John 10:17 cannot be used to support that the Father's love for the Son was conditional. Contexts like John 3:35, 5:20, 17:3-10, and Matthew 3:17 all help us to understand that love was an ongoing part of the eternal relationship between Father and Son. Reading theology into a passage in order to support that particular theology is always exegetically problematic, and can also be problematic with respect to logic.

16

Nine Steps for Biblical Exegesis and Exposition: (8) Secondary Verification

Technically only the first seven steps of this process are purely exegetical. In those steps we aren't using anything but the text itself (though because of our limitations in connecting with the languages, especially, it is expected that we will use tools like lexicons and perhaps even grammars). In those steps, we have avoided referring to commentaries, because we can't rely on the exegesis of others without ceasing to do exegesis on our own. So with as little external aid as possible, we have sought to draw out the meaning of the text. And if we have done our job well to this point, we have a good handle on the passage we are studying, and we are ready to test our hypothesis of meaning.

In this eighth step, secondary verification, our job is to use external sources including commentaries (preferably exegetical) in order to verify that we have asked and answered the right questions. The first seven steps are exegesis proper – primary verification. We verify meaning by appealing to the primary source: the text itself. Now we move on to secondary verification, where we appeal to external sources to test our work.

Primary verification (as worked out in previous steps) comes from the contextual examination of Scripture – first the immediate context in an exegetical verification, and then more far reaching contexts in a systematic verification. By this point primary verification should be effectively completed. Secondary verification offers a further opportunity to challenge one's exegetical work by comparing it to the exegetical work of other learned exegetes.

Valuable external resources at this stage include introductions (generally to Old or New Testament studies), surveys (generally offering overviews of Old and New Testaments or individual books), handbooks and dictionaries (providing general outlines and definitions), and exegetical commentaries (providing verse analysis and other key exegetical information).

First, we should utilize a number of resources covering the selected passage. Avoid locking into one commentator, but rather utilize a multiplicity. Comparing an exegesis with only one commentator generally does not offer enough of breadth to soundly test the exegetical process. The purpose of this process is not simply to find agreement with an esteemed commentator, but rather to provide a critical look at the exegetical work we have already done. *We are not trying to confirm our answers; rather we are trying to be sure we haven't missed any important observations.*

Next, we should identify the hermeneutic method of the commentators. This is a vital step, not only in assessing a commentary's validity and usefulness, but also in developing a critical approach to Biblical research literature. Developing an awareness of the commentator's presuppositions, theological bents, and methodologies is key in both areas. While this can be a painstaking process, usually there are litmus-test passages we can look at to quickly identify the commentator's interpretive approach.

As we become familiar with various external sources, we should summarize agreements and differences in the interpretations of the commentators. Exegetically and critically examine each commentator's agreements and differences. Have they covered key elements, or have they glossed over difficult or controversial issues? Particularly in light of the hermeneutic method utilized, certain conclusions can be expected. An allegorical approach will generally lead to replacement theology conclusions. Spiritualization will often de-emphasize primary applications. Theological hermeneutics can often lead to wild and unverifiable conclusions. Do those commentators, using similar methodologies, arrive at similar conclusions? Have any of the writers made observations or asked questions we haven't?

Armed with answers to these questions, we now can defend our interpretation or alter it in light of the findings. If the process of secondary verification uncovers holes in our exegetical conclusions, we need to go back and review our entire exegetical process to determine the cause. What we need is not only a refinement of the conclusions regarding the particular passage, but also a refinement in the overall process. We need to ensure that the next exegetical exercise is sounder than the previous. Ultimately, we simply need to observe well and answer questions properly. So we are using external sources to test whether we have been thorough, or whether we have left stones unturned.

I can't emphasize enough that the point of this stage is not simply to look at the conclusions of other writers and gain satisfaction in agreeing with them. The point is to focus on their process, not their product. Just as in our own exegesis our goal is not to manipulate the process to arrive at a certain product, our goal here is to uncover the process of these other sources, for the sake of assessing and testing our own. It is for this reason that we delay using these resources until after we have finished exegesis.

Once we have examined the secondary sources, hopefully we find they confirm that we have asked and answered the key questions – that our process has been sound. If so, we move on to the final step (exposition), and if not, we revisit our work to refine and correct any deficiencies.

17
Nine Steps For Biblical Exegesis And Exposition: (9) Development of Exposition

This is the step where we most often derail. Even if we have done our first seven steps well – handling the text accurately and comprehensively – and even if our eighth step has helped us to have confidence that we have grasped the meaning of the passage, there is still much possibility of error in our ninth and final step. The major problem is that we sometimes forget our purpose at this stage – and *we fail at this in two particular ways*.

Recall the four basic steps of Bible study: observation, interpretation, correlation (or verification), and application. The first seven steps of the (more detailed) exegetical process entail observation, interpretation, and primary verification. The eighth step completes the verification process. So the first eight steps of the exegetical process correlates, basically, with the first three steps of basic Bible study. By comparing the more complex process (exegetical) with the simpler process (basic or introductory Bible study), it is apparent that the final steps of both are to be very practical – meaning, having to do with *practice*. Once we have understood the meaning of the text, what are we supposed to *do* with it? James reminds us to be doers of the word and not just hearers only (Jam 1:22).

The first purpose of exegeting the text is so that we might understand what God has said and appropriately put it into practice. Of course, we must recognize the distinction between primary application (for the initial audience) and secondary application (for you and me). The Scriptures were written not only for the original audience, but also so that you and I might be equipped for every good work (2 Tim 3:16-17). Consequently, there is no passage of the Bible that we can't draw from in our own personal lives, we just need to draw correctly.

Consider, for example, Ezra, who, as is recorded in Ezra 7:10, sought to learn the law of God, to practice it and to teach it. Notice the order in Ezra's process: learn, do, teach. We mustn't learn simply so we can teach others. We must learn so we can grow closer to our Lord, understanding Him better. So this final step (exposition) is not first about preparing an explanation of the passage for someone else, it is about me putting the passage into use in my own life, and doing so with proper understanding of the passage in mind. *The first of two major ways we can fail at understanding the purpose of exposition is to focus on training up others before allowing ourselves to be trained.*

The second purpose of exposition is to communicate God's word to others, ultimately for the equipping of the saints for the work of service, to the building up of the body of Christ (Eph 4:12; 2 Tim 3:16-17). And here is where we often get it wrong: when we think that we are the ones equipping people, we have missed vital Biblical data. It is not you and I that equip others – it is the word of God. His word equips, and it is the task of exposition (after we *practice*) to help others understand how to handle God's word for themselves. Rather than create followers who are dependant upon us for their daily sustenance, we need to be helping disciples to grow in the ability to feed themselves.

Consider this: of all the instances the word *feed* is used in the

NT, it is never used as an imperative to pastors – or anyone – with respect to spiritually feeding others (the only exception is Jn 21:15, in which Peter is given specific direction from Christ). Even in the Lord's prayer, the disciples were to ask the Father for their daily bread (Mt 6:11). In short, our job is not to create dependants who have to come to us for feeding. Rather, it is to train up disciples who will have not only the ability to feed themselves, but also the ability to teach others to feed themselves as well (2 Tim 2:2). We must keep this goal in mind as we communicate the Bible to others.

If that goal is firmly in mind, then we can avoid *the second major mistake of exposition: the failure to show our work*. It is remarkable to me how many exposition textbooks describe accurately the exegetical process, and then when they move into the subject of exposition, they suggest the exegete hide his or her work from those they would teach: "Don't use Greek and Hebrew words." "Don't talk about grammar." "Don't get into the technicalities." "Just give them the big idea." "Don't exegete from the pulpit."

I can't emphasize enough just how completely wrongheaded these suggestions are. If the goal is to help people to develop their own abilities to handle the text, then *we absolutely must model these things in our own exposition*. If we don't, we are equally as guilty as the father who refuses to allow his children to see how a meal is prepared – *ever*. How will those children handle the responsibilities of life when they have no one around to feed them and they must do it themselves? Elsewhere, I have suggested that we are not chefs, preparing fancy meals for people's delight, but instead we are teaching people how to cook for themselves. If we don't show those we are training how to do the basic exegetical tasks necessary for their own feeding, then how effective can we possibly be at training them? It is a terrible travesty when anyone creates dependency in anyone else. And when we don't teach people to think, study, and function on their own, we are being very, very cruel.

Okay, so how do we do it right, then? *Show our work!* Exegete from the pulpit – from the dinner table, the sofa, and anywhere else you are given opportunity. Where there are people willing to learn, show your work in the text. Teach them how to do that work themselves. It's just that simple. And please, *please*…stop writing sermons, and let the Bible speak for itself. A sermon can't equip anyone. God's word can and does. Which would you rather provide?

Now that the dead horse has been sufficiently pummeled, let's move on to some specific methodology for communicating the Bible to others. Please keep in mind what follows is only a suggested way to prepare for communicating the Bible – it is certainly not the only acceptable form of delivery. The key is whether or not we are allowing the text to speak on its own terms and showing people how to handle it for themselves. That is the goal of the process that follows.

First, provide a verse analysis or a running commentary on the passage. Generally this can be as simple as basic summary of each passage in relation to the overall context, or it can be as complex as including every discovered element of exegetical insight. In either case (and all those in between), the content should be the direct result of the exegetical study.

Second, summarize principles (universal truths applicable to all), primary application (intended response of the initial audience), and secondary application (intended response of you and I). If a universal principle is evident in the passage, it should be noted as crucial to both primary and secondary application. Primary application relates directly to the original intended audience, while secondary application relates to later audiences, including the exegete. Principles and applications should be stated with clarity and conciseness to ensure that keys have been grasped.

Third, identify the impact of the passage on your own life

and begin to act upon it. Just as it is throughout the entire study process, the passage should have personal impact. Remember, James exhorts believers to be doers of the word and not merely hearers (Jam 1:22-27), and later cautions against being too "ready" to teach. Before the edification of others must come the application to one's self. Remember Ezra:

> For Ezra had set his heart to study the law of the Lord, and to practice it and to teach His statutes and ordinances in Israel (Ezra 7:10).

Ezra's priorities show a focus on (1) diligence necessary for study and learning, (2) being an effectual doer and practitioner of all that God had said, and (3) only then being a faithful teacher of Scripture. While it is easier to focus on how the passage will be delivered to a target audience or congregation than to consider its impact on ourselves, the godly examples of the Bible demonstrate how important personal devotion and godliness is to God. Practice comes before teaching. The adage says, "Them that can't do, teach," but in the context of Biblical teaching, it is more accurate to say, "Them that would teach (and even them that wouldn't) must *do*."

Fourth, develop a presentation of the passage for the edification of others. This component is considered in detail in the next section of this book, as we look at seven different approaches for exposition, distinguished primarily by method and audience:

(1) Informal Preaching
(2) Formal Preaching
(3) Informal Teaching
(4) Formal Teaching: The Synthetic Preview
(5) Formal Teaching: The Exegetical Journey
(6) Formal Teaching: The Analytical (Theological) Summary
(7) Formal Teaching: Teaching Topically

18

The Hermeneutic and Exegetical Implications Of Descriptive and Prescriptive

The short-form process of discerning and appropriating the meaning of a Biblical passage includes the four basic steps of (1) observation, (2) interpretation, (3) correlation, and (4) application. The more detailed exegetical process includes nine steps: (1) verify text and translation, (2) understand background and context, (3) identify structural keys, (4) identify grammatical and syntactical keys, (5) identify lexical keys, (6) identify Biblical context, (7) identify theological context, (8) secondary verification, and (9) exposition.

Steps one through seven of the detailed exegetical process correspond to observation and interpretation in the more summary process. Both methods include a verification element, and both culminate with appropriation (exposition and application).

Compared side by side, the processes coincide as follows:

Abbreviated Process	*Detailed Process*
Observation	Verify text and translation
	Understand background and context

>   Identify structural keys
>   Identify grammatical and syntactical keys
>   Identify lexical keys
>   Identify Biblical context
>   Identify theological context

Interpretation (The result of the seven observational steps)

Correlation   Secondary verification

Application   Exposition

As a result of the seven observational or exegetical steps, we can formulate and test our interpretation, and we can appropriate the passage properly. The exposition of a passage includes a discussion of the applications of a passage, and should include some consideration of primary and secondary application.[68]

Primary application refers to how the original audience was to respond to the passage, while secondary application references expected responses of later (i.e., secondary) readers.

The distinction between the two aspects (primary and secondary) is critical. Without acknowledging the distinction we would not be able to discern whether or not we (the modern readers), for example, are expected to go to a nearby village to obtain the colt of a donkey (Mt 21:2).

All seven observational steps help us differentiate between primary and secondary application, as we discover what is descriptive and what is prescriptive. Descriptive is that which describes, as in historical narrative. Acts 5:1-11, for example, describes what took place when Ananias and Sapphira lied in order

---

[68] Christopher Cone, *Prolegomena on Biblical Hermeneutics and Method*, 2nd Edition. (Hurst, TX: Tyndale Seminary Press, 2012), 263–264.

to make themselves look more spiritual. Prescriptive is that which prescribes, or commands. Prescriptive material is that which provides directions for the audience. Matthew 28:18-20 contains one prescription, the imperative make disciples (*matheteusate*).

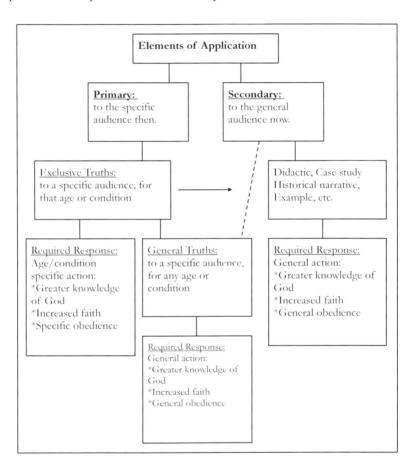

Further, because this imperative is in a descriptive context (the passage is describing what Jesus said to His disciples), we can recognize that the passage is describing a prescription for the disciples, and thus the primary application of the passage was a call for the disciples to obey the specific command. We can certainly draw a secondary application from this passage, from the description of the events that took place there, and from other Biblical contexts which focus on disciple making (eg., 2 Tim 2:2). But the primary application of this passage is for the disciples to whom Jesus was speaking – just as in Matthew 21:2, the primary application is for the specific disciples Jesus was addressing (thus we are not obligated to obtain the colt of a donkey).

In considering primary and secondary applications, the first question to be asked is whether or not the passage is descriptive or prescriptive. Next, if the passage is prescriptive, we need to ask for whom is it prescriptive? Consider Exodus 19:4-6, as an example:

> 'You yourselves have seen what I did to the Egyptians, and *how* I bore you on eagles' wings, and brought you to Myself. 'Now then, if you will indeed obey My voice and keep My covenant, then you shall be My own possession among all the peoples, for all the earth is Mine; and you shall be to Me a kingdom of priests and a holy nation.' These are the words that you shall speak to the sons of Israel."

These verses are descriptive, in that they are the record of what God said to Moses (see 19:3). They are also prescriptive in the sense that they contain information Moses was commanded to pass along to Israel. So in answer to the question regarding the recipient of the prescription, the answer is Moses. There appears to be another prescriptive layer here, as the content was to be heeded by Israel ("...hear My voice and keep My covenant..."), but it is not until the message is delivered that it becomes prescriptive for Israel. So we might identify the primary application as for Moses to communicate what God spoke. There are a number of secondary applications we might draw from this description of Moses' prescription, but only one primary application. Further in 19:7 we read a description of Moses fulfilling the prescription of 19:3, and delivering God's message to Israel. The primary application of 19:7

would be for Israel to respond to what was given them. Again, we might draw any number of secondary applications, but the primary application is limited to the initial audience.

In considering the distinction between descriptive and prescriptive, it is evident that we need to identify the direct recipient of any prescriptions so that we can properly apply (primary) the passage. Once we have done that we can move on to the more descriptive elements that would lead us to secondary applications. Let's examine one more example. Consider Acts 16:11-34, the account of the Philippian jailor coming to believe in Christ. The context is descriptive, as it is a narrative describing events that happened. This is most obvious from the use of past tense and the sequence of the events as they are described. However, in 16:31 we discover a prescriptive element in response to the jailor's question of what he must do to be saved. Paul and Silas responded that he should believe (*pisteuson*, aorist active imperative, second person singular) in the Lord Jesus.

In order to correctly apply the passage, we must identify who is the recipient of the prescription. In this case, it is the Philippian Jailor. The primary application of the prescription is then that the jailor needed to believe in order to be saved. It is not correct to apply the passage as a universal formula for salvation – even *if the conditions are universally applicable*. The primary application of the prescription is not to you and me; rather it was for the Philippian jailor. Now, of course we might draw many appropriate secondary applications, as we recognize that the formula is indeed universally applicable (all who believe in Jesus Christ have eternal life, see, Jn 6:47, for example), but we need to be careful to distinguish between the primary application and the secondary. In instances like these we must keep in mind that arriving at a proper conclusion (in this case, what one must do to be saved) does not justify misapplying a passage.

As part of the interpretation process, we must recognize

descriptive and prescriptive language, distinguishing between the two. In so doing we will have a much clearer understanding of primary and secondary applications in a given context.

19
Biblical Wordplay Doesn't Obfuscate Meaning

Years ago, inaugural Tampa Bay Buccaneers' Coach John McKay was asked after yet another loss about his team's execution. He quipped without hesitation, "I'm all for it." McKay had the ability to quickly recognize not only the original, intended meaning of a word, but also other meanings as well. This quick recognition helped him to be a master of wordplay. Former Yankee's manager, Yogi Berra was also skilled at this, once referring to a recurrence as "déjà vu all over again."

In communication we appreciate wordplay, but we often fail to consider that without initial, intended meaning, there could be no wordplay, puns, or discernible metaphor. Original meaning is vitally important, and it is an irony that without it we would lose the capacity to violate it in ways humorous or otherwise.

The Biblical writers are not strangers to wordplay, as we have several fine examples to consider. Paul's allegory in Galatians 4:22-31 wouldn't be useful at all if the original referents, Sarah and Hagar, weren't discussed at length in earlier Scripture. Paul doesn't change the meaning of the original texts (Gen 16), but rather he uses that original intended meaning to teach a new lesson to the Galatians, using Hagar to illustrate the mother of those born under law, and Sarah, the mother of those born in freedom. Paul's retasking of Genesis 16 comes with a transparent admission ("This is allegorically speaking," Gal 4:24) that he is borrowing the passage to illustrate something not discussed in the initial passage. In other words, Paul's wordplay is obvious, intentional, and transparently announced. Further, it makes no attempt to reinterpret or redefine the earlier passage. The later passage simply employs the earlier one as fodder for an object lesson.

Solomon personifies wisdom as a woman in Proverbs 3:13-18, adding that she has a right and left hand (3:16). He extends the metaphor further by objectifying "her" as a tree of life (3:18), using personification and objectification in the same phrase. The result is to make wisdom a very personal and desirable thing – an effective tool with which to begin a book of proverbs extolling and advocating wisdom.

In 1 Kings 18:27, Elijah mocks (*hatal*) the prophets of Baal with sarcasm, affirming that Baal is indeed a god (*elohim*), so the prophets must not be calling on him with a loud enough (great, *gadol*) voice. Adding insult to injury, Elijah suggests perhaps Baal is asleep and needs to be awakened (hence the need for loud voices). In this case, the text announces Elijah's wordplay (sarcasm). It is obvious Elijah does not view Baal as a deity.

Jesus gets in on the action, introducing parables in which the main characters are fictional by referencing people without the definite articles: "A man had two sons"(Lk 15:11), "Now, there was a rich man…"(Lk 16:1), "Now, there was a rich man…" (Lk 16:19). Notice especially the 16:19 reference, which introduces what some consider a historical narrative of Lazarus and the rich man. The introduction to the narrative is word-for-word identical to the previous one in 16:1 (*anthropos tis en plousios*) except for the word now or but (*de*), and that is different only because of the placement of the introduction to the story after the statement of setting in 16:1 ("Now He was also saying to the disciples…"). Jesus introduces the stories of 16:1 and 16:19 identically, showing the reader (or the listener, in the original setting) that the stories have the same weight, and are of the same literary kind. In other words, characteristics of Jesus' metaphorical storytelling help us to contrast Jesus' parables with His non-fiction statements – like the ones alluded to in Luke 24:27, "Then beginning with Moses and with all the prophets, He explained to them the things concerning Himself in all the Scriptures."

Like Solomon says, "The words of wise men are like goads, and masters of these collections are like well-driven nails; they are given by one Shepherd" (Ecc 12:11). The masterful use of words is helpful on many levels. But Solomon also adds a warning regarding excessiveness with respect to words: "But beyond this, my son, be warned: the writing of many books is endless, and excessive devotion to books is wearying to the body" (Ecc 12:12). As readers and Biblical interpreters, we need to keep things simple, appreciate meaning, and take the text as it was intended. Going beyond these simple principles provides fodder for voluminosity, but leaves little room for perspicuity.

20

Diversity, Biblical Interpretation, and Sunrise Over the Atlantic

In most contexts, diversity is a beautiful thing. Creation reflects an incredible array of diverse kinds of beauty. As I watch the sun begin to rise over the Atlantic Ocean, I see wispy clouds high above, with a thick puff of clouds just above the horizon. There is enough clear sky in between for the sun's gentle rays to cascade over the still, calm water – water that would normally be stirred up by the wind and currents. The gentle waves wash in to shore, barely audible, but still ever present. There are so many colors, shapes, sounds, and smells. It is almost too much to take in, and yet, it is all these things working in unison that makes the sunrise such a beautiful sight. God understands how to paint a scene, and diversity is one of His most remarkable tools – no one appreciates variety more than Him.

But there are also contexts where diversity is not a blessing. Let's say that I hand each of ten people a small piece of crumpled paper with a formula written on it: $31+X=86$. If I asked those ten people to tell me the meaning of X, and nine of them came up with answers other than fifty-five, we would recognize the answers to be diverse, but not necessarily beautiful. We would recognize those answers as wrong, at least within our basic mathematical system.

So it is with the Bible. God has communicated in such a way as to be understood, but we often fail to ascertain the Author's intent. As I peer over the horizon at the ever brightening sky I see His handiwork, and I recognize that the heavens declare His glory (Ps 19). As I peruse the pages of Scripture, I need to recognize that He is communicating a message – ultimately, for His glory (Eph 1), but understood by different interpretive methods.

In understanding Scripture, we observe what the text says, we interpret what it means, and we must apply it properly. This last point is where we often get it wrong. We must distinguish between primary and secondary application. Primary application refers to how the original audience was supposed to take action, based on what was said or written. Secondary application refers to what we – the non-original audience, many years later – are supposed to think or do based on what has been written. For example, in Matthew 26:18-19, Jesus tells His disciples to talk to a certain man. We seem to have no problem recognizing primary application here (have any of you attempted to talk to that specific man?), but when Jesus tells those same disciples to make disciples (Mt 28:19-20), we suddenly lose the ability to distinguish between primary and secondary application.

My point here is not to suggest that we shouldn't be making disciples, it is only to say that if we are not consistent in our interpretive methodology, then we will be inconsistent in our application of Scripture. If we don't distinguish between primary and secondary application, then who is to say what we should or should not do? There are passages that command people be stoned to death for touching a mountain (e.g., Ex 19:12-13), and other passages that mandate forgiveness (e.g., Mt 6:12-14). We should answer a fool according to his folly (Prov 26:5)…wait – no we shouldn't (Prov 26:4). In this way, we could cite passage after passage with confusing results, but I think the point is clear already – if we fail to interpret properly (seeking to understand what the

Author intended), and we fail to distinguish between primary and secondary application, then we will be confused at best and blasphemous at worst.

So let's consider this. How many of our opinions about who we are, how we should think, or what we should do are formulated on faulty interpretive method? These concepts are simple, but not easy. Are we willing to re-examine everything in light of His word? As simple as that process can be, it can also be painful. But it is so very necessary, and so very fruitful. Now the sun has risen beyond the clouds, and is shining directly upon me. The sunrise has passed, and a new day has begun. Today, how will we handle His word? Will we ignore it altogether? Will we abuse it to the point that it is unrecognizable? Or will we sit humbly before our Master, with the same patience as if awaiting the beauties of the new morning's sunrise?

SECTION III

OVERVIEW OF THE EXPOSITIONAL PROCESS

21

The Prerequisites of Passion and Love

A Brief Word About Passion

Many of the concepts presented in this book are done so in a fairly technical manner, so that pertinent information is not left out. In light of this mechanical approach in writing, it would not surprise me if some aspiring Biblical communicators might read what follows and be intimidated or discouraged, wondering who would want to listen to them communicate with such prescribed forms and precision. Some might perceive that following an ordered methodology is the first ingredient in a recipe for disinterested listeners. To those I offer a brief introductory word of encouragement, and to the rest, I beg your pardon for my covering here what you have already discovered.

What are the common traits of truly great Bible communicators? Reviewing Ezra 7:10 helps us answer this question: first, they are committed to the study of His word, second they are committed to being doers of His word, and third they are committed to sharing it with others as God provides opportunity. These traits are elementary. These we know. But what else? Are there other characteristics that contribute to effective Biblical communication? I suggest there is one additional trait that complements the commitment to truth in Biblical communication: *passion*.

In my own life and experience I have been privileged to learn from some absolutely outstanding Biblical communicators. Each of them exemplified Ezra 7:10, and each of them demonstrated *passion*. Now, I don't mean passion simply in the sense of emotion – it is a much bigger concept than that. For example, when the prophets of the Old Testament era were communicating to the Israelites and other nations, do you suppose they were monotone and boring, or would you think that they were passionately communicating as representatives of the Almighty God who had commissioned them? Or when John the Baptist was shouting in the wilderness (Is 40:3, Mk 1:3), can you imagine him doing that dispassionately, or was he driven by the conviction of his stewardship and by the desire that people should understand who this Messiah was that John was announcing? Or when Jesus was chastising the Pharisees as a "brood of vipers" (e.g., Mt 3:7, 12:34, 23:33), was He doing it insincerely and in a disinterested way, or was He locked in on these men addressing them in moments of powerful confrontation? Or when Peter addressed the Jews confidently proclaiming (e.g., Acts 2:29) who Jesus was, was Peter speaking with the disconnectedness of someone who is only addressing theories, or was he championing the truth? Or when Paul was trying to persuade the Jews and Greeks in the synagogue at Corinth (Acts 18:4), or solemnly testifying there (18:5), was there no indication that he *actually believed* in what he was proclaiming, or was he speaking with the sincerity of someone who knew that at any moment he might be arrested or stoned on account of his message?

These Biblical examples cry out to anyone who would wish to communicate God's word to others that *passion* is in order – a sincerity, genuineness, and personal investedness. We are people on a mission to represent the truth of the Almighty God to others.

What a privilege! What a stewardship! What a responsibility! If those that hear us are bored or disengaged, then perhaps we are either presenting them with boring material (and not God's word), or we are not engaged ourselves. Perhaps we are not demonstrating the passion that expectedly comes with having such a profound message to present.

Now, of course, there are those who are lukewarm, who will not respond to God's word with more than a yawn and an internal commitment not to waste anymore of their time in the Bible. There are also those who will so desire to have their ears tickled that they may be rather indifferent to what God actually has to say. Yet our responsibility is faithfulness regardless of the response and outcomes. The question is whether we are communicating the Bible for the wrong reasons – for our own pride or for our own gain – or whether we are fully invested in Him. Do we recognize that we are not our own but that we have been bought with a price (1 Cor 6:20)? Do we recognize that we have been crucified with Christ and it is no longer we who live, but Christ in us (Gal 2:20)?

As we communicate God's word, either to those who are not yet alive in Christ (preaching), or to those who are new creations (teaching), let us do so with our whole hearts, and not as dispassionate but as passionate for Him who saved us. Let us say, sincerely, with Paul, "Woe is me if I do not proclaim the gospel…" (1 Cor 9:16). While we are not called as apostles as he was, we are entrusted with the same gospel, which is God's power to save (Rom 1:16-17), and with the same word of God, which is His means of equipping believers (2 Tim 3:16-17). So as we examine in the following pages the nuts and bolts of communicating His word, let us not *get lost* in the technicalities, but rather let us *learn* the technicalities so that we can consider how to faithfully handle, live, and communicate His word.

A Brief Word About Love

Some have cited the need for "the speech before the speech,"[69] as an introductory expression of love for the listeners, without which the motivation for the communication may be unclear, and without which the perceived coldness of the messenger can stifle the life-affirming heat of the message. The introductory personal element is employed by a number of Biblical writers.

Luke addresses his letter to most excellent Theophilus (Lk 1:3) and explains his motivation – to provide certainty to Theophilus (1:4). Note that Luke's introduction to Acts is more abbreviated – he had already established (or at least acknowledged the personal connection). Paul introduces his letter to the Romans with an expression of his gratitude for them and for their testimony, and with an expression of his deep desire to fellowship with them (Rom 1: 8-15). Even in his first letter to the Corinthians – a letter in which he would vigorously chastise his audience – he expresses gratitude for God's grace toward them and for their ultimate future completion in Christ (1 Cor 1:4-9). After beginning his letter to the Ephesians with an extended doxology, Paul expresses gratitude and prays for their strengthening and growth in Him (Eph 1:16-23).

Peter's introduction includes a very personal discussion of his readers' difficulties and hope (1 Pet 1:3-9). That personal element is evident throughout both of Peter's letters. While John's Gospel and his first letter are addressed to broad audiences (John's Gospel, to unbelievers in general, and 1 John to believers), and thus aren't particularly personal in their introductions and overall content, his second letter begins with a very personal commendation and an expression of love (2 Jn 1-4). His third letter begins with a similar expression (3 Jn 1-6). Jude also introduces his letter both with an expression of love and with a transparent

---

[69] Calvin Miller, *Preaching: The Art of Narrative Exposition* (Grand Rapids, MI: Baker Book, 2006), 188.

discussion of his motivation and purpose (Jude 1-3).

Paul reminds us in 1 Corinthians 13:1-3 that if we do great things but otherwise lack love, we are nothing. He adds in 1 Timothy 1:5 that the goal of our instruction is love. If we are communicating the Bible to others, and we don't have deep rooted concern for their spiritual well being then we are missing the point. Jesus commissioned His disciples to love each other (Jn 13:34-35), and later He commissioned them to make disciples, teaching all that He commanded (Mt 28:20). How could they fulfill the discipleship mandate if they first weren't fulfilling the love mandate? If we aren't willing to love the people we are teaching, then we are just an unpleasant noise. Who wants to listen to a clanging cymbal, after all?

22
The Biblical Difference Between Preaching and Teaching

The Greek New Testament uses many different words to describe distinct methods of communicating. There are thirteen hundred and twenty-nine references in the Greek New Testament using forms of the word *lego*, which is to *say* or *speak*. Two hundred and ninety-six times the word *laleo* is used, denoting *saying* or *speaking*. One hundred and nine times *parakaleo* is used to reference *exhorting*, *urging*, or *encouraging*. Ninety-seven times *didasko* or *teach* is employed. Sixty-one times we find *kerusso*, which is typically translated as *preach* or *proclaim*. Fifty-four times *euangellizo* appears, sometimes translated as *preach*, but referencing specifically the *telling of good news*.

Eighteen times *katangello* is utilized (all in Acts, Romans, 1 Corinthians, Philippians, and Colossians) to denote *speaking out* or *intently proclaiming*. Seventeen times *elencho* denotes *rebuking* or *correcting*. Thirteen times *dialegomai* is used to describe a process of engagement and participating in dialogue. Ten times reference is made, with the word *apologeomai*, to *making a defense*. Ten times *suzeteo* is used to reference *arguing* or *disputing*. Nine times *parresiazomai* is used for *speaking boldly*. Three times *diangello* communicates a *speaking through* or *giving notice*. There are other communication words utilized in the GNT, but these verb roots (and their represented forms) make up the vast majority.

> 1329 – *lego* – say, speak
> 296 – *laleo* – speak
> 109 – *parakaleo* – exhort, urge, encourage
> 97 – *didasko* – teach
> 61 – *kerusso* – preach, proclaim
> 54 – *euangellizo* – speak good news
> 18 – *katangello* – speak out, speak intently
> 17 – *elengcho* – rebuke, correct
> 13 – *dialegomai* – speak through, dialogue
> 10 – *apologeomai* – make a defense
> 10 – *suzeteo* – argue, dispute
> 9 – *parresiazomai* – speak boldly
> 3 – *diangello* – speak through, give notice

In addition to these verbs, two nouns are particularly helpful for the current discussion. *Didaskalia*, the noun form of the word *teaching* is used twenty-one times, while *kerugma*, generally translated as *preaching* (noun form), appears nine times.

> 21 – *didaskalia* – teaching, doctrine, instruction (noun)
> 9 – *kerugma* – message, preaching (noun)

In every instance of the word *kerugma*, the content of the preaching is for unbelievers – i.e., the Gospel, or a message of sin and repentance.[70] The post-pentecost[71] instances of the term *didaskalia* are very pointed:

---

[70] Mt 12:41; Mk 16:8; Lk 11:32; Rom 16:25; 1 Cor 1:21, 2:4, 15:14; 2 Tim 4:17; Tit 1:3.
[71] The two pre-pentecost references, Mt 15:9 and Mk 7:7, are general uses of the term, and not indicative of audience-specific content.

Romans 12:7 – *teaching* within the body of Christ
Romans 15:4 – written for our (believers) *instruction*
Ephesians 4:14 – so that we as believers may not be carried about by every *doctrine*
Colossians 2:22 – contrasts sound teaching with human *precepts*
1 Timothy 1:10 – contrasts with sound *doctrine*
1 Timothy 4:1 – *teachings* of demons
1 Timothy 4:6 – sound *doctrine*
1 Timothy 4:13 – exhortation and *teaching*
1 Timothy 4:16 – pay close attention to yourself and to your *teaching*
1 Timothy 5:17 – in speaking (preaching) and *teaching*
1 Timothy 6:1 – our *doctrine*
1 Timothy 6:3 (twice) – a different *doctrine*…and with the *doctrine* conforming to godliness
2 Timothy 3:10 – Timothy followed Paul's *teaching*
2 Timothy 3:16 – all Scripture is profitable for *teaching*
2 Timothy 4:3 – they will not endure sound *doctrine*
Titus 1:9 – sound *doctrine*
Titus 2:1 – sound *doctrine*
Titus 2:7 – purity in *doctrine*
Titus 2:10 – the *doctrine* of our God and Savior

In every post-pentecost use of *didaskalia*, there is one of two characteristics of teaching evident: either the teaching is false and is to be avoided, or else it is sound and is for believers to heed. In comparing the two terms *kerugma* and *didaskalia*, *kerugma* is for unbelievers and sound *didaskalia* is for believers. Additionally, all but four of the uses of *didaskalia* appear in Paul's letters to Timothy and Titus – two pastoral letters intended for the promotion of orthodoxy and spiritual growth in the church.

There are thirty-three instances of *kerusso* in the pre-pentecost NT, with all of them occurring in the Synoptics, and none in John's Gospel. The remaining twenty-eight NT appearances are post-pentecost. Note the audience or recipients of the post-pentecost forms of *kerusso*:

> Acts 8:5 – *proclaiming* Christ to the city of Samaria
> Acts 9:20 – *proclaiming* in the synagogue that Jesus is the Son of God
> Acts 10:37 – the Baptism John *proclaimed*
> Acts 10:42 – to *preach* about Jesus to the people
> Acts 15:21 – those who *preach* Moses
> Acts 19:13 – Jesus, whom Paul *preaches*
> Acts 20:25 – Paul *preaching* the kingdom among the Ephesians (implied, prior to the founding of the church there)
> Acts 28:31 – *preaching* the kingdom of God (Paul welcomed all who came, and some he was teaching, to others he was preaching)
> Romans 2:21 – *preach* that one should not steal
> Romans 10:8 – the word of faith which we are *preaching*
> Romans 10:14 – a *preacher*, leading to hearing, leading to belief
> Romans 10:15 – someone must be sent, to *preach*
> 1 Corinthians 1:23 – *preach* Christ crucified
> 1 Corinthians 9:27 – I have *preached* to others
> 1 Corinthians 15:11 – we *preach* (the Gospel, as in 15:3-4), and so you believed
> 1 Corinthians 15:12 – Christ is *preached*
> 2 Corinthians 1:19 – Christ *preached* among you
> 2 Corinthians 4:5 – *preach* Christ Jesus our Lord
> 2 Corinthians 11:4 – *preaches* another Jesus whom we have not preached
> Galatians 2:2 – the gospel which I *preach*

> Galatians 5:11 – *preach* circumcision
> Philippians 1:15 – *preaching* Christ
> Colossians 1:23 – the *faith*....which was proclaimed
> 1 Thessalonians 2:9 – we *proclaimed* to you the gospel of God
> 1 Timothy 3:16 – He...*proclaimed* among the nations
> 2 Timothy 4:2 – *preach* the word
> 1 Peter 3:19 – He made *proclamation* to the spirits
> Revelation 5:2 – a strong angel *proclaiming*

In each of these instances *kerusso* (most commonly translated *preach*) refers either to the proclamation of the gospel to unbelievers, or to proclamation in the generic sense (as in Rev 5:2). It does appear at first glance that 2 Timothy 4:2 is an exception – that Paul is exhorting Timothy to preach the word as part of his pastoral function, and that this is an instance of preaching to believers. However, Paul's usage of terms and the near context of Paul's command indicates that 2 Timothy 4:2 is not an exception.

Paul writes five imperatives for Timothy in 2 Timothy 4:2: preach (keruxon), be ready (*epistethi*), reprove (*elenchon*), rebuke (*epitimeson*), and exhort (*parakaleson*). The imperatives are needed because there will come a time when sound doctrine will be abandoned, and teachers will be accumulated that are not consistent with sound doctrine (4:3). In light of the teaching focus in 4:3, it would seem appropriate to assume that all the content of 4:2 is in a teaching context. However, 4:5 adds the imperative to *work* the work of an evangelist (*ergon poison euangelistou*). Earlier Paul differentiates between the role of evangelist and pastor–teacher (Eph 4:11), and in all other of the seventeen Pauline instances of the word *kerusso* and its forms, Paul refers to either the preaching of the gospel to unbelievers or to proclaiming something in a generic sense (as in Rom 2:21). Further, in 1 Corinthians 15:2, Paul refers to "the *word* (*logo* – same root as in 2 Tim 4:2) which *I preached* (*euengelisamen*)," as that which resulted in belief, not edification. If 2

Timothy 4:2 was an indication that Paul was mandating the preaching of the word to believers, it would represent a departure from his normal usage, and would be the only instance in the NT that such an imperative appears. Rather than take the *hapax legomena* interpretation, it seems more accurate to consider that Timothy's preaching of the word had to do with the work of an evangelist rather than the pastoral component of communicating God's word to believers.

Finally, it is worth considering in this context that there are fifty-four post-pentecost usages of the word *preach* (NASB) that are not rendered from the word *kerusso*. Forty-five of those instances are rendered from forms of *euangelizo*, which is a verb form of the phrase *good message*. Each of these instances have some reference to the proclaiming of the gospel.

> Acts 5:42 – teaching and *preaching (euangelizomenoi)* Jesus as the Christ
> Acts 8:4 – *preaching the good news (euangelizomeno)*
> Acts 8:25 – *preaching the gospel (euangelizonto)*
> Acts 8:35 – *preached (euangelisato)* Jesus
> Acts 8:40 – *preaching the gospel (euangelizeto)*
> Acts 10:36 – *preaching (euangelizomenos)* peace through Jesus Christ
> Acts 11:20 – *preaching (euangelizomenoi)* the Lord Jesus
> Acts 13:32 – we *preach (euangelizomenoi)* to you the good news
> Acts 14:7 – *preach the gospel* (euangelizomenoi)
> Acts 14:15 – *preach the gospel* (euangelizomenoi)
> Acts 14:21 – *preached the gospel (euangelisamenoi)*
> Acts 15:35 – teaching and *preaching (euangelizomenoi)*
> Acts 16:10 – *to preach the gospel (euangelisasthai)*
> Acts 17:18 – *preaching (euangelizeto)* Jesus
> Romans 1:9 – *preaching of the gospel (euangelio)*

Romans 1:15 – *to preach the gospel* (*euangelisasthai*)
Romans 15:20 – *to preach the gospel* (*euangelisasthai*)
1 Corinthians 1:17 – *to preach the gospel* (*euangelisasthai*)
1 Corinthians 9:16 (twice) – *preach the gospel* (*euangelizomai*)…*preach the gospel* (*euangelisomai*)
1 Corinthians 9:18 – *preach the gospel* (*euangelizomenos*)
1 Corinthians 15:1 – the gospel which *I preached* (*euengelisamen*)
1 Corinthians 15:2 – the word which *I preached* (*euengelisamen*)
2 Corinthians 10:16 – *to preach the gospel* (*euangelisasthai*)
2 Corinthians 11:7 – *preached the gospel* (*euangelisamen*)
Galatians 1:8 (twice) – preach to you a *gospel* (*euangelizetai*)…what we have *preached* (*euangelisametha*) to you
Galatians 1:9 – *preaching* to you *a gospel* (*euangelizetai*)
Galatians 1:11 – *gospel which was preached* (*euangelisthen*)
Galatians 1:16 – that *I might preach* (*euangelizomai*) Christ
Galatians 1:23 – *preaching* the faith (*euangelizetai*)
Galatians 3:8 – *preached the gospel beforehand* (*proeuangelisato*)
Galatians 4:13 – *I preached the gospel* (*euengelisamen*)
Ephesians 2:17 – *preached* (*euengelisato*) peace
Ephesians 3:8 – *to preach* (*euangelisasthai*) to the Gentiles
Philippians 4:15 – *preaching of the gospel* (*euangeliou*)
Hebrews 4:2 – *good news preached* (*euangelismenoi*)
Hebrews 4:6 – *good news preached* (*euangelisthentes*)
1 Peter 1:12 – *preached the gospel* (*euangelisamenon*)
1 Peter 1:25 – which *was preached* (*euangelisthen*)
1 Peter 4:6 – *gospel…has been preached* (*euengelisthe*)
Revelation 10:7 – as He *preached* (*euengelisen*) to His servants the prophets
Revelation 14:6 – gospel *to preach* (*euangelisai*)

The remaining nine post-pentecost non-*kerruso* renderings of *preach* in the NASB are as follows:

> Acts 21:28 – this is the man who *preaches* (*didaskon*) against (Acts 21:28 actually uses the word typically translated *teach*, though the NASB translates it as *preach*. It is worth noting that the people making the statement are not apostles, nor those heralding sound doctrine, but those attempting to have Paul harmed. This verse offers no data on whether or not teaching and preaching are distinct; it is simply the record of what was said by some ill-motivated individuals.)
> Romans 15:19 – *fully preached* (not rendered) *the gospel* (*peplerokenai to euangelion, or completed the gospel*)
> Romans 16:25 – the *preaching* (*kerugma*) of Jesus Christ
> 1 Corinthians 1:21 – foolishness of the *preaching* (*the message preached, tou kerugmatos*)
> 1 Corinthians 2:4 – *and my preaching* (*kai to kerugma mou*)
> 1 Corinthians 15:14 – *our preaching* (*kerugma emon*)
> Colossians 1:25 – the *preaching* – added, not rendered.
> 1 Timothy 5:17 – who work hard at *preaching* (not rendered, so better translated who work hard *in the word*) and teaching
> 1 Timothy 6:2 – teach and *preach* (*parakalei*, better *to exhort or encourage*)

Four of these instances render forms of *kerugma* (Rom 16:25, 1 Cor 1:21, 2:4, 15:14), and reference the proclaiming of the gospel. Two render words better translated as either teaching (as in Acts 21:28) or encouraging or exhorting (as in 1 Tim 6:2). 1 Timothy 6:2 is a context of encouraging or exhorting believers. The NASB's translation of the imperative as *preach* confuses the technical aspect of preaching for encouraging or exhorting. This particular rendering is the equivalent of referencing the Holy Spirit in John 14:16 as the *Preacher*, rather than the Helper (or Encourager, or

Exhorter). The final three occurrences (Rom 15:19, Col 1:25, and 1 Tim 5:17) add the term *preached* or *preaching* to the translation, but do not render the word from any Greek equivalent. In short, *preach* is not in any of these three passages. Most notable is the NASB reference of 1 Timothy 5:17 to elders as working hard at preaching and teaching. This passage is not advocating preaching as part of the elder/pastor role, but it is advocating instead the elder/pastor's diligent labor *in the word* and in teaching.

These hundreds of words and passages all present a unified message: that the primary mechanism for disseminating information to the body of Christ is *teaching*, and to those outside the body, the primary tool is *preaching*. This is not to say that a pastor should not be preaching the gospel within the church. In fact, three times Peter refers in his second letter (2 Pet 1:12, 1:13, 3:1) to reminders grounded in the gospel, but these reminders were secondary to the broad teaching of content throughout Peter's letters. Also, as in Timothy's case, it would seem very fitting and appropriate to the pastoral role that there be an emphasis on doing the work of an evangelist.

However, in our seeking to understand what is the work of an evangelist, we must examine the many Biblical instances of evangelism. The results of such an inquiry show that in the early church era evangelism was primarily conducted outside of the corporate meeting of the church. Preaching the gospel within those gatherings is certainly not prohibited, but there is another emphasis for the body that is mandated: *teaching*. While both activities of preaching and teaching are vital and commanded in their own contexts, there is definite and measurable distinction between the two. Confusing the two creates a significant imbalance in our understanding and in our practice. Perhaps it is time to revisit the pastor-as-preacher culture that has become so prevalent. The pastor's primary function (as in Ephesians 4:11) is to shepherd by teaching.

The Close Proximity of Teaching and Preaching

While there is a clear distinction between teaching and preaching, the two activities are not necessarily to be completely divorced from each other in practice. There are several post-pentecost instances where the two are practiced in close proximity. In Acts 5:42 the apostles are "teaching (*didaskontes*) and preaching (*euangelizomenoi*) Jesus the Christ." Later Paul and Barnabas, along with many others, are teaching (*didaskontes*) and preaching (*euangelizomenoi*) the word of the Lord (15:35). During his imprisonment at Rome, Paul is preaching (*kerusson*) and teaching (*didaskon*) (28:31). While in the earlier references there is no mention of distinctive content for the preaching and teaching, in this particular instance, the content is specified: Paul is preaching the kingdom of God and teaching about the Lord Jesus Christ.

While there are three other post-pentecost instances in the NASB of teaching and preaching appearing in close proximity, the term *preaching* is not rendered from an equivalent Greek word in two of those instances. In 1 Timothy 5:17, the elders are working hard *in word* (*en logo*) and *teaching*. In 1 Timothy 6:2 Timothy is told to teach and *exhort* (*parakalei*) these principles. In the instance in which the term *preach* is more precisely rendered, the content considered is not the word of God or the gospel, but simply how some are presenting ethical mandates (Rom 2:21).

What these close proximity instances of teaching and preaching show us is that while there are specific purposes and audiences intended for each activity, the two can be so closely related as to be used in the same context. While we shouldn't confuse the two terms and activities, we shouldn't neglect either one.

Priority in Communicating to Mixed Audiences

In any number of settings, a Bible communicator will not be aware of the spiritual/positional status of the listeners. In fact, only the

Lord has the capacity to truly understand what is in the heart of man (1 Cor 4:5). Consequently, while we do observe a clear conceptual distinction between preaching and teaching, it may be very helpful in practice for the two to share a close proximity. Peter grounds his exhortations to spiritual progress on reminders of the basic truths of the gospel (2 Pet 1:12, 1:13, 3:1). Paul recounts the gospel and how the Corinthians received it (1 Cor 15), and moves from that elementary reminder to more complex teaching of the eschatological hope of resurrection. In both of these examples, the writers are addressing believers, so they don't provide a model for communicating with a positionally mixed audience. Still they show how the gospel can be effectively (and necessarily) interwoven into a didactic situation. In cases like these preaching the gospel becomes an organic part of a teaching moment.

It is worth noting that not a single New Testament book is directly addressed to a mixed audience of unbelievers and believers (Hebrews is understood by some as written to mixed recipients, but this writer suggests the internal evidence supports the epistle's having been crafted for believers). In fact, John's Gospel is the only book directly addressing unbelievers (Jn 20:30-31). So, we don't have a book-level model for addressing mixed audiences.

Within a narrower context we have an important exchange between Jesus and his disciples – some of who were believing and some of who were unbelieving (Jn 6:60-66). Jesus used this opportunity to draw a sharp division between believers and unbelievers among his disciples by *teaching* (6:59) profound truths about Himself (6:53-55), the Father (6:57, 65), and the Spirit (6:63). The result of His teaching was that those who did not believe had no desire to listen to Him any further, and they simply stopped walking with Him from that point further (6:66). This episode is not within the church context, but nonetheless it provides a helpful example of teaching in a mixed-audience scenario. Here, Jesus taught hard truths (6:60) while communicating vividly the condition for eternal life (6:53-58). Some disciples were willing to remain and learn (6:68-69), while others weren't. In this instance, the priority is *teaching* – even in a setting in which Jesus knew there were some who were in unbelief (6:64) – and yet He incorporates basic gospel truths, creating a moment of decision for His listeners.

Within the context of believers assembling, there is an obvious priority of teaching over preaching. But the local church is often accompanied by unbelievers – some rather obvious and some not. If we are handling the word well, we will find many opportunities, even within teaching settings, (1) to ground exhortations for maturity of believers in gospel truth, as Peter and Paul modeled, and (2) to draw connections between taught material and the expected response for both believers and unbelievers. Thus, a teaching ministry in the church context can very naturally include gospel proclamation. The danger to avoid is in failing to challenge believers to grow past basic gospel truths:

> Therefore leaving the elementary teaching about the Christ, let us press on to maturity, not laying again a foundation of repentance from dead works and of faith toward God, of instruction about washings and the laying on of hands, and the resurrection of the dead and eternal judgment (Heb 6:1-2)…

When engaging with brothers and sisters in Christ, if we are not prioritizing growth to maturity, then we are missing the point of what is expected even of new believers: to be transformed by the renewing of our minds (Rom 12:1-2), to set the mind on things above (Col 3:1-4), and to allow the word of Christ to dwell in us (Col 3:16), just to name a few aspects. These points reflect the development of the ability to handle solid food, rather than a continuing dependence on milk (1 Cor 3:2).

23
Seven Informal and Formal Methods for Preaching and Teaching: (1) Informal Preaching

There are essentially seven different methods for communicating the Bible. (1) Informal preaching is addressed typically to unbelievers, is responsive to the unbeliever, and is generally not guided by rhetorical structure but rather by dialogue. (2) Formal preaching is also addressed to unbelievers, but is initiated by the preacher, and is more rhetorically structured. (3) Informal teaching is addressed to believers, typically in a casual setting, focusing on smaller groups and even individuals, and is not guided by rhetorical structure but by dialogue. (4-7) Formal teaching is also addressed to believers in a more formal setting, and can be effective with audiences of all sizes. Formal teaching generally fits into one of four categories. (4) Synthetic teaching is an overview or survey of a book or large section of Scripture. (5) Exegetical teaching is a verse-by-verse handling of a particular passage in context. (6) Analytical teaching is a topical or systematic handling of an aspect of Biblical doctrine (theology). (7) Topical teaching is very similar to analytical teaching, but might be employed for different purposes and in different contexts. Each of these modes of communication can be very effective if we follow the patterns provided in the Bible.

Understanding that there is a measurable Biblical distinction between preaching and teaching, we can also recognize that there are distinct Biblical models for formal and informal preaching and teaching. An examination of the various oratories of Jesus' ministry and of the apostolic era that followed shows that Jesus and the apostles valued both structured, formal, pre-intended delivery as well as less structured, informal, responsive delivery.

Paul illustrates both of these models in Acts 17. First we discover that Paul had a custom (17:2) of entering the synagogue – unsolicited – on a series of Sabbaths, and reasoning with the Jews from the Scriptures. He explains and gives evidence of Christ's identity and work (17:3). Paul's communication in this setting at Thessalonica was more formal, was deliberate, and involved explanation and presentation of evidence. Later Paul was in Athens, engaging in the same formal approach (17:16-17), when an opportunity arose. The philosophers requested a special audience with Paul, asking in 17:19, "May we know what this new teaching is which you are proclaiming…?" While Paul's address to them was certainly well structured and thought out, his preaching at Athens serves as an example of a less formal and more responsive model. Paul went where the questions were, and he addressed the questions directly. The content of his presentation to the Athenian philosophers was perhaps not dramatically different than that of his reasoning in the synagogues, but the presentations themselves differed in that one was pre-planned and initiated by Paul, the other was responsive to expressed needs. One was more formal and structured to best fit the context of the synagogue, the other was extemporaneously developed to meet the need of the moment. This is the essential difference between formal and informal preaching of God's word: it is formal if the speaker is initiating the presentation, informal if the audience is initiating.

Consider, for example, the elements of Peter's exhortation in 1 Peter 3:15:

> ...but sanctify Christ as Lord in your hearts, always being ready to make a defense to everyone who asks you to give an account for the hope that is in you, yet with gentleness and reverence...

(1) The imperative to believers: *sanctify or set apart Christ as Lord in your hearts* – this process begins with a commitment to the lordship of Jesus Christ.
(2) The adjective and adverb: *always ready* – the expectation here is self-evident. There needs to be such a level of preparation and understanding so as to be always primed for action.
(3) The direct object: *to a defense (apologian)*.
(4) The indirect object: *to all who are asking you*.
(5) The content of the request: *a word about the in-you hope*.

It is worth noting that this is the only imperative related to *apologetics* for believers, consequently Biblical apologetics is not an offensive task, but a responsive one. It is not formal, but informal. Biblical apologetics equals the informal preaching of the gospel – or more specifically, a word about the hope that is within us (which, of course, stems from the gospel). From this context we can say that not all evangelism is apologetic, but all apologetics – at least according to Peter's mention here – is evangelism.

Case Study: Contending for the Faith Without Being Contentious

Paul's words echo as if exclaimed from a canyon, yet we often fail to hear them. *"If possible, so far as it depends on you, be at peace with all men"* (Rom 12:18). At the same time if we listen closely, we can hear the resolve in Jude's voice as he urges believers to *"contend earnestly for the faith which was once for all handed down to the saints"* (Jude 3).

We are at war, but we are to be peaceful. This is no contradiction. Jude urges vigilance against false teachings within the church. Paul urges that we be as peaceful toward people as possible.

Paul illustrates both when he contends vigorously against different gospels and their teachers within the church (Gal 1:6-9). His contention extends even so far as a public rebuke of Peter because of his legalistic error (2:11ff). Peter's later response illustrates that Paul's efforts were unifying not divisive (2 Pet 3:15). Paul provides another example in Acts 17, when he interacts in a very peaceful and respectful way with unbelievers who were steeped in paganism. Paul labors to expose them to the truth, but does not force their hand – nor even condemn them. The response to his efforts was mixed: some sneered, others were eager to learn more, and some believed (17:32-34). Paul didn't expect that everyone would respond well, and his approach was not determined by the response he expected.

Paul illustrates that Christians *can* fulfill both mandates. When interacting with believers, he teaches them and reproves, holding them to the high ethical standards God prescribed for Christians. When interacting with unbelievers, Paul never appeals that they change their behavior. Instead he turns their eyes toward Jesus that they might understand who He is and what He had done for them. Paul models an opportunistic, rather than offensive evangelistic style.

Peter likewise advocates for opportunistic interaction with unbelievers when he reminds believers to be "always ready to make a defense to everyone who asks you to give an account for the hope that is in you…" (1 Pet 3:15). Peter's apologetic mandate is a response to those who ask (αἰτοῦντι). Peter does not prescribe for Christians to take an offensive, but rather a defensive stance. He is certainly not prohibiting believers from initiating conversations, but apologetics is responsive, rather than initiatory. Peter adds an important qualifier for our apologetic responses – that they should always be "with gentleness and reverence" (1 Pet 3:15).

Contending without being contentious is an example of how if we simply consider contextual factors we can understand that some apparent contradictions are not contradictions at all. Solomon illustrates this exact principle, when he gives guidance to readers that they "Do not answer a fool according to his folly" (Prov 26:4). In the very next verse, he seemingly contradicts that statement, saying, "Answer a fool according to his folly" (26:5). But there is more to it than that. 25:4 adds, "or you will also be like him." In that context, one should be careful in responding to a fool's folly, lest the responder find him or herself in the same foolishness they are answering. 26:5 adds, "that he not be wise in his own eyes." There is an appropriate time to answer a fool, and there is an inappropriate time for such responses. Solomon doesn't contradict himself; he explains how one can discern the right response for the situation. Rightly assessing the situation helps us respond properly. Sometimes we should contend. Other times we should not be contentious. At other times still, we should be both. As Paul implies, sometimes whether we are at peace is dependent on us, and sometimes it isn't. We need to discern the difference.

24

Seven Informal and Formal Methods for Preaching and Teaching: (2) Formal Preaching

It is interesting that we don't have any obvious New Testament instances of formal (or speaker initiated) preaching or presentation of the gospel. We don't have record of the structure and content of Paul's messages in the synagogues, for example. However, there are some hints as to what and how Paul communicated in those more formal settings. The crux of his proclamation was that Jesus is the Son of God (Acts 9:20). In that context he was confounding the Jews and proving (presumably by the Scriptures) that Jesus is the Christ (9:22). He proclaimed (*katangellon*) the word of God (13:5). He sat down and subjected himself to the culture of the day, waiting for the opportunity to make proclamation (13:14-16).

The expectation on the part of his listeners was that he would proclaim the word of the Lord (13:44). Paul spoke in such a manner as to appeal to both Jews and Greeks (14:1). His custom was to reason from the Scriptures (17:2, 17; 18:4, 19), and to explain and give evidence for the Person and work of Christ (17:3). His reasoning and persuading included content about the kingdom of God (19:8). Finally, his manner of communication was peaceful, so as not to cause a riot within the context of the synagogue (24:12).

Extracting what we are told of Paul's synagogue ministry provides the following characteristics of Paul's more formal preaching:

(1) The content was the word of God.
(2) The focus was the Person and work of Christ.
(3) The method was proving, reasoning, explaining, and persuading using the Scriptures.
(4) The message was reasonable and persuasive.
(5) The delivery was peaceful (insofar as the message allowed).

Perhaps one reason we don't have any further detail on the formal model is perhaps Jesus' charge to the disciples that they make up their minds not to prepare beforehand to defend themselves, because He would give them utterance and wisdom that their opponents would not be able to refute (Lk 21:12-15). In part due to this exhortation, we observe the apostles taking a responsive rather than initiatory stance. Still we can glean from apostolic evangelistic encounters some helpful structural patterns. After all, the apostles encouraged the next generation to "preach the word" (2 Tim 4:2). Peter's first address in Jerusalem, while responsive, was structured and well crafted, and as such provides an example for more formal proclamation.

Peter first accounts for human experience by appealing to Scripture (Acts 2:15-21). Second, he draws a necessary connection from human experience to Jesus Christ (2:22-24) and justifies that connection by Scripture (2:25-28). Third, he returns to human experience, appealing to the reality of who Christ is and what He did (2:29-36). When asked about what is the appropriate response to such truth (2:37), Peter prescribes repentance[72] – a change of

---

[72] Note that the imperative to repent (aorist active imperative second person) is set apart from the imperative to be baptized (aorist active imperative third person), the pronoun for forgiveness of *your* sins and the verb *to receive* the Holy Spirit are both in the second person. Repentance was the only condition, in this context, baptism was prescribed but not resulting in the two conditions.

mind (2:37). The model here is as follows:

(1) Connect the experience of the listener to Scripture.
(2) Demonstrate by the Scriptures the Person and work of Christ.
(3) Communicate the expected response.

Again in Acts 4, Peter answers the amazement of the people by appealing to Biblical history – specifically how God related historically to the listeners (3:13), how they had responded to Him (3:14-15), an explanation of the Person and work of Christ, along with a mention of the appropriate response (faith) to that truth (3:16), a specific statement of the expectation (repent and return, 3:17-19), and a reminder of God's promised response (3:19-20). The model here looks like:

(1) Discuss God's identity and historical intervention (the Sovereign, Creator).
(2) Discuss the human response (rebellion).
(3) Discuss the prescribed response (repent and return).
(4) Discuss result of receiving grace (kept promises).

In this particular instance, Peter is addressing Jews, and has in mind a specific response on the part of the Jews (repent and return), as well as a prophesied response from God – that the times of which Jeremiah spoke might come upon the people of Israel (e.g., Jer 29:11-13). Consequently, while we can borrow Peter's rhetorical structure, we need to be careful not to impose a prescription for Israel and the requisite blessing upon someone other than those to whom it was promised.

Acts 4 records yet another preaching of Peter, this one also informal and responsive, yet we observe a pattern that we can employ in formal evangelism. First is a connection of human experience to Christ (4:9-10), an emphasis of the Person and work of Christ (4:11-12), then a statement of His exclusivity in the salvific event (4:12). While there is no specific statement of the expected response, that which was to be responded to was the name of Jesus Christ. Peter's formula here is:

(1) Connect human experience to Christ.
(2) Specify His identity and His work.
(3) Acknowledge that He is the only Way of salvation.

Stephen provides another informal example of the preaching of the Gospel, simply recounting Israel's history from the Abrahamic covenant, to Jacob, to Joseph, to Moses and the Mosaic covenant, to David, and the Davidic covenant, to the prophets and Stephen's listeners' rejection of those prophets, and ultimately of Christ. This address seems more focused on indicting Stephen's listeners than on offering them repentance. It is more a pronouncement of judgment than an offer of grace through faith. Still, Stephen's historical narrative approach is a helpful model to give context to the Person and work of Christ.

Paul's preaching at the synagogue Pisidian Antioch was a response to an invitation to share *any* word of exhortation (13:15), and it is notable the approach Paul employed when he seemingly had the freedom to address any topic. He appealed to those Israelites who feared God (13:16), reminded them of God's deliverance of Israel at the exodus (13:17), recounted the history of Israel from the wilderness wandering (13:18), the conquest of Canaan (13:19), the period of the judges (13:20), the beginning of the monarchy with Saul's kingdom (13:21), to David's uniqueness and God's choosing of him (13:22), with a view to the arrival of the Messiah in the line of David, and as preannounced by John (13:23-25). After providing the historical context for the Person and work of Christ, Paul reminds his listeners of the rejection of Jesus, His death, burial, resurrection, and post resurrection appearances (13:27-31). Finally, Paul reminds of the Messiah's unique identity and position (13:32-37), and that it is through Him that the forgiveness of sins is proclaimed something the Law of Moses could not accomplish (13:38-39). Paul exhorts his listeners to heed the message so as not to miss the prophesied coming of Messiah (13:40-41). Paul's preaching in this instance can be broken down as follows:

(1) Recounting of history, to set the context for Christ.
(2) Explanation of the Person and work of Christ.
(3) Explanation of salvation through Him.
(4) Exhortation to respond properly, so as not to miss the opportunity.

Paul's preaching to the Athenians at Mars Hill (Acts 17:22-31) provides a slightly different approach, as this is the first of the accounts considered here in which the audience is predominantly gentile rather than Jewish. First, Paul acknowledges the Athenians' spirituality (17:22), and offers to provide them certainty where they are uncertain (17:23). He begins with the account of creation (17:24), acknowledging God's sovereign rights as Creator (17:24-25), His creation of and sovereignty over humanity (17:26), and the human seeking for the God who is not far off (17:27). He emphasizes the human connection to God (17:28-29), and the resulting expectation that humanity should come to the truth about God via repentance (17:30), because God will judge the world through Christ, whom He raised from the dead (17:31). The basic formula Paul models here is:

(1) To presuppose God's existence.
(2) To offer certainty.
(3) To state the sovereignty of God as Creator, and to

acknowledge His relationship with His creation.
(4) To acknowledge the disconnection of humanity from God.
(5) To prescribe the method for reconciliation (repentance).
(6) To emphasize the centrality of the Person and work of Christ, both now and in the future, as demonstrated in His resurrection.

Finally, we consider Paul's concise statement of the gospel in 1 Corinthians 15:3-5. Christ died for our sins according to the Scriptures (15:3), and that He was buried and raised on the third day according to the Scriptures (15:4), and that He appeared to Cephas, then to the twelve (15:5). Paul adds that Jesus appeared to more than five hundred, then again to James and all the apostles, and then finally to Paul, himself (15:6-7). This gospel presentation includes at least the elements of His substitutionary death for sins, His burial, and His resurrection. From the repetition of the *kai hoti* phrase, it appears that Paul is also including Jesus' appearance to the apostles as part of the gospel presentation, though from the *kata tas graphas* phrases, we might conclude that the gospel includes only the death, burial and resurrection. But either way, what is very apparent from Paul's gospel reminder here is the centrality of the Person and work of Christ. While Paul only directly mentions the work of Christ, it is apparent that in order to effectively accomplish the work, the Person must be properly qualified. For example, in order to accomplish a substitutionary death, Jesus could not have been dying to pay for His own sin. Thus, implicit in this gospel claim is the sinlessness (and thus, deity) of Jesus Christ. So when trying to reduce the gospel to its most basic elements, we are clearly left with the Person and work of Christ, and the prescribed response to Him (i.e., faith).

In each of the above examples, we see consistently four elements: (1) an assumption of the existence of God, (2) a historical context setting and/or relating to human experience, (3) the central focus on the Person and work of Christ, (4) a statement of (or at least implication of) the prescribed response. Obviously, we have no Biblical prescription or limitation regarding how a formal proclamation of the gospel should be structured and presented, but these evangelistic instances give us models that are well grounded, and thus, in the estimation of this writer, highly recommended. Consequently, when developing a formal preaching of the gospel, it is recommended that we follow one or more of the formulas provided here, or in examination of other evangelistic episodes in Scripture, we follow the patterns evident in those contexts. Either way, it is best to recognize that the Scriptures provide sufficient models for the formal proclamation of the gospel, even if those models are extracted from instances wherein the gospel was presented in an informal way.

Jonathan Edwards' "Sinners in the Hands of an Angry God" is one of the best known extra-Biblical evangelistic messages. Delivered initially to his own church at Northampton, Massachusetts, he presented it by invitation a second time (as recorded below) on July 8th, 1741 in Enfeld, Connecticut. Compare Edwards' methodology and theological breadth with some of the Biblical examples discussed above. Edwards typically wrote out his messages, and this particular manuscript remains useful for thinking through how one addresses the contemporary culture with the truth of God's word. Edwards certainly pulled no punches, and his listeners suffered no lack of theological depth in his words. Edwards sternly challenged them to think about who God is, what He requires, and how they should respond.

One analyst of Edwards' communication noted five characteristics present in Edwards' messages: (1) his messages generally were composed of three divisions – text, doctrine, and application, (2) his message idea was derived from Scripture (in the case of "Sinners in the Hands of an Angry God," the primary passage was Deuteronomy 32:35), (3) his messages were infused with Scriptural references, with a general balance of Old and New Testament passages, (4) his messages included frequent appeals to the phrase "in Scripture," in order to remind his listeners that the message was grounded in Scripture, and thus had implications for their lives, and (5) his messages were rooted in the authority and inerrancy of Scripture.[73]

Case Study: Jonathan Edwards, "Sinners in the Hands of an Angry God"[74]

Their foot shall slide in due time. Deuteronomy 32:35

In this verse is threatened the vengeance of God on the wicked unbelieving Israelites, who were God's visible people, and who lived under the means of grace; but who, notwithstanding all God's wonderful works towards them, remained (as verse 28.) void of counsel, having no understanding in them. Under all the cultivations of heaven, they brought forth bitter and poisonous fruit; as in the two verses next preceding the text. – The expression I have chosen for my text, their foot shall slide in due time, seems to imply the following things, relating to the punishment and destruction to which these wicked Israelites were exposed.

That they were always exposed to destruction; as one that stands or walks in slippery places is always exposed to fall. This is implied in the manner of their destruction coming upon them, being represented by their foot sliding. The same is expressed, Psalm 73:18. "Surely thou didst set them in slippery places; thou castedst them down into destruction."

---

[73] Jayoung Cho, "A Critical Examination of Jonathan Edwards's Theology of Preaching," (Ph.D Diss., New Orleans Baptist Theological Seminary, 2012), 39-47.
[74] From Christian Classics Ethereal Library, Jonathan Edwards, "Sinners in the Hand of an Angry God, " July 8, 1741, Enfeld, Connecticut, viewed at http://www.ccel.org/ccel/edwards/sermons.sinners.html.

It implies, that they were always exposed to sudden unexpected destruction. As he that walks in slippery places is every moment liable to fall, he cannot foresee one moment whether he shall stand or fall the next; and when he does fall, he falls at once without warning: Which is also expressed in Psalm 73:18,19. "Surely thou didst set them in slippery places; thou castedst them down into destruction: How are they brought into desolation as in a moment!" Another thing implied is, that they are liable to fall of themselves, without being thrown down by the hand of another; as he that stands or walks on slippery ground needs nothing but his own weight to throw him down.

That the reason why they are not fallen already and do not fall now is only that God's appointed time is not come. For it is said, that when that due time, or appointed time comes, their foot shall slide. Then they shall be left to fall, as they are inclined by their own weight. God will not hold them up in these slippery places any longer, but will let them go; and then, at that very instant, they shall fall into destruction; as he that stands on such slippery declining ground, on the edge of a pit, he cannot stand alone, when he is let go he immediately falls and is lost.

The observation from the words that I would now insist upon is this. – "There is nothing that keeps wicked men at any one moment out of hell, but the mere pleasure of God." – By the mere pleasure of God, I mean his sovereign pleasure, his arbitrary will, restrained by no obligation, hindered by no manner of difficulty, any more than if nothing else but God's mere will had in the least degree, or in any respect whatsoever, any hand in the preservation of wicked men one moment. – The truth of this observation may appear by the following consideration.

There is no want of power in God to cast wicked men into hell at any moment. Men's hands cannot be strong when God rises up. The strongest have no power to resist him, nor can any deliver out of his hands. – He is not only able to cast wicked men into hell, but he can most easily do it. Sometimes an earthly prince meets with a great deal of difficulty to subdue a rebel, who has found means to fortify himself, and has made himself strong by the numbers of his followers. But it is not so with God. There is no fortress that is any defence from the power of God. Though hand join in hand, and vast multitudes of God's enemies combine and associate themselves, they are easily broken in pieces. They are as great heaps of light chaff before the whirlwind; or large quantities of dry stubble before devouring flames. We find it easy to tread on and crush a worm that we see crawling on the earth; so it is easy for us to cut or singe a slender thread that any thing hangs by: thus easy is it for God, when he pleases, to cast his enemies down to hell. What are we, that we should think to stand before him, at whose rebuke the earth trembles, and before whom the rocks are thrown down?

They deserve to be cast into hell; so that divine justice never stands in the way, it makes no objection against God's using his power at any moment to destroy them. Yea, on the contrary, justice calls aloud for an infinite punishment of their sins. Divine justice says of the tree that brings forth such grapes of Sodom, "Cut it down, why cumbereth it the ground?" Luke 13:7. The sword of divine justice is every moment brandished over their heads, and it is nothing but the hand of arbitrary mercy, and God's mere will, that holds it back.

They are already under a sentence of condemnation to hell. They do not only justly deserve to be cast down thither, but the sentence of the law of God, that eternal and immutable rule of righteousness that God has fixed between him and mankind, is gone out against them, and stands against them; so that they are bound over already to hell. John 3:18. "He that believeth not is condemned already." So that every unconverted man properly belongs to hell; that is his place; from thence he is, John 8:23. "Ye are from beneath:" And thither he is bound; it is the place that justice,

SECTION III: OVERVIEW OF THE EXPOSITIONAL PROCESS 169

and God's word, and the sentence of his unchangeable law assign to him.

They are now the objects of that very same anger and wrath of God, that is expressed in the torments of hell. And the reason why they do not go down to hell at each moment, is not because God, in whose power they are, is not then very angry with them; as he is with many miserable creatures now tormented in hell, who there feel and bear the fierceness of his wrath. Yea, God is a great deal more angry with great numbers that are now on earth: yea, doubtless, with many that are now in this congregation, who it may be are at ease, than he is with many of those who are now in the flames of hell.

So that it is not because God is unmindful of their wickedness, and does not resent it, that he does not let loose his hand and cut them off. God is not altogether such an one as themselves, though they may imagine him to be so. The wrath of God burns against them, their damnation does not slumber; the pit is prepared, the fire is made ready, the furnace is now hot, ready to receive them; the flames do now rage and glow. The glittering sword is whet, and held over them, and the pit hath opened its mouth under them.

The devil stands ready to fall upon them, and seize them as his own, at what moment God shall permit him. They belong to him; he has their souls in his possession, and under his dominion. The scripture represents them as his goods, Luke 11:21. The devils watch them; they are ever by them at their right hand; they stand waiting for them, like greedy hungry lions that see their prey, and expect to have it, but are for the present kept back. If God should withdraw his hand, by which they are restrained, they would in one moment fly upon their poor souls. The old serpent is gaping for them; hell opens its mouth wide to receive them; and if God should permit it, they would be hastily swallowed up and lost.

There are in the souls of wicked men those hellish

principles reigning, that would presently kindle and flame out into hell fire, if it were not for God's restraints. There is laid in the very nature of carnal men, a foundation for the torments of hell. There are those corrupt principles, in reigning power in them, and in full possession of them, that are seeds of hell fire. These principles are active and powerful, exceeding violent in their nature, and if it were not for the restraining hand of God upon them, they would soon break out, they would flame out after the same manner as the same corruptions, the same enmity does in the hearts of damned souls, and would beget the same torments as they do in them. The souls of the wicked are in scripture compared to the troubled sea, Isa. 57:20. For the present, God restrains their wickedness by his mighty power, as he does the raging waves of the troubled sea, saying, "Hitherto shalt thou come, but no further;" but if God should withdraw that restraining power, it would soon carry all before it. Sin is the ruin and misery of the soul; it is destructive in its nature; and if God should leave it without restraint, there would need nothing else to make the soul perfectly miserable. The corruption of the heart of man is immoderate and boundless in its fury; and while wicked men live here, it is like fire pent up by God's restraints, whereas if it were let loose, it would set on fire the course of nature; and as the heart is now a sink of sin, so if sin was not restrained, it would immediately turn the soul into fiery oven, or a furnace of fire and brimstone.

It is no security to wicked men for one moment, that there are no visible means of death at hand. It is no security to a natural man, that he is now in health, and that he does not see which way he should now immediately go out of the world by any accident, and that there is no visible danger in any respect in his circumstances. The manifold and continual experience of the world in all ages, shows this is no evidence, that a man is not on the very brink of eternity, and that the next step will not be into another world. The unseen, unthought-of ways and means of persons going suddenly out of the world are innumerable and inconceivable. Unconverted men walk over the pit of hell on a rotten covering, and there are innumerable places in this covering so weak that they will not bear their weight, and these places are not seen. The arrows of death fly unseen at noon-day; the sharpest sight cannot discern them. God has so many different unsearchable ways of taking wicked men out of the world and sending them to hell, that there is nothing to make it appear, that God had need to be at the expense of a miracle, or go out of the ordinary course of his providence, to destroy any wicked man, at any moment. All the means that there are of sinners going out of the world, are so in God's hands, and so universally and absolutely subject to his power and determination, that it does not depend at all the less on the mere will of God, whether sinners shall at any moment go to hell, than if means were never made use of, or at all concerned in the case.

Natural men's prudence and care to preserve their own lives, or the care of others to preserve them, do not secure them a moment. To this, divine providence and universal experience do also bear testimony. There is this clear evidence that men's own wisdom is no security to them from death; that if it were otherwise we should see some difference between the wise and politic men of the world, and others, with regard to their liableness to early and unexpected death: but how is it in fact? Eccles. 2:16. "How dieth the wise man? even as the fool."

All wicked men's pains and contrivance which they use to escape hell, while they continue to reject Christ, and so remain wicked men, do not secure them from hell one moment. Almost every natural man that hears of hell, flatters himself that he shall escape it; he depends upon himself for his own security; he flatters himself in what he has done, in what he is now doing, or what he intends to do. Every one lays out matters in his own mind how he shall avoid damnation, and flatters himself that he contrives well for himself, and that his schemes will not fail. They hear indeed that there are but few saved, and that the greater part of men that have died heretofore are gone to hell; but each one imagines that he lays out matters better for his own escape than others have done. He does not intend to come to that place of torment; he says within himself, that he intends to take effectual care, and to order matters so for himself as not to fail.

But the foolish children of men miserably delude themselves in their own schemes, and in confidence in their own strength and wisdom; they trust to nothing but a shadow. The greater part of those who heretofore have lived under the same means of grace, and are now dead, are undoubtedly gone to hell; and it was not because they were not as wise as those who are now alive: it was not because they did not lay out matters as well for themselves to secure their own escape. If we could speak with them, and inquire of them, one by one, whether they expected, when alive, and when they used to hear about hell, ever to be the subjects of misery: we doubtless, should hear one and another reply, "No, I never intended to come here: I had laid out matters otherwise in my mind; I thought I should contrive well for myself – I thought my scheme good. I intended to take effectual care; but it came upon me unexpected; I did not look for it at that time, and in that manner; it came as a thief – Death outwitted me: God's wrath was too quick for me. Oh, my cursed foolishness! I was flattering myself, and pleasing myself with vain dreams of what I would do hereafter; and when I was saying, Peace and safety, then sudden destruction came upon me."

God has laid himself under no obligation, by any promise to keep any natural man out of hell one moment. God certainly has made no promises either of eternal life, or of any deliverance or preservation from eternal death, but what are contained in the covenant of grace, the promises that are given in Christ, in whom all the promises are yea and amen. But surely they have no interest in the promises of the covenant of grace who are not the children of the covenant, who do not believe in any of the promises, and have no interest in the Mediator of the covenant.

So that, whatever some have imagined and pretended about promises made to natural men's earnest seeking and knocking, it is plain and manifest, that whatever pains a natural man takes in religion, whatever prayers he makes, till he believes in Christ, God is under no manner of obligation to keep him a moment from eternal destruction.

So that, thus it is that natural men are held in the hand of God, over the pit of hell; they have deserved the fiery pit, and are already sentenced to it; and God is dreadfully provoked, his anger is as great towards them as to those that are actually suffering the executions of the fierceness of his wrath in hell, and they have done nothing in the least to appease or abate that anger, neither is God in the least bound by any promise to hold them up one moment; the devil is waiting for them, hell is gaping for them, the flames gather and flash about them, and would fain lay hold on them, and swallow them up; the fire pent up in their own hearts is struggling to break out: and they have no interest in any Mediator, there are no means within reach that can be any security to them. In short, they have no refuge, nothing to take hold of; all that preserves them every moment is the mere arbitrary will, and uncovenanted, unobliged forbearance of an incensed God.

Application
The use of this awful subject may be for awakening unconverted persons in this congregation. This that you have heard is the case of every one of you that are out of Christ. – That world of misery, that lake of burning brimstone, is extended abroad under you. There is the dreadful pit of the glowing flames of the wrath of God; there is hell's wide gaping mouth open; and you have nothing to stand upon, nor any thing to take hold of; there is nothing between you and hell but the air; it is only the power and mere pleasure of God

that holds you up.

You probably are not sensible of this; you find you are kept out of hell, but do not see the hand of God in it; but look at other things, as the good state of your bodily constitution, your care of your own life, and the means you use for your own preservation. But indeed these things are nothing; if God should withdraw his hand, they would avail no more to keep you from falling, than the thin air to hold up a person that is suspended in it.

Your wickedness makes you as it were heavy as lead, and to tend downwards with great weight and pressure towards hell; and if God should let you go, you would immediately sink and swiftly descend and plunge into the bottomless gulf, and your healthy constitution, and your own care and prudence, and best contrivance, and all your righteousness, would have no more influence to uphold you and keep you out of hell, than a spider's web would have to stop a falling rock. Were it not for the sovereign pleasure of God, the earth would not bear you one moment; for you are a burden to it; the creation groans with you; the creature is made subject to the bondage of your corruption, not willingly; the sun does not willingly shine upon you to give you light to serve sin and Satan; the earth does not willingly yield her increase to satisfy your lusts; nor is it willingly a stage for your wickedness to be acted upon; the air does not willingly serve you for breath to maintain the flame of life in your vitals, while you spend your life in the service of God's enemies.

God's creatures are good, and were made for men to serve God with, and do not willingly subserve to any other purpose, and groan when they are abused to purposes so directly contrary to their nature and end. And the world would spew you out, were it not for the sovereign hand of him who hath subjected it in hope. There are the black clouds of God's wrath now hanging directly over your heads, full of the dreadful storm, and big with thunder; and were it not for the restraining hand of God, it would immediately burst forth upon you. The sovereign pleasure of God, for the present, stays his rough wind; otherwise it would come with fury, and your destruction would come like a whirlwind, and you would be like the chaff on the summer threshing floor.

The wrath of God is like great waters that are dammed for the present; they increase more and more, and rise higher and higher, till an outlet is given; and the longer the stream is stopped, the more rapid and mighty is its course, when once it is let loose. It is true, that judgment against your evil works has not been executed hitherto; the floods of God's vengeance have been withheld; but your guilt in the mean time is constantly increasing, and you are every day treasuring up more wrath; the waters are constantly rising, and waxing more and more mighty; and there is nothing but the mere pleasure of God, that holds the waters back, that are unwilling to be stopped, and press hard to go forward. If God should only withdraw his hand from the flood-gate, it would immediately fly open, and the fiery floods of the fierceness and wrath of God, would rush forth with inconceivable fury, and would come upon you with omnipotent power; and if your strength were ten thousand times greater than it is, yea, ten thousand times greater than the strength of the stoutest, sturdiest devil in hell, it would be nothing to withstand or endure it.

The bow of God's wrath is bent, and the arrow made ready on the string, and justice bends the arrow at your heart, and strains the bow, and it is nothing but the mere pleasure of God, and that of an angry God, without any promise or obligation at all, that keeps the arrow one moment from being made drunk with your blood. Thus all you that never passed under a great change of heart, by the mighty power of the Spirit of God upon your souls; all you that were never born again, and made new creatures, and raised from being dead in sin, to a state of new, and before altogether unexperienced light and life, are in the hands of an angry God. However you may have reformed your life in many things, and may have had religious affections, and may keep up a form of religion in your families and closets, and in the house of God, it is nothing but his mere pleasure that keeps you from being this moment swallowed up in everlasting destruction. However unconvinced you may now be of the truth of what you hear, by and by you will be fully convinced of it. Those that are gone from being in the like circumstances with you, see that it was so with them; for destruction came suddenly upon most of them; when they expected nothing of it, and while they were saying, Peace and safety: now they see, that those things on which they depended for peace and safety, were nothing but thin air and empty shadows.

The God that holds you over the pit of hell, much as one holds a spider, or some loathsome insect over the fire, abhors you, and is dreadfully provoked: his wrath towards you burns like fire; he looks upon you as worthy of nothing else, but to be cast into the fire; he is of purer eyes than to bear to have you in his sight; you are ten thousand times more abominable in his eyes, than the most hateful venomous serpent is in ours. You have offended him infinitely more than ever a stubborn rebel did his prince; and yet it is nothing but his hand that holds you from falling into the fire every moment. It is to be ascribed to nothing else, that you did not go to hell the last night; that you was suffered to awake again in this world, after you closed your eyes to sleep. And there is no other reason to be given, why you have not dropped into hell since you arose in the morning, but that God's hand has held you up. There is no other reason to be given why you have not gone to hell, since you have sat here in the house of God, provoking his pure eyes by your sinful wicked manner of attending his solemn worship. Yea, there is nothing else that is to be given as a reason why you do not this very moment drop down into hell.

O sinner! Consider the fearful danger you are in: it is a great furnace of wrath, a wide and bottomless pit, full of the fire of wrath, that you are held over in the hand of that God, whose wrath is provoked and incensed as much against you, as against many of the damned in hell. You hang by a slender thread, with the flames of divine wrath flashing about it, and ready every moment to singe it, and burn it asunder; and you have no interest in any Mediator, and nothing to lay hold of to save yourself, nothing to keep off the flames of wrath, nothing of your own, nothing that you ever have done, nothing that you can do, to induce God to spare you one moment. – And consider here more particularly, Whose wrath it is: it is the wrath of the infinite God. If it were only the wrath of man, though it were of the most potent prince, it would be comparatively little to be regarded. The wrath of kings is very much dreaded, especially of absolute monarchs, who have the possessions and lives of their subjects wholly in their power, to be disposed of at their mere will. Prov. 20:2. "The fear of a king is as the roaring of a lion: Whoso provoketh him to anger, sinneth against his own soul." The subject that very much enrages an arbitrary prince, is liable to suffer the most extreme torments that human art can invent, or human power can inflict. But the greatest earthly potentates in their greatest majesty and strength, and when clothed in their greatest terrors, are but feeble, despicable worms of the dust, in comparison of the great and almighty Creator and King of heaven and earth. It is but little that they can do, when most enraged, and when they have exerted the utmost of their fury. All the kings of the earth, before God, are as grasshoppers; they are nothing, and less than nothing: both their love and their hatred is to be despised. The wrath of the great King of kings, is as much more terrible than theirs, as his majesty is greater. Luke 12:4,5. "And I say unto you, my friends, Be not afraid of them that kill the body, and after that, have no more that they can do. But I will forewarn you whom you shall fear: fear him, which after he hath killed, hath power to cast into hell: yea, I say unto you, Fear him."

It is the fierceness of his wrath that you are exposed to. We often read of the fury of God; as in Isa. 59:18. "According to their deeds, accordingly he will repay fury to his adversaries." So Isa. 66:15. "For behold, the Lord will come with fire, and with his chariots like a whirlwind, to render his anger with fury, and his rebuke with flames of fire." And in many other places. So, Rev. 19:15, we read of "the wine press of the fierceness and wrath of Almighty God." The words are exceeding terrible. If it had only been said, "the wrath of God," the words would have implied that which is infinitely dreadful: but it is "the fierceness and wrath of God." The fury of God! the fierceness of Jehovah! Oh, how dreadful that must be! Who can utter or conceive what such expressions carry in them! But it is also "the fierceness and wrath of almighty God." As though there would be a very great manifestation of his almighty power in what the fierceness of his wrath should inflict, as though omnipotence should be as it were enraged, and exerted, as men are wont to exert their strength in the fierceness of their wrath. Oh! then, what will be the consequence! What will become of the poor worms that shall suffer it! Whose hands can be strong? And whose heart can endure? To what a dreadful, inexpressible, inconceivable depth of misery must the poor creature be sunk who shall be the subject of this!

Consider this, you that are here present, that yet remain in an unregenerate state. That God will execute the fierceness of his anger, implies, that he will inflict wrath without any pity. When God beholds the ineffable extremity of your case, and sees your torment to be so vastly disproportioned to your strength, and sees how your poor soul is crushed, and sinks down, as it were, into an infinite gloom; he will have no compassion upon you, he will not forbear the executions of his wrath, or in the least lighten his hand; there shall be no moderation or mercy, nor will God then at all stay his rough wind; he will have no regard to your welfare, nor be at all careful lest you should suffer too much in any other sense, than only that you shall not suffer beyond what strict justice requires. Nothing shall be withheld, because it is so hard for you to bear. Ezek. 8:18. "Therefore will I also deal in fury: mine eye shall not spare, neither will I have pity; and though they cry in mine ears with a loud voice, yet I will not hear them." Now God stands ready to pity you; this is a day of mercy; you may cry now with some encouragement of obtaining mercy. But when once the day of mercy is past, your most lamentable and dolorous cries and shrieks will be in vain; you will be wholly lost and thrown away of God, as to any regard to your welfare. God will have no other use to put you to, but to suffer misery; you shall be continued in being to no other end; for you will be a vessel of wrath fitted to destruction; and there will be no other use of this vessel, but to be filled full of wrath. God will be so far from pitying you when you cry to him, that it is said he will only "laugh and mock," Prov. 1:25,26, etc.

How awful are those words, Isa. 63:3, which are the words of the great God. "I will tread them in mine anger, and will trample them in my fury, and their blood shall be sprinkled upon my garments, and I will stain all my raiment." It is perhaps impossible to conceive of words that carry in them greater manifestations of these three things, viz. contempt, and hatred, and fierceness of indignation. If you cry to God to pity you, he will be so far from pitying you in your doleful case, or showing you the least regard or favour, that instead of that, he will only tread you under foot. And though he will know that you cannot bear the weight of omnipotence treading upon you, yet he will not regard that, but he will crush you under his feet without mercy; he will crush out your blood, and make it fly, and it shall be sprinkled on his garments, so as to stain all his raiment. He will not only hate you, but he will have you in the utmost contempt: no place shall be thought fit for you, but under his feet to be trodden down as the mire of the streets.

The misery you are exposed to is that which God will inflict to that end, that he might show what that wrath of Jehovah is. God hath had it on his heart to show to angels and men, both how excellent his love is, and also how terrible his wrath is. Sometimes earthly kings have a mind to show how terrible their wrath is, by the extreme punishments they would execute on those that would provoke them. Nebuchadnezzar, that mighty and haughty monarch of the Chaldean empire, was willing to show his wrath when enraged with Shadrach, Meshach, and Abednego; and accordingly gave orders that the burning fiery furnace should be heated seven times hotter than it was before; doubtless, it was raised to the utmost degree of fierceness that human art could raise it. But the great God is also willing to show his wrath, and magnify his awful majesty and mighty power in the extreme sufferings of his enemies. Rom. 9:22. "What if God, willing to show his wrath, and to make his power known, endured with much long-suffering the vessels of wrath fitted to destruction?" And seeing this is his design, and what he has determined, even to show how terrible the unrestrained wrath, the fury and fierceness of Jehovah is, he will do it to effect. There will be something accomplished and brought to pass that will be dreadful with a witness. When the great and angry God hath risen up and executed his awful vengeance on the poor sinner, and the wretch is actually suffering the infinite weight and power of his indignation, then will God call upon the whole universe to behold that awful majesty and mighty power that is to be seen in it. Isa. 33:12-14. "And the people shall be as the burnings of lime, as thorns cut up shall they be burnt in the fire. Hear ye that are far off, what I have done; and ye that are near, acknowledge my might. The sinners in Zion are afraid; fearfulness hath surprised the hypocrites," etc.

Thus it will be with you that are in an unconverted state, if you continue in it; the infinite might, and majesty, and terribleness of the omnipotent God shall be magnified upon you, in the ineffable strength of your torments. You shall be tormented in the presence of the holy angels, and in the presence of the Lamb; and when you shall be in this state of suffering, the glorious inhabitants of heaven shall go forth and look on the awful spectacle, that they may see what the wrath and fierceness of the Almighty is; and when they have seen it, they will fall down and adore that great power and majesty. Isa. 66:23,24. "And it shall come to pass, that from one new moon to another, and from one sabbath to another, shall all flesh come to worship before me, saith the Lord. And they shall go forth and look upon the carcasses of the men that have transgressed against me; for their worm shall not die, neither shall their fire be quenched, and they shall be an abhorring unto all flesh."

It is everlasting wrath. It would be dreadful to suffer this fierceness and wrath of Almighty God one moment; but you must suffer it to all eternity. There will be no end to this exquisite horrible misery. When you look forward, you shall see a long for ever, a boundless duration before you, which will swallow up your thoughts, and amaze your soul; and you will absolutely despair of ever having any deliverance, any end, any mitigation, any rest at all. You will know certainly that you must wear out long ages, millions of millions of ages, in wrestling and conflicting with this almighty merciless vengeance; and then when you have so done, when so many ages have actually been spent by you in this manner, you will know that all is but a point to what remains. So that your punishment will indeed be infinite. Oh, who can express what the state of a soul in such circumstances is! All that we can possibly say about it, gives but a very feeble, faint representation of it; it is inexpressible and inconceivable: For "who knows the power of God's anger?"

How dreadful is the state of those that are daily and hourly in the danger of this great wrath and infinite misery! But this is the dismal case of every soul in this congregation that has not been born again, however moral and strict, sober and religious, they may otherwise be. Oh that you would consider it, whether you be young or old! There is reason to think, that there are many in this congregation now hearing this discourse, that will actually be the subjects of this very misery to all eternity. We know not who they are, or in what seats they sit, or what thoughts they now have. It may be they are now at ease, and hear all these things without much disturbance, and are now flattering themselves that they are not the persons, promising themselves that they shall escape. If we knew that there was one person, and but one, in the whole congregation, that was to be the subject of this misery, what an awful thing would it be to think of! If we knew who it was, what an awful sight would it be to see such a person! How might all the rest of the congregation lift up a lamentable and bitter cry over him! But, alas! instead of one, how many is it likely will remember this discourse in hell? And it would be a wonder, if some that are now present should not be in hell in a very short time, even before this year is out. And it would be no wonder if some persons, that now sit here, in some seats of this meeting-house, in health, quiet and secure, should be there before tomorrow morning. Those of you that finally continue in a natural condition, that shall keep out of hell longest will be there in a little time! your damnation does not slumber; it will come swiftly, and, in all probability, very suddenly upon many of you. You have reason to wonder that you are not already in hell. It is doubtless the case of some whom you have seen and known, that never deserved hell more than you, and that heretofore appeared as likely to have been now alive as you. Their case is past all hope; they are crying in extreme misery and perfect despair; but here you are in the land of the living and in the house of God, and have an opportunity to obtain salvation. What would not those poor damned hopeless souls give for one day's opportunity such as you now enjoy!

And now you have an extraordinary opportunity, a day wherein Christ has thrown the door of mercy wide open, and stands in calling and crying with a loud voice to poor sinners; a day wherein many are flocking to him, and pressing into the kingdom of God. Many are daily coming from the east, west, north and south; many that were very lately in the same miserable condition that you are in, are now in a happy state, with their hearts filled with love to him who has loved them, and washed them from their sins in his own blood, and rejoicing in hope of the glory of God. How awful is it to be left behind at such a day! To see so many others feasting, while you are pining and perishing! To see so many rejoicing and singing for joy of heart, while you have cause to mourn for sorrow of heart, and howl for vexation of spirit! How can you rest one moment in such a condition? Are not your souls as precious as the souls of the people at Suffield, where they are flocking from day to day to Christ?

Are there not many here who have lived long in the world, and are not to this day born again? and so are aliens from the commonwealth of Israel, and have done nothing ever since they have lived, but treasure up wrath against the day of wrath? Oh, sirs, your case, in an especial manner, is extremely dangerous. Your guilt and hardness of heart is extremely great. Do you not see how generality persons of your years are passed over and left, in the present remarkable and wonderful dispensation of God's mercy? You had need to consider yourselves, and awake thoroughly out of sleep. You cannot bear the fierceness and wrath of the infinite God. – And you, young men, and young women, will you neglect this precious season which you now enjoy, when so many others of your age are renouncing all youthful vanities, and flocking to Christ? You especially have now an extraordinary opportunity; but if you neglect it, it will soon be with you as with those persons who spent all the precious days of youth in sin, and are now come to such a dreadful pass in blindness and hardness. – And you, children, who are unconverted, do not you know that you are going down to hell, to bear the dreadful wrath of that God, who is now angry with you every day and every night? Will you be content to be the children of the devil, when so many other children in the land are converted, and are become the holy and happy children of the King of kings?

And let every one that is yet out of Christ, and hanging over the pit of hell, whether they be old men and women, or middle aged, or young people, or little children, now hearken to the loud calls of God's word and providence. This acceptable year of the Lord, a day of such great favour to some, will doubtless be a day of as remarkable vengeance to others. Men's hearts harden, and their guilt increases apace at such a day as this, if they neglect their souls; and never was there so great danger of such persons being given up to hardness of heart and blindness of mind. God seems now to be hastily gathering in his elect in all parts of the land; and probably the greater part of adult persons that ever shall be saved, will be brought in now in a little time, and that it will be as it was on the great out-pouring of the Spirit upon the Jews in the apostles' days; the election will obtain, and the rest will be blinded. If this should be the case with you, you will eternally curse this day, and will curse the day that ever you was born, to see such a season of the pouring out of God's Spirit, and will wish that you had died and gone to hell before you had seen it. Now undoubtedly it is, as it was in the days of John the Baptist, the axe is in an extraordinary manner laid at the root of the trees, that every tree which brings not forth good fruit, may be hewn down and cast into the fire.

Therefore, let every one that is out of Christ, now awake and fly from the wrath to come. The wrath of Almighty God is now undoubtedly hanging over a great part of this congregation. Let every one fly out of Sodom: "Haste and escape for your lives, look not behind you, escape to the mountain, lest you be consumed."

Case Study: When Faith Goes to College What Comes Home? Communicating Components of a Biblical Worldview

The Barna Group indicated recently that only 20% of young adults

SECTION III: OVERVIEW OF THE EXPOSITIONAL PROCESS 185

maintain a level of spiritual activity consistent with that of their high-school years.[75] If this study may be used to predict, only one in five who were spiritually attentive during high school will remain that way into adulthood. This is more significant, I think, than studies that show young adults leaving the church because they never really engaged. So, why the migration from spiritually serious to spiritually apathetic? I would suggest that a significant component for the departure is Christians' general unpreparedness for what they will face at university. Friedrich Nietzsche famously wrote "Once did people say God, when they looked out upon distant seas, now however, have I taught you to say Superman."[76] In keeping with Nietzsche's "God is dead" theme, Bertrand Russell observed,

> Religion is based, I think, primarily and mainly upon fear. It is partly the terror of the unknown and partly, as I have said, the wish to feel that you have a kind of elder brother who will stand by you in all your troubles and disputes. Fear is the basis of the whole thing — fear of the mysterious, fear of defeat, fear of death. Fear is the parent of cruelty, and therefore it is no wonder if cruelty and religion have gone hand in hand. It is because fear is at the basis of those two things. In this world we can now begin a little to understand things, and a little to master them by help of science, which has forced its way step by step against the Christian religion, against the churches, and against the opposition of all the old precepts. Science can help us to get over this craven fear in which mankind has lived for so many

---

[75] Barna Group "Most Twentysomethings Put Christianity on the Shelf following Spiritually Active Teen Years," http://www.barna.org/teens-next-gen-articles/147-most-twentysomethings-put-christianity-on-the-shelf-following-spiritually-active-teen-years, published 9/11/2006.
[76] Friedrich Nietzsche, *Thus Spoke Zarathustra*, (Pennsylvania: Penn State University, 1999), 82.

generations. Science can teach us, and I think our own hearts can teach us, no longer to look around for imaginary supports, no longer to invent allies in the sky, but rather to look to our own efforts here below to make this world a better place to live in, instead of the sort of place that the churches in all these centuries have made it.[77]

Just as Nietzsche described self-sufficiency as the means of deriving independence from God (and thereby "killing" Him), Russell understood that science was the ultimate means of self-sufficiency. As *Pirates of the Caribbean* character Lord Cutler Beckett proclaimed to the metaphysically enhanced Davey Jones, "The immaterial has become immaterial."[78]

Historian of philosophy W.K.C. Guthrie recognizes early influences of naturalism in science and philosophy. He notes, "Philosophy and science start with the bold confession of faith that not caprice but an inherent orderliness underlies the phenomena, and the explanation of nature is to be sought within nature itself."[79] In other words, the rise of philosophy and science is admittedly rooted in faith that only the natural realm is reality. The Greek natural philosophers were the predecessors to the modern scientific movement, and the defining factor (faith in the exclusivity of the material) has remained central through the years.

Wendell Berry describes the purpose of the university as follows:

> The thing being made in a university is humanity. Given the current influence of universities, this is merely inevitable.

---

[77] Bertrand Russell, "Why I Am Not a Christian," March 6, 1927, http://www.users.drew.edu/~jlenz/whynot.html.
[78] Ted Elliott and Terry Rossio, *Pirates of the Caribbean: At World's End*, theatrical release, directed by Gore Verbinski, Disney, 2007.
[79] WKC Guthrie, *A History of Greek Philosophy, Volume I: The Earlier Presocratics and the Pythagoreans* (New York, NY: Cambridge University Press, 1962), 44.

> But what universities, at least the publicly supported ones, are mandated to make or to help to make is human beings in the fullest sense of those words – not just trained workers or knowledgeable citizens but responsible heirs and members of human culture...Underlying the idea of a university – the bringing together, the combining into one, of all the disciplines – is the idea that good work and good citizenship are the inevitable by-products of the making of a good – that is, a fully developed – human being. This, as I understand it, is the definition of the name university.[80]

Berry's comments illustrate the interdisciplinary design of university – that knowledge and applications are integrative and connected. Consequently there are significant implications when the university is successful, as Berry describes, at making humanity. Here is the key question then: if the science and philosophy that undergirds university curriculum is decidedly anti-metaphysical, then how does the student survive the inculcation of an anti-God worldview?

Sadly, many don't, for their own theistic faith often goes unexamined and unsupported, and is easily abandoned when challenged. People don't often realize what they believe until those beliefs are countered. Sometimes the arguments against Christianity, for example, are so convincing that we may abandon it with little resistance. But for those willing to examine Biblical Christianity and contrast it fairly with the atheistic roots of contemporary science and philosophy (so-called), the process of engaging atheism as a worldview – in all its glory – can be a very productive process.

In other words, Christians should not be afraid of engaging other views – but we should engage those views from a vantage

---

[80] Wendell Berry, *Home Economics* (New York: North Point Press, 1987), 77.

point of knowledge, rather than ignorance. We should understand not just what is believed, but why. We should understand the implications of what is believed. We should have a basic framework of worldview that allows us to fairly compare and contrast the diverse worldviews.

I suggest at least the following six components for such a framework, to the end that we can have confidence in what we believe, that we can challenge each other and refine where we need refining, and ultimately so that we can think and walk as we ought. We ought to (1) understand that everyone begins with faith, (2) understand the basis of truth, (3) understand the conflict of worldviews, (4) understand our position in Christ, (5) understand our equipment for growing and walking, and (6) understand our responsibility to unbelievers.

Understand That Everyone Begins With Faith

Proverbs 1:7 and 9:10 describe the fear of the Lord as the beginning of wisdom, knowledge, and understanding. Psalm 114:1 describes those who proclaim in their hearts that there is no God as foolish. Everyone begins with a first step of faith (a presupposition). Atheists, like theists, are indeed people of faith. The difference between the two is simply the object of their faith, and their methods for justifying it. To illustrate, Carl Sagan began his groundbreaking *The Cosmos* with the words "The cosmos is all that is or ever was or ever will be."[81] This is not a scientific statement (the scientific method requires observation), rather it is a faith statement, and one that undergirds all of Sagan's scientific pursuit. Ultimately, for Sagan, the cosmos is the only god there is. By contrast, the Bible begins with the presupposition that God exists – and never attempts to defend that presupposition (e.g., see Rom 1 and Heb 11:6). Everyone's first step of investigation is a step of

---

[81] Carl Sagan, *The Cosmos* (New York: Ballantine, 1980), 1.

faith. From that first step, all other steps are grounded and their scope is defined. In other words, that first step of faith defines the rules of the game – what is allowed and what isn't. There is no neutral ground.

Understand the Basis of Truth
If everyone begins with faith, then the Christian need not feel uneasy being a person of faith – if the object of the faith is worthy of that faith. One major distinguishing point between Biblical theist and atheist is how the object of faith can be known – how the data is to be interpreted. We are all dealing with the same data (atheist and theist alike), but how we interpret the data leads to very diverse conclusions.

In the seventeenth century, Rene Descartes concluded that the only way to have true knowledge was by the guided use of reason. He developed a method whereby, he believed he could guide his reason into truth. Unfortunately, Descartes did not seem to account for the finitude of human reason, and thus his rationalism is not a flawless vehicle for gaining knowledge.

David Hume, in the eighteenth century, argued that the senses were the key to the discernment of knowledge. Sensory experience was guided and was superior to reason. Hume's epistemology did not allow for any metaphysical reality, however, as only that which can be sensed can be considered to be real.

Whereas Descartes' rationalism considered reason as the ultimate arbiter of truth, and Hume's empiricism relied solely on sensory experience, the Bible acknowledges that the message of God and His work of salvation is foolishness to those who have not been saved by Him (e.g., 1 Cor 1:18-25). Nonetheless, it asserts that the resurrection of Jesus, for example, occurred (e.g., Mt 28, Mk 16, Lk 24, Jn 20, 1 Cor 15). The Bible presents this event as both rational (Lk 24:44-46) and empirically verified at the time (Jn 20:24-29, 1 Cor 15:6-8). Still the Bible does not present either of those aspects (rational or empirical) as final arbiters of truth.

These three approaches to truth (rationalism, empiricism, and what I will call Biblicism) all have to deal with the same data – for example, there is a cosmos, that all three approaches have to interact with, but they interpret that cosmos differently. If the first step of faith is that there is nothing beyond the cosmos, then an explanation of God as creator is not allowed. The question, then, is not the data itself, but rather what we consider our final authority for ascertaining the truth about the data.

Understand the Conflict of Worldviews
If we begin with a first step of faith, and then interpret the data based on that first step of faith, then clearly, certain conclusions are not allowed – they would violate the rules of the game. Both the atheist and the theist have to come to grips with this reality. Consequently, when an atheist defines science, the definition might be as follows:

> ...science being the scientific methodology — the method and practices used by scientists to acquire reliable knowledge about the world around us. The superiority of science over other attempts to acquire knowledge lies in that methodology. Developed over the course of many decades, the scientific method provides us with information that is more consistently reliable and useful than any other system that humans have ever tried to develop — including especially faith, religion, and intuition.[82]

By contrast, consider this description of science by theistic thinkers,

The first issue needed to be covered is whether or not the

---

[82] Austine Cline, "Defining Science – How is Science Defined?" from http://atheism.about.com/od/philosophyofscience/a/DefineScience.htm.

definition of science even allows for theistic cosmology. But what is science? The National Science Teachers Association decided its standards for science with a position statement adopted in 2000. In the statement, the organization laid out that "science, by definition, is limited to naturalistic methods and explanations and, as such, is precluded from using supernatural elements in the production of scientific knowledge," (Nature). To say then that the natural world was created by God's hand completely contradicts this organization's central doctrine, nullifying the value of any reasoning for creation. If one decides to agree with the NSTA, then of course it is going to be impossible to give evidence that the world has a divine creator. One must be open to the possibility that God made the world in order to accept scientific evidence for creationism. To simply say scientists must only value the natural world is to limit oneself from the possibility of discoveries that support theism. In other words, only an open-minded individual will be able to interpret data that contradicts evolutionism.[83]

These two perspectives of science are totally incompatible with one another. Likewise, the implications of these perspectives are also often mutually exclusive. There is a conflict of worldviews evident at every level of inquiry, because the rules of the game have been defined with the very first presupposition. Again, there is no neutral ground.

Understand Our Position in Christ
As Biblical Christians we need to understand the impact of our position in Christ. We have been saved from the world system (Eph 2:1-10) and the spiritual blindness associated with it (Rom 6:1-11,

---

[83] "Theistic Cosmology" viewed at http://www.spiritualmilk.com/id27.html.

Col 2:20-3:7). We are blessed with every spiritual blessing in Christ (Eph 1:3). All that we are and have is rooted in Christ. Consequently, we are not bound by the anti-metaphysical rules demanded by atheism. Further, in the process of engaging worldviews contradictory to the Biblical one, our standing as children of God (1 Jn 3:1) allows us to approach God as a child would a father (Rom 8:15). It is OK to examine, to evaluate, and even to question. The Bible presents many examples of people who questioned God – some did it in rebellion, others did it as children seeking to understand the truth.

If we understand our position in Him, then the inquiry has a purpose. We are trying to understand Him better – to know Him more closely (e.g., Jn 17:3). Consider Job. He certainly questioned God, yet he was not condemned for it. He was corrected – he was given knowledge of things he didn't previously understand, but never is he rebuked for engaging the process. Christians, we should not fear engaging the questions. We should engage, but we should do so from a good understanding of where we stand in Him.

Understand Our Equipment for Growing and Walking

It is also very important that we understand the tools at our disposal. What equipment has God given us in order to understand truth? Romans 1:16-17 characterizes the gospel as something of which we should not be ashamed, for it is God's power to save. 2 Corinthians 10:3-5 describes our warfare as not against people, but as spiritual and as against speculations and falsehood. Ephesians 6:10-18 presents the reality of spiritual warfare and considers our equipment for it. The only offensive weapon in the arsenal is the word of God. 2 Timothy 3:16-17 speaks with specificity on the authority of God's word, and its usefulness for every area of our lives, so that we can be equipped for every good work. 2 Peter 1:3 informs us that we have been given everything pertaining to life and godliness.

In this process of walking and growing, of engaging and learning, God's word is our final authority. It claims for itself the sufficiency for every area of life. Consequently, if we are trying to walk as Christians, but we use methods grounded in atheistic presuppositions (e.g., Darwinian evolution, empirical science as the highest method for determining truth), then we are sure to be confused. We need to keep our walk consistent with our calling (Eph 4:1).

Understand Our Responsibility to Unbelievers
Finally, we need to understand our responsibility to those who don't agree with the Biblical worldview. Peter prescribes in 1 Peter 3:15-16 that believers should, "Sanctify Christ as Lord in your hearts, always ready to make a defense to everyone who asks you to give an account for the hope that is in you, yet with gentleness and reverence, and keep a good conscience so that in the thing in which you are slandered those who revile your good behavior in Christ may be put to shame." Our responsibility, as Peter outlines here, is: (1) to always be operating with proper perspective to Christ, (2) to always be prepared to make a defense (apologia) to those who ask about our hope, and (3) to give an account, when asked, with gentleness and reverence. Notice first the centrality of Christ in all this – He is the reason for our standing, and He is the motivation and help for our walk. Also, notice that "apologetics" as Peter uses the term is not an offensive thing, but rather it is a responsive evangelism – sharing the truth about our hope with those who ask.

Consequently, as we encounter and engage worldviews contrary to the Bible, and especially the atheistic presuppositions so prevalent at university, we need to be unafraid, having certainty about the Bible and its representations. In order to have that confidence, we need to be diligent workers in the Bible – worthy students (2 Tim 2:15) who understand that if we want to walk with

Him, we need to get to know Him. We need to recognize that our strength is in Him. Additionally, we need to be aware that defeating unbelievers in debate is not our goal or responsibility. We are not aggressors going to university to conquer all who would disagree with our views. Instead, we are interacting with those who don't know God for the purpose that they might get a glimpse of His love, that they might see His character in us, and that they might be drawn to the hope that He offers freely through Jesus Christ.

Conclusion

When faith goes to college, what comes home? The answer to that question has more to do with the object and content of that faith than it does with the university process itself. As an atheistic professor and scholar, whom I greatly respect, once told me, "Atheism is a faith, and here (at university), my faith rules." I would hope that Christians at university would understand that we are in unsympathetic territory, that we need to be prepared and well equipped with the word of God, that we must be always ready to explain our hope, and that we must be always gentle and respectful. Perhaps then those who go to university without any knowledge of God can find Him even there. If we are who we are supposed to be – confident in His word – then God can use us, if He so desires, to help others find what they aren't looking for.

25
Seven Informal and Formal Methods for Preaching and Teaching: (3) Informal Teaching

Informal teaching refers here primarily to one-on-one, non-systematic teaching, such as might be prominent in a discipleship relationship. Jesus modeled this by discipling men in an informal, and generally non-systematic way. He used daily circumstances as teaching opportunities, and He responded to questions, all with a view toward training up the apostles in His word and in Him. The process was largely Jesus doing life together with His disciples, and utilizing the moments to help His followers progress in the process of their maturing. While the records of Jesus' instruction of His disciples show a focus on who He was and what He would accomplish, the Biblical call for replication includes that focus and more. Paul, for example, challenges Timothy to entrust the things he had heard from Paul to faithful men who would then be able to teach others (2 Tim 2:2). The things Timothy heard from Paul were broader than simply Christological, though of course they were built on the cornerstone of Christ (Eph 2:20).

Essentially, as we move from Jesus' pedagogy to that of the disciples, as unique as that setting was, to the pedagogy Paul prescribed for Timothy, we see that informal teaching is essentially taking advantage of the opportunities that non-systematic pedagogy provides, all while having the preparation and intentionality of the more formal approach. Consequently, in such a discipleship relationship we must have a desired outcome (that the disciple will mature to the point of being able to disciple others), and a systematic plan to achieve that, even if the content is delivered in a non-systematic way.

To illustrate, when a teacher enters the classroom, there is an agenda that must be accomplished. There is a quantifiable amount of data that must be communicated by the teacher to the students. But more importantly, that data needs to be processed effectively by the students, if it is to have any transformative impact on their lives. Sometimes a lecture is not the best way to effect that processing. In some cases it is best to incite questions and dialogue that allows students to be directly and actively involved in the shaping of the discussion. In this pedagogy, the teacher allows the questions and dialogue to guide the class, but does so in such a way as to maintain enough control so as to accomplish the teaching agenda. This type of class has a very informal feel, but in fact is very carefully planned and structured. In the same way, strategy is needed in order to effectively teach with an informal pedagogy.

In the case of replication through discipleship, the leader should have a detailed roadmap, rooted in Scripture and grounded on Christ. Because the goal is the overall maturity of the believer, with a view to replication, there should be a systematic preparation for communicating truths needed for maturity. Remember, in order to have effective informal teaching, there must be a foundation of formal preparation. The following is a sample outline of elementary components of each of the eleven areas of Biblical theology, systematically organized to provide the structured backdrop for informal pedagogy. This approach offers a roadmap (chronology included, but not prerequisite), while allowing for a high degree of flexibility in delivery.

Case Study: A Formal Discipleship Outline for Informal or Formal Discipleship Pedagogy

New Life in Christ: Weeks 1-14
Week 1
(1) The Gospel – Romans 1:16-17, 3:23, 5:12, 6:23, 1 Corinthians 15:1-8, Isaiah 6:3, 53:5-6, 64:6-7, Acts 16:31, John 3:16, Ephesians 2:8-10, John 17:3.
(2) The Importance of:
    a. Bible Study – 2 Timothy 3:16-17, 2:15, Psalm 119, Colossians 3:16.
    b. Prayer – Ephesians 6:18, 1 Thessalonians 5:17.
    c. Fellowship – 1 Corinthians 12:13-27, Hebrews 10:23-25.

Week 2
(3) The Doctrine of the Trinity – Isaiah 48:11, 12, 16, Ephesians. 1:1-14, 2:18.

Week 3
(4) Basics of Salvation – Ephesians 2:8-10, 1 Peter 1:3-5.
    a. Positional – John 3:16, 5:24, Colossians 1:13, Romans 8.
    b. Redemption and Forgiveness – Romans 3:24, 1 Corinthians 1:30, Ephesians 1:7, Colossians 1:14.
    c. Justification – Romans 3:20, 3:28, 4:25, 5:1, 5:9, 5;16-18, 8:1, 30, Galatians 2:16, 3:11, Titus 3:7.
    d. Regeneration – John 3:16, 17:3, 20:30-31, Romans 6:1-13, 2 Corinthians 5:17, Galatians 2:20, Titus 3:5.

Week 4
    e. Reconciliation – Romans 5:1,11, 2 Corinthians 5:18-19, Ephesians 2:13-18, Colossians 1:22.
    f. Sanctification – Acts 26:18, 1 Corinthians 1:2, 30, Ephesians 5:25-26, Colossians 1:22, Hebrews 2:11, 10:10, 14.

      g. Baptism – Romans 6:4, 1 Corinthians 12:13, Galatians 3:27, Ephesians 4:5, Colossians 2:12, Titus 3:5, 1 Peter 3:21.
      h. Sealing – 2 Corinthians 1:22;, Ephesians 1:13, 4:30.

Week 5
      i. Sonship – John 1:12, Romans 8:15, Galatians 3:26, 4:5-6, Ephesians 1:5.
      j. Security – John 1:12, 3:16, 10:28-30, Romans 8:28-39, 11:29, Galatians 3:29, Ephesians 1:1-14, 2:8-10, Philippians 1:6; Hebrews 13:5, 1 Peter 1:3-5, 1 John 3:1-2, 5:11-12.
      k. Spiritual Blessing – Ephesians 1:3.

Week 6
(5) Practical, Progressive Salvation
      a. Purpose – John 17:3.

Week 7
      b. Sanctification – Romans 12:1-2, Ephesians 2:10, 2 Peter 3:18.

Week 8
      c. Assurance – John 20:30-31, 1 John 2:3, 3:24, 4:13-15, 5:13.

Week 9
      d. Children – Ephesians 5:1, 1 John 3:10, Proverbs 3:11-12.

Week 10
      e. Subject to the Effects of Sin – Romans 7:14-25, 1 Corinthians 3:1-3, 5:5, 10:12, Ephesians 2:1-3, 1 John 1:8.

Week 11
      f. Fruitbearing – Matthew 3:8, John 15, Romans 7:4, Galatians 5:22, Ephesians 5:9, Philippians 1:11, Colossians 1:10.

Week 12
(6) Ultimate – Free from the penalty, power, presence, and effects of sin.
   a. Christlikeness – Romans 8:28-30, 1 John 3:2.
Week 13
   b. Glorification – Romans 8:28-30, Colossians 3:3-4.
Week 14
   c. At Home With The Lord – John 14:1-3, 2 Corinthians 5:6-8, Philippians 1:21-26.

Walking in the Spirit: Weeks 15-18
Week 15
(7) Personal Bible Study: Being Filled With the Spirit – Ephesians 5:18, 2 Timothy 3:16-17, 1 Peter 2:2.
   a. Hearing – Romans 10:17, Galatians 3:2-5.
   b. Reading – 2 Corinthians 1:13, Ephesians 3:4, Colossians 4:16, 1 Thessalonians 5:27.
   c. Studying – Acts 17:10-11, 2 Timothy 2:15.
   d. Memorizing – Psalm 119:9-11.
   e. Considering – 2 Timothy 2:7, Hebrews 3:1.
   f. Reminding – 2 Peter 1:13.
Week 16
(8) Prayer – Matthew 5:44, 6:5-6, 6:9-13, Romans 12:12, Ephesians 6:18, Philippians 4:6, Colossians 4:2, 1 Thessalonians 5:17, James 5:13, 16, 1 Peter 3:12, 4:7.
Week 17
(9) Fellowship With Believers – Acts 2:42, Hebrews 10:25.
   a. Purposes For Assembling Together – 1 Corinthians 14:12, Ephesians 3:21, 4:11-12, 1 Timothy 2:8, 4:12.
   b. Role in the Church – Romans 12:4-8, 1 Corinthians 12, 1 Peter 4:10-11.

Week 18

(10) Evangelism – Matthew 28:19, 2 Corinthians 5:20-21, Romans 10:1, 13-15, 2 Timothy 4:2.

Developing Christian Character: Weeks 19-25

Week 19

(11) Lordship of Christ: Proper Perspective of God and Man – Romans 6:23, 1 Corinthians 15:57, Philippians 2:10.

Week 20

(12) The Cost of Discipleship – Luke 14:26-27, 2 Timothy 2:3-6, 3:12.

Week 21

(13) Understanding God's Will – Romans 12:2, Ephesians 5:17, 1 Thessalonians 4:13.

Week 22

(14) Stewardship.
   a. Spiritual Gifts – Romans 12:1-8, 1 Corinthians 12, 1 Peter 4:10-11.

Week 23
   b. Physical Gifts
      i. OT Giving (tithing) – Numbers 18:24.
      ii. Church Age Giving – 2 Corinthians 9:7-8, James 2:14-17, 1 John 3:17, 1 Corinthians 9:23, 10:31.

Week 24

(15) Living as a Servant – Galatians 5:13, Ephesians 5:21, Philippians 2:2-4.

Week 25

(16) Accountability – 1 Thessalonians 5:11, James 5:16.

(17) Forgiveness – Matthew 6:12-1, 18:21-35, 2 Corinthians 2:7, Ephesians 4:32.

Christian Hope: Weeks 26-27
    Week 26
    (18) Prophetic Implications – Daniel 9, Matthew 24, John 14:1-3, Romans 9-11, 1 Thessalonians 4:13-18, Revelation 19, 20.
    Week 27
    (19) Handling Death – 1 Thessalonians 4:13-18, 1 Corinthians 3:10-15, 15:50-58, 2 Corinthians 5:6-9, Hebrews 9:27.

Christian Maturity: Weeks 28-36
    Week 28
    (20) The Four Kinds of People – 1 Corinthians 2:14-15, 3:1 (14:20), Galatians 5:22-24.
    Week 29
    (21) Walking in Love – John 13:34-35, Romans 12:10, 13:8, Ephesians 4:2, 1 Thessalonians 3:12, 1 Peter 1:22, 4:8, 1 John 3:11, 23, 4:7, 11.
    Week 30
    (22) Walking in Purity: Warfare of the Believer (Dealing with Testing and Temptation)
        a. Opponents: the World, the Devil, and the Flesh – Ephesians 2:1-3.
    Week 31
        b. Defense: 1 Corinthians 10:12-13, Ephesians 6:10-18, 2 Timothy 2:22.
    Week 32
        c. Forgiveness – Ephesians 1:7, 1 John 1:9.
    Week 33
        d. Discipline – Proverbs 3:12, Hebrews 12:6-13.
    Week 34
        e. Growth and Victory – Ephesians 4:15, 1 Peter 2:2,

2 Peter 3:18, 1 John 5:4.

Week 35

(23) Walking in Integrity – Ephesians 4:15, 24-25.

Week 36

(24) Discipling Others – Matthew 28:19, 1 Corinthians 4:15-16, 2 Timothy 2:2, Titus 2:2, Hebrews 10:24.

26

Seven Informal and Formal Methods for Preaching and Teaching: (4) Formal Teaching – The Synthetic Preview

Introduction: The Forest and the Trees

Perhaps you have heard the expression "can't see the forest for the trees." The expression denotes being so focused on details that the larger picture does not come into focus. Borrowing that concept and applying it to Biblical exegesis and exposition, we recognize that there is indeed a forest made up of individual trees, and that those trees can be classified into various categories within the larger whole of the forest. Because we desire to learn, to practice, and to teach the whole counsel or purpose of God, as Paul modeled in Acts 20:27, we need to recognize the importance of the trees, their classifications, and the entire forest.

Synthesis is the bringing together of ideas to form a system. In Biblical exposition, synthesis pertains to the overview of books or large sections of Scripture, and directly corresponds to viewing the entire forest, perhaps from a bird's eye vantage point. The synthetic preview helps us to evaluate the big picture, and to conduct our more detailed study, practice, and communication within the context of the greater whole.

While our entire process must be exegetical (drawing

meaning from the text rather than reading meaning into the text), in the context of the forest and the trees we can characterize the closer examination of the details as exegetical. In the forest and trees metaphor, the exegetical study is the examination of the details of the trees – perhaps at any given time we might be making observations of the smallest leaf on the smallest tree. If we viewed the forest only from its most detailed components, it would be very difficult for us to ever arrive at a conclusion of what the entire forest has to offer. Consequently, while the exegetical pursuit of the details is extremely vital, it is not the only necessary and worthwhile pursuit.

Further, in our examination of the forest and its contents, we discover that there are a finite number of *kinds* of trees represented there. By a process of analysis or systematization, we can quantify the kinds of trees and classify each tree in the forest by those kinds. In Biblical exposition this is the function of systematic theology – to classify Biblical truths by topic. This analysis complements the synthetic and exegetical processes, helping us to arrive at an accurate picture of the forest and its contents.

Each of these three processes are necessary, each must be exegetically grounded, and each must be given appropriate attention, not only in the exegetical process, but also in the expositional. In the process of exegesis we cover the synthetic elements in identifying structural keys (Step #3) and in examining Biblical context (Step #6). We cover the analytic or systematic aspects, especially, in examining theological context (Step #7). Exegetical components are considered throughout, since, after all, the process is exegetical at its core.

The central premise of integrating exegesis and exposition is that in exposition the exegetical processes should be manifest – the method being communicated along with the content in order to help the learners to develop exegetical capabilities that are necessary to the development of the spiritual life. Consequently, as we examine these three expositional elements (synthetic, exegetical, analytical) in practice, we keep in mind that we must show our work and be transparent about how we derive our conclusions.

The Synthetic Preview

Imagine that you have just purchased a bicycle, but it is completely unassembled, and you have to put it together. You open the large box containing all the parts, including nuts and bolts, but there are no instructions. By detailed examination of each of the parts (exegesis) and categorization of the kinds of parts (analysis, systematization) you would eventually be able to figure out how to put things together. But imagine how much more quickly you would be able to understand where the parts fit and how, if you simply had a set of directions. In the expository process, the synthetic preview is the instructions.

Very helpful especially in launching a book study, the synthetic preview helps learners understand the big picture of why and how the particular book of the Bible fits in the larger context. The synthetic preview introduces background and context, but primarily corresponds with the identification of structural keys and the resulting outlining of the book (Step #3). Simply put, the synthetic preview is an introduction, a bird's-eye level preview, of the more detailed study to follow. This type of presentation requires discipline on the part of the teacher – both to keep things concise, and to present a sufficient level of data for the necessary understanding of the book or group of books.

The synthetic method of teaching includes individual (1) book overviews, (2) overviews of major sections of Scripture – such as the Old Testament chronological books or the Gospels and Acts, and (3) surveys of the Old and New Testaments. Each of these has an important place in the pedagogy of the church, whether for teaching in large groups, small groups, or one-on-one settings. Yet sadly, as lamentably rare as is exegetical handling of the Scriptures in churches, perhaps even more rare is the synthetic preview. Even in churches that do focus on book studies and verse-by-verse teaching, there is often insufficient emphasis on thinking synthetically for the learners to have the broad understanding of Scripture that they need in order to press on to maturity. Despite this tendency to de-emphasis in our practice, there is actually Biblical precedent for introducing the more detailed book examination with synthetic preview material.

Revelation 1:19 is a notable application of a synthetic preview. While we read the book and recognize that particular passage as outlining the structure of Revelation, we should note that this structure is given to John by way of introduction. This introductory classification is designed to guide John and to help him classify material as he writes. In the same way, the synthetic preview provides context that helps guide the reader throughout the process of engaging the text.

Luke 1:1-4 previews Luke's Gospel synthetically, providing (1) the distinctives of this particular account in comparison to others, (2) the occasion for the account, (3) the method of development, (4) the flow or layout of the account, (5) the initial audience of the account, and (6) the purpose of the account.

Proverbs 1:1-3 is a synthetic preview of sorts, as the passage provides key background information, including (1) literary type (which offers a clue as to the structural keys), (2) the author of that particular section, (3) his background, (4) and his purpose in writing.

Amos 1:1 provides some important information for constructing the synthetic preview: (1) the literary type, (2) the author, (3) his background, and (4) the chronological setting. The following is a sample synthetic overview of Amos.

Case Study: A Synthetic Preview of Amos

Slide #1

> Overview
> of Amos
> (755 BC)
>
> Judgment on the Nations
> and on Israel

Rationale

The title slide provides some introductory data to try to help set the context in the minds of learners. Four elements are included here: the book title, the characterization of this study as an overview, the approximate dating of the prophecy, and a brief summary of the content of the prophecy. These four elements are included based on the principle of repetition as beneficial for learning. All of the data on this slide will be reproduced within the presentation.

208 INTEGRATING EXEGESIS AND EXPOSITION

Slide #2

```
                    Intro to Amos

  • Shepherd and fig-        • 1:1 The words of Amos,
    grower from Tekoa          who was among the
    (near Bethlehem)           sheepherders from
                               Tekoa, which he
  • During Uzziah of           envisioned in visions
    Judah, Jeroboam II         concerning Israel in the
    of Israel (2 Kin           days of Uzziah king of
    14-15)                     Judah, and in the days
                               of Jeroboam son of
  • Two years before           Joash, king of Israel,
    earthquake of              two years before the
    Zechariah 14:5, so         earthquake.
    about 755 BC
```

Rationale

We begin with a reading of the internal introduction to the book (generally found in the first few verses, and sometimes complemented by the concluding words of the book), and noting a few key points. Here the author is identified, as is the timing of the prophecy. In this case, the timing is determinable based on (external) historical verification of an earthquake that happened in the middle of the eighth century, B.C.[84] Notably, the historical date is derived from the secondary verification stage (Step #8) – meaning it is obviously not exegetical material but is sourced outside the Biblical text. If time permits, it is always good to cite any extra-Biblical sources from which data is referenced, so as not to imply that it is the direct fruit of the exegetical process. Again,

---

[84] The earthquake is discussed in sources such as Austin, S.A., G.W. Franz, and E.G. Frost, "Amos's Earthquake: An extraordinary Middle East seismic event of 750 B.C." in International Geology Review: 42(7), 2000: 657-671.

transparency regarding how the conclusions are derived is of the utmost importance if the learner is going to develop the ability to do such a study independently.

Slide #3

> ### Intro to Amos
>
> - A shepherd, fig-grower
> - Commissioned as a prophet to the Northern Kingdom
> - Pronounced God's judgment on nations and on Israel
>
> - 7:14 Then Amos replied to Amaziah, "I am not a prophet, nor am I the son of a prophet; for I am a herdsman and a grower of sycamore figs.
> - 15 "But the Lord took me from following the flock and the Lord said to me, 'Go prophesy to My people Israel.'

Rationale

An examination of background and context elements further into the book confirm what was discovered in the introduction – that Amos was a herdsman and grower of figs. This context also adds that Amos was commissioned and sent to prophecy specifically to the Northern Kingdom, even thought the content extends far beyond just the northern ten tribes. In context, the timing indicates that this was an eleventh-hour warning for the Northern Kingdom to change its approach, and to prepare for what was soon to come.

Slide #4

```
         Outline of Amos

  • Judgment on Nations 1:2-2:3

  • Judgment on Israel 2:4-9:15
```

Rationale

Based on the structural keys (which in this case are geographical in the early chapters), we present a simple and non-detailed outline of the major divisions of the book. Greater detail, by way of sub points comes a bit further into the presentation.

The bulk of the work for this stage is done in Step #3, and at this point the usefulness of integrating the exegetical and the expositional processes is apparent. It is the actual exegetical work that provides the backdrop for the expositional presentation, and the more transparent the expositor can be regarding the exegetical task, the more effective the presentation.

In this case we discover that while Amos is from the South, his prophetic ministry engages also (and primarily) the nations and Israel. Not only is the message applicable to those particular nations, but it also provides an important warning to Judah. Both explicitly (e.g., 2:4-5) and by way of secondary application.

Slide #5

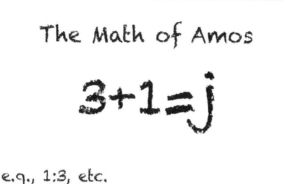

Rationale

This slide provides a mnemonic based on the "for three even for four...I will not revoke..." passages. Three plus one equals judgment. It is helpful to think in terms of mnemonic tools and visual devices especially in the synthetic preview, as the goal here is first to give a contextual grounding of key points related to the book, and second to teach listeners to think observationally and critically about what they are reading.

In the synthetic preview we can include engaging and challenging ways to think about the text as a whole, not only to help with the understanding of the content, but to promote an excitement regarding what the study has in store. It is an exciting thing to study God's word, and just because we are being deliberate about the processes of observation and presentation doesn't mean the study has to be dry. If it is boring, it is because we make it so, not because the text is irrelevant or non-engaging.

Slide #6

Outline of Amos

- Judgment on Nations 1:3–2:3
- (structural keys: geographical)

  – Damascus 1:3-5
  – Gaza 1:6-8
  – Tyre 1:9-10
  – Edom 1:11-12
  – Ammon 1:13-15
  – Moab 2:1-3

Rationale

After providing a general outline, we begin to specify just a bit. Working from the structural keys uncovered in Step #3, we observe divisions in the text, units of thought that help us to understand the purpose and flow of the book. Because of the geographical nature of the outline of this early section of the book, a map is included to help the learner gain a perspective of the proximity of these nations to Israel.

Particularly when discussing geography, visual tools are especially helpful. It can be a challenge for the uninitiated to remember the often unfamiliar names and places of the Hebrew Bible (or of the New Testament world). A simple map here or there can go a long way in simplifying things. Even a map crudely drawn on a whiteboard can help the learner get a feel for direction, dimension, and distance.

SECTION III: OVERVIEW OF THE EXPOSITIONAL PROCESS 213

Slide #7

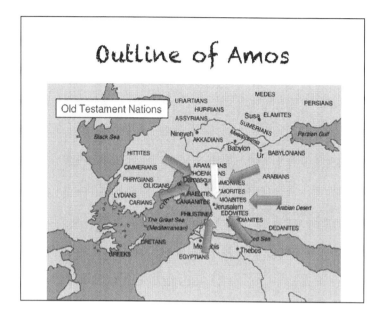

Rationale

This slide underscores the significance of the geographical proximity to Israel of the nations being judged. Much of the judgment coming upon those nations was as a result of their mistreatment of Israel. This map shows how surrounded Israel was by nations who were unsympathetic to Israel's well-being, and the map helps learners to visualize the insecurities that Israel faced during this era. Israel and Judah during the Divided Kingdom were never free from the ongoing threat of violence at the hand of aggressors. In large part this was due to Israel's early failure to drive out the nations and separate from them as God had commanded (e.g., Josh 23:11-13, Judg 1:18-35).

Pedagogically the slide adds a visual component that is so helpful to the process of the synthetic preview. Largely, the synthetic preview ought to provide simple mental images to give the later exegetical study a contextual grounding.

Slide #8

> # Outline of Amos
>
> - Judgment on Israel 2:4-9:15
>
>   – Judah 2:4-5
>   – Israel 2:6-5:3
>   – Avoidable 5:4-15
>   – The Day of the Lord 5:16-20

Rationale

Considering the first four units of the Judgment on Israel section, this slide continues the narration of the secondary outline points, and introduces the Day of the Lord, which could be an area for more in-depth discussion in the format of the analytical summary, as time allows.

Even at this point it is not too early to introduce listeners to the components to follow: the exegetical journey – which will take us through each section, verse by verse, and the analytical summary, which will help us to understand major ideas and relate them to other passages that discuss those same ideas. At this point it should be apparent that the three components of formal teaching (synthetic preview, exegetical journey, and analytical summary) are not independent, but rather complement each other in such a way as to present a more comprehensive picture of the book and passage than would be possible if only one component was considered.

Slide #9

Outline of Amos

- Judgment on Israel 2:4-9:15

    - God rejects 5:21-27
    - For arrogance 6
    - Amos intercedes, Amaziah rejects 7
    - Judgment unavoidable 8:1-9:10
    - Restoration assured 9:11-15

Rationale

This slide is a continuation of the second major outline point (Judgment on Israel), and by this time we are observing some repeated themes that deserve emphasis. For example, we see that the judgment was earlier mentioned as possibly avoidable (see 5:14-15), by chapter 8, the judgment is unavoidable (8:1-9:10), though a remnant will be delivered, just as in the earlier context (compare 5:15 and 9:8). Likewise, along with the judgment, there is coming a certain restoration for Israel.

In the major and minor divisions of this and other books, we begin to see repeated themes emphasizing the character and activity of God, inviting the learner to delve deeper, and to anticipate the exegetical journey to follow.

Slide #10

```
           Character of God in Amos

   • He has sworn by              נִשְׁבַּע אֲדֹנָי  –
     His holiness 4:2              יְהוִה בְּקָדְשׁוֹ

   • He has sworn by              נִשְׁבַּע אֲדֹנָי  –
     Himself 6:8                       יְהוִה

   • He has sworn by             נִשְׁבַּע יְהוָה  –
     the pride of                   בִּגְאוֹן יַעֲקֹב
     Jacob 8:7
```

Rationale

In anticipation of the later exegetical work, there are some themes that deserve attention in the synthetic preview. Here we take a brief look at the character of God as revealed in Amos, noting that three times in the book God swears. First, by His holiness, that judgment is coming, next, by Himself, that judgment is coming, and finally, by the pride of Jacob (an ironic and sad reference) that judgment is coming.

From these repeated mentions of God's oaths, we learn much about how seriously God takes sin, and this context provides an excellent opportunity to introduce some elementary aspects of phrasing (perhaps the learner discovers by brief mention that Hebrew is read right to left, and the learner is also introduced to some key words used in this context, such as the name *Yahweh* in 8:7). Once again, the process for the learner is secondary to the content itself, but introducing and explaining the process will help learners to discover the content for themselves.

SECTION III: OVERVIEW OF THE EXPOSITIONAL PROCESS   217

Slide #11

```
Character of God in Amos

• He relents from            – נִחַם יְהוָה עַל־
  judgment at times             זֹאת
  7:3, 6

• His name is YHWH          –יְהוָה שְׁמוֹ
  5:8

• He controls how
  and when He
  speaks 8:11
• He judges and He
  restores 9:14-15
```

Rationale

A continuation of the previous slide, this one provides some hope, as God does not only judge, but He also restores. This is an aspect of His character introduced in this synthetic preview, to be confirmed in the exegetical journey and tested in the analytical summary. The inclusion of a few pertinent Hebrew phrases are not necessary, but as in the previous slide, that inclusion can help visually introduce the significance of the Biblical languages, and can help create a comfort level on the part of learners with a pursuit by which they might otherwise be intimidated. At this juncture the benefit of mentioning the Biblical languages is in simplifying and not complicating. The expositor must be cautious not to come across as overly academic or prideful in the use of the languages. The desire is to gently introduce some linguistic concepts to encourage deeper study, not to discourage it.

Slide #12

> ## Primary Application
>
> - God is just, therefore judgment is coming because they had not returned to Him (e.g., 4:6,8,9,10,11).
>
> - Israel is to prepare (be firm) to meet Him (4:12).
>
> - Israel is to seek Him so that they may live (5:4,6).
>
> - Seek good and not evil that you may live; and thus may the Lord God of hosts be with you just as you have said! Hate evil, love good, and establish justice in the gate! Perhaps the Lord God of hosts may be gracious to the remnant of Joseph. (5:14-15)

Rationale

At this early stage of exposition it is appropriate to introduce the important hermeneutical principles of primary and secondary application. In this case, we observe specific primary applications for Israel, and in keeping with the concept that all Scripture is God-breathed and useful for the equipping of every believer (2 Tim 3:16-17), we recognize that we must distinguish between action points for Israel and those for the secondary reader. Israel was expected to respond, in light of impending judgment on the nation at the hands of other nations, and in fulfillment of the curses and blessings aspect of the Mosaic Covenant (e.g., Deut 28-30).

Slide #13

> # Secondary Application
>
> ...Considering God's character, demonstrated in His dealings with the nations and with Israel...
> ...how will we live???
>
> - Are we ready to meet Him?
> - Are we seeking Him?
> - Are we seeking good and not evil?

Rationale

Contemporary readers are not bound by the particular conditions of the Mosaic Covenant as Israel was. Still, we are interacting with the same God as was Israel, and His character is unchanged. While there essentially is only one primary application (in this case, Israel was to acknowledge God in light of the coming judgment), there can be many secondary applications, so it is wise not to dwell too long on any one secondary application.

The Holy Spirit can use His word in our lives in many ways – the meaning doesn't change, but the secondary applications are so varied that if we spend extended time dealing with secondary application to the neglect of the meaning of the text, then we have shortchanged the learner, because they leave with a secondary application and not the meaning of the text, and certainly not an understanding of how to handle the next section of the text for themselves.

In this case, we list a few brief secondary application questions paralleling the imperatives that constitute the primary application for Israel. Here we are modeling for the learner the distinction between primary and secondary application, and at the same time we are emphasizing that all believers are to respond appropriately to these passages, for spiritual growth and maturity – ultimately for a closer walk with Him.

The synthetic preview is the introduction to in-depth Bible study, and should be engaging, exciting, and helpful. If our presentation fails in any of these areas, then we need to assess how we are handling the process, because this stage of exposition sets the tone for the exegetical journey to follow and the analytical summary that helps tie it all together.

27
Seven Informal and Formal Methods for Preaching and Teaching: (5) Formal Teaching – The Exegetical Journey

Whereas the synthetic preview covers whole books at a time, and the analytical summary consolidates theological themes of the book, the exegetical journey is the verse-by-verse examination of individual passages in context. This is the core of Bible study, and should be given the greatest emphasis and time allotment of the three processes. If the book study is introduced by the synthetic preview and concluded with the analytical summary, the body of the study is the exegetical journey.

For a Biblical pattern, we consider the exposition recorded in Nehemiah 8:1-12. Note in particular the emphases regarding both the content and the response. The content – the textbook – was the word of God (8:1). It was prayerfully considered (8:6). It was opened and it was read (8:3, 5). It was explained, to ensure that the hearers understood (8:8), and it provided calls to action and encouragement (8:10). In response, the people gathered to hear it (8:1). It was heard attentively (8:3) and respectfully (8:5). It was received as true (8:6). It was received patiently (8:7). It elicited personal response (8:9). It resulted in worship of God (8:6). It was understood and acted upon (8:12). Of course, this expository episode is descriptive rather than prescriptive, and we have substantial freedom in how we structure communicating the word. However, we want to try to follow the Biblical pattern as closely as we can. Here is an outline following key components of that pattern for the structure and delivery of a verse-by-verse exposition:

(1) Read the entire passage to be covered.
(2) Pray for guidance in study.
(3) Summarize background and context
(4) Read each individual section (sentence, verse, or paragraph).
(5) Relate section to the overall context.
(6) Summarize each section's verse analysis and exegetical key points (repeat this for each section covered).
(7) Highlight principles and applications at appropriate points.
(8) Offer a brief summary of overall exegetical context, highlights, and principles and applications.
(9) Pray for wisdom and strength in order to be an effectual doer of the word for His glory.

Let's examine this presentation method in more detail. For consideration here, we will assume a time frame of roughly thirty minutes is available for this presentation. We quantify each activity with a time (listed at the end of each header below). Now, if that is just too mechanical for you, feel free to ignore that aspect. It is merely provided to help give perspective for how to budget and structure time in order to cover all that is intended.

As a communicator becomes more practiced in the art and discipline of communication, there is less need for such restrictive structure. An experienced communicator probably would not think in terms of such precise time controls, but through practice would have developed the internal clock needed for proper pacing.

(1) Reading of the Passage (1 minute)

To demonstrate respect for the word, to set the tone of Biblical focus, and to give room for the Holy Spirit to use His word in our lives and the lives of listeners, reading all or a portion of the passage to be covered is an excellent habit to develop. If we are covering an extensive passage we might not be able to read the entire passage. If that is the case we can read a few verses from the section. When God's word is read, there is a purpose accomplished (Is 55:8-11). That in itself is significant enough to make worthy the investment of time.

(2) Prayer (1 minute)

Hopefully we have been in prayer throughout the process, but this particular moment allows learners to come humbly before God with us. An opening prayer also demonstrates humility, as we ask for His guidance and wisdom, and as we communicate our desire to handle His word well.

(3) Summary of Background and Context (3 minutes)

Here we spend a few moments setting the stage for the passage covered, providing background information and introducing the context. It is worth considering that many of the most memorable stories are those that paint such a vivid picture at the outset that the reader feels like they are right there with the main characters as the story is told.

If we are continuing an exegetical study from a previous instance (such as continuing a book study over the course of several weeks or even months), then it is helpful to also give a brief explanation of what was covered last time in order to refresh the memories of those who participated in the previous study and to orient those who, for whatever reason, didn't.

(4) Reading of Each Individual Section (3 minutes)

Steps 1-3 of this process introduce the teaching as a whole. Steps 4, 5, 6, 7 are each to be repeated as needed, depending on how many verses or sections are being handled. We repeat these steps as necessary until we finish the entire passage to be covered. The whole passage is a pizza, let's say. Steps 4, 5, 6 and 7 are individual pieces. So we are eating individual pieces until the entire pericope-pizza is devoured.

We need to handle each individual passage with a predictable structure so that the learners will be able to anticipate and understand where the passage is going, and ultimately they can begin to see patterns they can follow in their own Bible study. We can't forget the priorities in teaching. We are teaching not to position ourselves as some kind of spiritual gurus upon whom learners should be dependant. We are teaching for teaching for spiritual growth and maturity, that they might grow to independence, to a mature walk with the Lord, and to the ability to make disciples as well.

(5) Relating of Each Section to the Overall Context (4 minutes)

Here we explain how our chosen passage relates to the broader context. For example, if we are considering Ephesians 2:8-9, we need to at least refer to 2:1-2, as these are near-context verses that provide the grounding of the later verses. While 2:8-9 describes the solution, 2:1-2 describes the problem.

Further, 2:8-9 fits within the context of the first three chapters of the letter, which consider the position of the believer, while the last three chapters of the letter describe the expectations for the believer's walk. A few explanatory notes on the passages relation to its contexts goes a long way in helping learners understand not only the passage we are teaching, but the next one as well.

(6) Summary of Each Section's Verse Analysis (12 minutes)

Let's say we are teaching Ephesians 1, and so far we have completed the first five steps:

> We have read Ephesians 1:1-14.
> We have prayed for guidance in study.
> We have given a basic summary of the background and context of Ephesians.
> We have read each individual section, considering 1:1-2, then 1:3-4a, then 1:4b-5, and so on.

At this sixth step, we would summarize each section's verse analysis and exegetical key points, so we would do Step 6 for 1:1-2, then again for 1:3-4a, then again for 1:4b-5, etc., through the entire passage. This way we are handling the verse itself, explaining it, drawing attention to key ideas in the text.

For example, in Ephesians 1 we observe four occurrences of the word *will* (*thelematos*):

1:1	Paul, an apostle of Christ Jesus by the **will** of God, To the saints who are at Ephesus and *who are* faithful in Christ Jesus:	Παῦλος ἀπόστολος Χριστοῦ Ἰησοῦ διὰ **θελήματος** θεοῦ τοῖς ἁγίοις τοῖς οὖσιν [ἐν Ἐφέσῳ] καὶ πιστοῖς ἐν Χριστῷ Ἰησοῦ,
1:5	He predestined us to adoption as sons through Jesus Christ to Himself, according to the kind intention of His **will**,	προορίσας ἡμᾶς εἰς υἱοθεσίαν διὰ Ἰησοῦ Χριστοῦ εἰς αὐτόν, κατὰ τὴν εὐδοκίαν τοῦ **θελήματος** αὐτοῦ,
1:9	He made known to us the mystery of His **will**, according to His kind intention which He purposed in Him	γνωρίσας ἡμῖν τὸ μυστήριον τοῦ **θελήματος** αὐτοῦ, κατὰ τὴν εὐδοκίαν αὐτοῦ ἣν προέθετο ἐν αὐτῷ
1:11	also we have obtained an inheritance, having been predestined according to His purpose who works all things after the counsel of His **will**,	Ἐν ᾧ καὶ ἐκληρώθημεν προορισθέντες κατὰ πρόθεσιν τοῦ τὰ πάντα ἐνεργοῦντος κατὰ τὴν βουλὴν τοῦ **θελήματος** αὐτοῦ

This is emphasis by repetition. So in handling each specific section or passage we might focus on that emphasis as an exegetical key point.

Further, it is important that we don't just talk about the verse or that we don't simply use the verse as a launching pad for our opinions and ideas. Listeners don't need our opinions or ideas, they need to understand what the verse is saying, and how they can handle the next one. If we are not transparent about how we arrived at the conclusions we are discussing – if we are not transparent about exegetical keys in the passage, then all we are accomplishing is communicating to our listeners that they simply have to trust us because they will have no idea how we got the information. We need to be accountable. We need to show our work, in part so that others will observe and develop the ability to do the same work.

(7) Highlighting of Principles and Application as Appropriate (3 minutes)

As we are repeating Steps 4, 5, 6, and 7 per section, we need to communicate principles and applications *as the text warrants*. In this, as in all other components, we must submit to the text as God's word, and thus as capable of accomplishing its purpose of equipping believers for every good work (2 Tim 3:17). Consequently, we have no need to artificially derive applications or relevancies, nor do we want to overemphasize application in general.

Recall that there is one primary application of a passage – that expected response of the original audience, and that there are many secondary applications of any given passage. In other words, while the meaning of a passage never changes, the Holy Spirit can use a passage in many ways in our lives. It can be helpful to mention one or two of these as the text warrants. Doing so *appropriately* can serve as a model for learners to think about how they can be doers of the word.

(8) Concluding Summary and Implications (2 minutes)

A good presentation (1) communicates to the listener in the introduction what will be said throughout, (2) communicates the content of what needs to be said, and then (3) communicates a summary of what was said. This tested formula is effective for helping to drive home the taught content by the use of repetition. After we have repeated Steps 4, 5, 6 and 7, as needed, Step 8 gives us a broader focus, to allow a final glimpse of the big picture. This conclusion includes a summary of overall exegetical context, highlights, principles and applications. Finally, at this point it is helpful to provide an exhortation to further study and to taking action, to being faithful doers of the word.

(9) Concluding Prayer (1 minute)

It is helpful to ask the Lord specifically to strengthen and provide wisdom to be doers of the word. In addition to making the request on its own merits, such a prayer reminds us all of our dependence on Him.

Why do we study the Bible? Why should we allow it to abide richly in us? Why should we be doers of it? Why should we teach it to others? The answers to these questions go a long way in helping us to understand *how* to do these things. Let's not forget our purpose as we engage in the process. God has a purpose in communicating His word. Let's not stand in His way by doing a poor job of understanding it, a poor job of obeying it, or a poor job of communicating it.

> For as the rain and the snow come down from heaven, and do not return there without watering the earth and making it bear and sprout, and furnishing seed to the sower and bread to the eater, so will My word be which goes forth from My

mouth. It will not return to Me empty, without accomplishing what I desire, and without succeeding in the matter for which I sent it (Is 55:10-11).

Case Study: An Exegetical Analysis of Matthew 18:15-20: The Purpose and Nature of Correction in the Church

Introduction

Because of its detail and sequence, Matthew 18:15-20 has long been recognized as a central passage in dealing with sin, conflict resolution, and discipline in the church. In these verses Jesus provides His disciples a pattern for dealing with a sinning brother, and describes a process to facilitate the desired outcome of a sinning brother's repentance and restoration. The discussion also considers the undesirable possibility that the sinning brother will not be penitent, and prescribes action to be taken under those less than ideal circumstances.

As this is the only Biblical passage outlining a step-by-step process in the church for dealing with sin, conflict, and discipline, it is regularly applied in churches that hold to Biblical authority. Furthermore, the details provided in the passage help us to assess and measure whether the process has been engaged correctly or not. And that ability to assess and measure is vitally important, because any missteps in applying the process can have profound negative impact not only on the individuals involved, but also on the broader health of the church.

This analysis of Matthew 18:15-20 includes a brief exegesis (employing the literal grammatical-historical hermeneutic, which has been, in large part, the church's historical interpretive method), and a consideration of the present-day implications of Jesus' teaching on these matters. Because this is a textual argument, there is not substantial appeal in the argument to historical or theological sources. Churches that admit dependence on the Biblical text (such as by assertion within the statement of faith to the effect that the Bible is authoritative) will rely more heavily on textual arguments than historical or theological ones, and will be governed more transparently by Biblical teachings.

Text and Translation

While the New American Standard Bible is a close word-for-word translation from the original Greek New Testament, there are some textual issues we need to consider in these verses before proceeding. For each verse we catalog significant manuscript variants and translation issues (from Greek to English, as represented in the NASB). The earlier readings (Sinaiticus and Vaticanus, for example) are given more weight here than are the later, but more numerous manuscripts of the Majority Text in this writer's translation.

18:15

"If your brother sins, go and show him his fault in private; if he listens to you, you have won your brother" (Mt 18:15, NASB). Ἐὰν δὲ ἁμαρτήσῃ [εἰς σὲ] ὁ ἀδελφός σου, ὕπαγε ἔλεγξον αὐτὸν μεταξὺ σοῦ καὶ αὐτοῦ μόνου. ἐάν σου ἀκούσῃ, ἐκέρδησας τὸν ἀδελφόν σου·

Notable Variants

Sinaiticus and Vaticanus do not include the phrase εἰς σὲ (unto or against you: i.e., if your brother sins *against you*), though the Majority Text does.

Translation

But if sins the brother of you, you go correct him between you and him alone. If you he hears, you have gained the brother of you.

18:16

"But if he does not listen *to you,* take one or two more with you, so that BY THE MOUTH OF TWO OR THREE WITNESSES EVERY FACT MAY BE CONFIRMED" (Mt 18:16, NASB). ἐὰν δὲ μὴ ἀκούσῃ, παράλαβε μετὰ σοῦ ἔτι ἕνα ἢ δύο, ἵνα ἐπὶ στόματος δύο μαρτύρων ἢ τριῶν σταθῇ πᾶν ῥῆμα·

Notable Variants
The phrase μετὰ σοῦ ἔτι ἕνα ἢ δύο (with you also one or two) has some minor transposition in P44 and Vaticanus, but is as written above in Sinaiticus and the Majority Text. The phrase δύο μαρτύρων ἢ τριῶν (two witnesses or three) has some slight transposition in Sinaiticus.

Translation
But if not he hears, take with you additionally one or two, in order that upon a mouth of two witnesses or three every word is established.

18:17
"If he refuses to listen to them, tell it to the church; and if he refuses to listen even to the church, let him be to you as a Gentile and a tax collector" (Mt. 18:17, NASB). ἐὰν δὲ παρακούσῃ αὐτῶν, εἰπὲ τῇ ἐκκλησίᾳ· ἐὰν δὲ καὶ τῆς ἐκκλησίας παρακούσῃ, ἔστω σοι ὥσπερ ὁ ἐθνικὸς καὶ ὁ τελώνης.

Notable Variants
The word ὡς (like) is inserted between καὶ and ὁ in Bezae Cantabrigiensis.

Translation
But if he is not listening of them, speak to the assembly (or church), but if even of the church he is not listening, he is to be to you (singular) as the Gentile and the tax collector.

18:18

"Truly I say to you, whatever you bind on earth shall have been bound in heaven; and whatever you loose on earth shall have been loosed in heaven" (Mt 18:18, NASB). Ἀμὴν λέγω ὑμῖν· ὅσα ἐὰν δήσητε ἐπὶ τῆς γῆς ἔσται δεδεμένα ἐν οὐρανῷ, καὶ ὅσα ἐὰν λύσητε ἐπὶ τῆς γῆς ἔσται λελυμένα ἐν οὐρανῷ.

Notable Variants

The phrase ἔσται δεδεμένα ἐν οὐρανῷ, καὶ ὅσα ἐὰν λύσητε ἐπὶ τῆς γῆς (it will be having been bound in heaven, and whatever has been loosed upon the earth) is omitted in Bezae Cantabrigiensis. The first occurrence of οὐρανῷ (in heaven) is replaced with τοῖς οὐρανοῖς (in the heavens) in Sinaiticus, and with τω ουρανω in the Majority Text. The second occurrence is replaced with τοῖς οὐρανοῖς in Bezae Cantabrigiensis.

Translation

Truly I say to you, if whatever you bind upon the earth, it will be having been bound in heaven, and whatever has been loosed upon the earth it will be having been loosed in heaven.

18:19

"Again I say to you, that if two of you agree on earth about anything that they may ask, it shall be done for them by My Father who is in heaven" (Mt 18:19, NASB). Πάλιν [ἀμὴν] λέγω ὑμῖν ὅτι ἐὰν δύο συμφωνήσωσιν ἐξ ὑμῶν ἐπὶ τῆς γῆς περὶ παντὸς πράγματος οὗ ἐὰν αἰτήσωνται, γενήσεται αὐτοῖς παρὰ τοῦ πατρός μου τοῦ ἐν οὐρανοῖς.

Notable Variants

Sinaiticus omits ἀμὴν (truly), while Vaticanus and the Majority Text include it. Vaticanus' συμφωνήσωσιν ἐξ ὑμῶν (if they agree of you) is slightly altered in several manuscripts.

Translation
Again I say to you that if they agree two of you upon the earth about everything of the matter that they ask it will be done for them from the Father of the Me in heavens.

18:20
"For where two or three have gathered together in My name, I am there in their midst" (Mt 18:20, NASB). οὗ γάρ εἰσιν δύο ἢ τρεῖς συνηγμένοι εἰς τὸ ἐμὸν ὄνομα, ἐκεῖ εἰμι ἐν μέσῳ αὐτῶν.

Notable Variants
The phrase οὗ γάρ εἰσιν (for where they are) is slightly altered in a few manuscripts.

Translation
For where they are two or three having gathered together in the name of me, there I am in amidst of them.

Implications of Variants and Working Translation
The only variant in this section that might have an impact in the final application of the passage is the omission of εἰς σὲ in 18:15. The Majority Text reading is reflected in the King James (KJV) rendering, "if thy brother shall trespass against thee…," whereas Sinaiticus and Vaticanus are represented by the NASB, which reads, "if your brother sins…"

The implication of the KJV reading is that the process should only be engaged if a sin is committed against the one engaging the process. In other words, if your brother sins, but it isn't against you, then this process is not applicable. The NASB rendering does not carry this implication, and does not seem to limit the process to be engaged only by the offended. This issue is discussed further in the final section of this analysis.

Working Translation

But if sins the brother of you, you go correct him between you and him alone. If you he hears, you have gained the brother of you. But if not he hears, take with you additionally one or two, in order that upon a mouth of two witnesses or three every word is established. But if he is not listening of them, speak to the assembly (or church), but if even of the church he is not listening, he is to be to you (singular) as the Gentile and the tax collector.

Truly I say to you, if whatever you bind upon the earth, it will be having been bound in heaven, and whatever has been loosed upon the earth it will be having been loosed in heaven. Again I say to you that if they agree two of you upon the earth about everything of the matter that they ask it will be done for them from the Father of the Me in heavens. For where they are two or three having gathered together in the name of me, there I am in amidst of them.

Background and Context

Matthew's Gospel centers on Jesus Christ as Israel's Davidic King-in-waiting, and this account bears a strong Hebrew cultural flavor. Jesus' first public proclamation recorded in Matthew introduces the theme: "Repent, for the kingdom of the heavens is at hand" (Mt 4:17). As we discover in the Gospel, Jesus is announcing that God's eternal, spiritual kingdom will come to earth in a physical manifestation, through the line of David, as was initially introduced in 2 Samuel 7. The famed Sermon on the Mount (Mt 5-7) is an exhortation by Jesus to the Jewish people (and His disciples) regarding the qualities needed for one to enter the promised kingdom. The way of entry was not external following of the Mosaic Law, but rather was an internal spiritual humility that went far beyond what the Law required – hence, the call to repent (or change the mind). Matthew 8-11 included a period of consideration, wherein Jesus demonstrated His qualifications and warrant for the Davidic throne, and Matthew emphasizes that Jesus fulfilled messianic prophecy.

Nonetheless, the forerunner and herald who announced the kingdom – John the baptist – was rejected, imprisoned, and ultimately murdered. Likewise the King that he proclaimed was also rejected in Matthew 12-13. From that moment forward, Jesus spoke in parables in order to veil the truth from the rejecting leaders and masses, and He turned to privately explaining the parables and teaching His disciples, preparing them for what was to come. The kingdom would be postponed, and the King would give His life as a ransom, even on behalf of those who had rejected Him. Even amidst the proclamations of judgment in Matthew 14-15, Jesus still demonstrated His power and His mercy.

In Matthew 16 Jesus introduces the assembly (τὴν ἐκκλησίαν, translated by the NASB as *the church*), which would be built upon Himself (Mt 16:18; 1 Pet 2:4-10), and specifically so in that His identity and His prescribed means of righteousness for those who would enter the kingdom would be a stumbling block to the nation of Israel. This is the first indication in the entire Bible that there would be a temporary shift of God's focus from the nation of Israel to *the church* (Rom 9-11 explains the reasons for the shift and how God would, at the time of His choosing, return His focus to the nation of Israel and save the nation). Matthew 17 adds yet more confirmation of His identity and qualification as King, and yet in that passage Jesus predicts His own death and resurrection. In this context Jesus is preparing His disciples for their challenging task ahead – for a time when He will no longer be physically with them.

Matthew 18 begins with the disciples' query regarding who would be the greatest in the kingdom of the heavens. Jesus responds by emphasizing the importance of childlike humility, and the importance to Him of those who demonstrate that humility of faith. Invoking the example of a shepherd who would leave his many sheep in order to find one lost one, Jesus describes how His Father does not wish for any of these *little ones* to perish. It is in this context that Jesus introduces the process for restoring a brother who is in sin.

There is an important correlation between the brother in sin (18:15) and the sheep that has strayed (18:12-13). Just as there is joy at the sheep's finding, there is joy at the restoration of the straying brother. The process Jesus describes must be understood in that light – as a part of God's design for restoration, and not for judgment. As the process is engaged, that goal must remain in view, even if it will not always be reflected in the outcome.

Immediately following 18:15-20 is a dialogue between Peter and Jesus, in which Peter inquires how often he should forgive a stumbling brother. Jesus' thorough response leaves no doubt of the centrality of forgiveness in the daily lives of His followers.

Structural Keys

As Matthew's Gospel belongs to the genre of historical narrative, the structure of the book is readily identifiable by sequential flow of narrative. Matthew introduces his record as "a book of genealogy of Jesus Christ, son of David, son of Abraham" (Mt 1:1). Jesus' connections to those two men is vital in order for the Abrahamic and Davidic covenants to be fulfilled in Him, and Matthew chooses historical narrative as the vehicle for demonstrating those necessary connections. After the brief statement of genealogy, we are told in narrative form that, "the birth of Jesus Christ was as follows…" (1:18), and that "all this took place…" (1:22).

Matthew continues with the frequent use of chronological terms throughout, and leaves the reader with no doubt that what is written is presented as a truthful historical narrative – even to the final paragraph. The structural keys, or building blocks of the book – and the keys to recognizing transitions – are found in the chronological and sequential terms that are so often found in narrative.

In light of the transparency of structural keys in Matthew, there is clarity in reckoning the major and minor divisions of the book, so that when we arrive at a pivotal passage like 18:15-20, we can have confidence that we are able to discern its proper placement and context within the greater narrative. In short, both the broader context and the passage itself are simple to ascertain because of Matthew's chosen genre and writing style.

Within the immediate context is an additional structural key that is vitally important for understanding 18:15-20. In 18:3, Jesus begins his exhortation with the phrase, "Truly I say to you" (ἀμὴν λέγω ὑμῖν). He repeats the phrase again to introduce the pericope of 18:18-20. This discursive tool is commonly used by Jesus and indicates a transition in subject matter. It is especially important to recognize that the transition occurs after the resolution process is given in 15-17, and introduces a unique authority and empowerment of the disciples in 18-20.

Grammatical and Syntactical Keys

In 8:15 the phrase *the brother of you* (ὁ ἀδελφός σου) contains a noun and pronoun – both singular. Further, the imperative verb (ὕπαγε) translated *go*, is also singular. This is describing a situation in which individual is dealing directly with another. At this stage, there is no third party involved, whatsoever. That condition is accentuated by the qualifier *between you and him alone* (μεταξὺ σοῦ καὶ αὐτοῦ μόνου). At this point, the matter is exclusively private, between only the two parties, and if the brother responds well, then the brother has been won and the matter is closed, never to see the light of expanded discussion (at least in regards to the specific application of the process described here). The lost sheep has been found and there is joy as a result.

However, if the brother does not hear, 18:16 adds another

step: take with you one or two (παράλαβε μετὰ σοῦ ἔτι ἕνα ἢ δύο). The imperative verb and pronoun is still singular. This second step can only be engaged by the one who initiated the first step, and the initiator must remain actively involved in the process. The one or two others are included for the purpose of confirming, or adding weight to what was originally discussed. They are not the central figures in this step, but they are required. While there is no discussion of the possibility of a positive outcome to this step (i.e., that the brother listens and heeds), the implication from the initial goal is that if the brother listens, then the brother has been won and the matter is closed – with no further discussion, just as in the case of the first step.

Yet again, if the second step does not conclude with a positive response by the offending brother, the initiator is himself prescribed (as indicated by the aorist active imperative, second person, singular εἰπὲ) to bring the matter to the attention of the assembly. At this point, the assembly becomes involved verbally in the correction process. While there is not imperative (second or third person) given to the assembly, the desired outcome of this third step is that the brother will listen to the assembly. If the brother does respond positively by listening to the assembly, then the brother has been won, and the matter is concluded with no further discussion.

If the third step does not yield a positive response from the offending brother, then a fourth step – a consequence of sorts is meted out. *He is to be to you* (ἔστω σοι)…with this phrase including the singular pronoun, the process is no longer about the one or two additional witnesses nor the assembly, but rather we are back to the original two parties: the offending brother and the initiator of the Matthew 18 process. There is not here any specific discussion of an assembly-wide response to the offending brother (though one might infer that the broader response should be the same as the specifically identified individual response), instead what is stated restores focus to the interaction between the two individuals: He (singular) is to be to you (singular) as the Gentile (singular) and the tax collector (singular).

Regarding the binding and loosing of 18:18, Jesus had already announced to Peter that He would give to Peter "the keys of the kingdom of heaven, and whatever you bind on earth shall have been bound in heaven and whatever you loose on earth shall have been loosed in heaven" (16:19). Jesus repeats the second half of this statement in 18:18 in addressing the disciples (plural). There is a subtle but important shift from the singulars used in 15-17 to the plurals used in 18-20. This transition indicates that a general and broadly applicable principle is identified in 15-17, and a more narrow primary application is intended for the disciples in 18-20. In short, 15-17 is phrased in such a way that the entire church can follow the clearly delineated instructions, and 18-20 provides for the disciples a unique authority and empowerment for their ministry ahead.

Lexical Keys

The occasion for the Matthew 18 resolution process is when (if) a brother sins. The verb *sins* (ἁμαρτήσῃ) in 18:15 indicates a transgressing or doing of wrong.[85] The object or recipient of the wrongdoing is not readily apparent in Sinaiticus and Vaticanus, while the Majority Text adds the object (εἰς σὲ). If the earlier readings are preferred (as it is by this writer), the occasion could include not only an offense against the initiator of the process, but any offense of which the initiator is aware. On the one hand this broader application allows for a heightened degree of accountability and concern among brethren, on the other hand this

---

[85] W. Bauer, W. Arndt, F.W. Gingrich, and F. Danker, "ἁμαρτάνω" in *A Greek-English Lexicon of the New Testament and Other Early Christian Literature*, 2nd Edition (Chicago: University of Chicago Press, 1964), 54. This source is hereafter referred to as BDAG.

broader application could encourage an overly critical spirit. Balance seems important at this juncture, but in either case – whether the earlier or later reading is preferred, there has clearly been a measurable wrong done.

The desired outcome is that the offending brother listens or hears (ἀκούσῃ). Evidently the term connotes more than simple auditory perception. BDAG cites the Matthew 18:15 usage as an instance of listening *and* following.[86]

If the offending brother does not respond positively to the first two steps, the matter is only then to be communicated to the assembly (τῇ ἐκκλησίᾳ). The term is rendered as church in the NASB, the KJV, and the ESV[87] – three prominent translations following formal equivalence. While the term is used in the LXX[88] to indicate various assemblies, the term is first used[89] in the NT in Matthew 16:18, and refers to a new entity to be built (οἰκοδομήσω, future) by Jesus, on Himself. It is possible that James's Epistle preceded Matthew's Gospel chronologically, and therefore, it is possible that James' lone usage of the term in James 5:14 referred to a general assembly, rather than to the new assembly that Jesus would build, however, James wrote at least a decade after Jesus predicted the new assembly, and as James was a prominent elder in the church at Jerusalem (Acts 15), it is far more likely that James' reference was specifically to the new assembly that is the church, rather than to a generic assembly.

Matthew's second reference to the term, in 18:17, seems a decisive reference to that assembly predicted just two chapters

---

[86] BDAG, " ἀκούω," 42.
[87] English Standard Version.
[88] The Septuagint, an early Greek translation of the Hebrew Bible.
[89] Both chronologically and sequentially, if the early authorship (circa 45) of Matthew's Gospel is accepted. James' Epistle was probably written in near chronological proximity, and probably after Matthew, as Eusebius implies (P. Schaff and H. Wace, *Nicene and Post-Nicene Fathers, Vol. I: Eusebius: Church History, Life of Constantine the Great, and Oration in Praise of Constantine* (Peabody, MA: Hendrickson, 1995), 152-153).

earlier. Hereafter, the term is always used in the NT to reference "the church or congregation as the totality of Christians living in one place"⁹⁰ or to other more specific designations of the Christian assembly. Consequently, this is a passage with direct application to the church throughout its generations, including the modern era.

That Jesus would use the term *tax collector* (τελώνης) in 18:17 is understandable if His intent was to communicate that the offending and unheeding brother should be considered as one who has a different agenda than the rest of the assembly. Further, it is notable that Matthew included the term – being a former tax collector himself (Mt 9:9). Matthew would have recognized firsthand the cultural stigma against tax collectors, who were noted for their unfair practices. Also of importance in this context is how Jesus treated tax collectors. Matthew observes that they were seeking Jesus out and were dining with Him and His disciples (9:10). In this context, Jesus did not seek them out, but was receptive when they came to Him (presumably) with a teachable spirit. Of course, in Matthew's case, Jesus did seek out a tax collector (9:9). The implication in this context is that the offending and unheeding brother is not to be ostracized to the point of rudeness or cruelty, but is not to be sought out for fellowship unless there is openness, a submissiveness, and arguably a change of mind that would lead to the brother hearing and receiving the chastisement.

That Jesus employs the word ἐθνικὸς is a bit more difficult because of the ethnic connotations. The NASB and ESV render the term as *Gentile*, while the KJV opts for *heathen man*. Note that the KJV reading removes any ethnic association, instead rendering the word in such a way as to focus more on the spiritual condition. The KJV's is a difficult translation to justify, for, while there is extrabiblical precedent for the term's spiritual connotation,⁹¹ the word,

---

⁹⁰ BDAG, "ἐκκλησία," 293.
⁹¹ BDAG, "ἐθνικός," 267.

naturally understood, has a definitive ethnic connotation. There are four NT instances of the term, including this one, and none give any decisive indication regarding which translation would be best. In 5:47, Jesus contrasts expectations for His primarily Jewish audience with the actions of the Gentiles. In 6:7, He contrasts the prayers of that same audience with the meaningless repetitions of the Gentiles. In 3 John 7 there is a simple statement that brethren did not accept anything by way of provision from the Gentiles.

If the term here is best translated *heathen*, then the offending unheeding brother is to be treated as an unbeliever. Once again, never is it justifiable for a believer to treat an unbeliever with rudeness or cruelty. Rather it should be understood that there are different worldviews in play, and the believer, it would seem, is not encouraged to seek out the offender until and unless there is an openness to correction. If the term is best translated *Gentiles*, the meaning is not far different, as Jesus is communicating to an entirely Jewish audience (His disciples, 18:1) who indeed had some cultural aversion to non-Jews. Importantly, Jesus does not advocate such an aversion to Gentiles, but rather this may be an instance where He utilizes an existing cultural stigma to indicate the kind of stigma that should be associated with a lack of repentance in the church. In short, Jesus is not advocating racism, but is advocating a kind of discrimination against the unrepentant brother.

Exposition and Implications

Matthew 18:15-20 introduces a corrective and restorative process to the disciples for application in the soon-to-be formed church. Jesus outlines specific steps, whereby that correction and restoration can take place. Equally as important as the outcome is the process, as Jesus directly prescribed it. His process is as follows:

Step 1: But if sins the brother of you, you go correct him between you and him alone. The condition for the process is a sinning brother (SB) and an individual who has either been sinned against, or who has observed the sin – this is the correcting brother (CB), and can be any individual in the church. CB is directed to go to SB and meet with him *alone*. That this meeting happens in private only between the two parties is a necessary and prescribed element of the process, and if this privacy is betrayed in any way, the entire process is undermined and cannot be engaged as designed.

Step 1, Possible Outcome 1: If you he hears, you have gained the brother of you. If SB is receptive, the matter is resolved and closed, the goal having been achieved. The process is complete.

Step 1, Possible Outcome 2: But if not he hears... if Step 1 does not result in the desired outcome, move to Step 2.

Step 2: take with you additionally one or two, in order that upon a mouth of two witnesses or three every word is established. CB is to initiate another meeting, including one or two more. By definition of the numbers prescribed, privacy during this step is again required and vitally important. In practical terms, privacy at this point allows for individuals to fail, repent (change their minds), and be restored without public spectacle. In this step the matter is confirmed by the additional one or two, offering yet another private setting wherein the matter can be resolved.

Step 2, Possible Outcome 1 is implied, but not stated: If you he hears, you have gained the brother of you. If SB is receptive, the matter is resolved and closed, the goal having been achieved. The process is complete.

*Step 2, Possible Outcome 2: But if he is not listening of them...*if Step 2 does not result in the desired outcome, move to Step 3.

*Step 3: speak to the assembly (or church)...*Sadly, SB's actions and negative response demands that the matter be made public (within the context of the church). At this point CB is now to communicate the matter to the church. At this point the entire assembly becomes involved for the purpose of restoration. Perhaps the many can impress upon SB the error of his ways, and the need for resolution.

Step 3, Possible Outcome 1 is implied but not stated: If you he hears, you have gained the brother of you. If SB is receptive, the matter is resolved and closed, the goal having been achieved. The process is complete.

*Step 3, Possible Outcome 2: but if even of the church he is not listening...*if Step 3 does not result in the desired outcome, move to Step 4.

Step 4: he is to be to you (singular) as the Gentile and the tax collector. At this point, and only if the first three steps have been undertaken as prescribed, CB is to acknowledge a different relationship with SB. This step is not a repudiation of SB's status as a brother. It represents broken fellowship, but not a severed relationship (positionally speaking). The goal here, though implied but not stated, remains restoration, and the hope would be that the loss of fellowship would cause SB to reconsider, and move toward (public, at this point) repentance and restoration. If this happens, CB should apply the infinite forgiveness described in 18:21-35.

It is worth noting that while 18:18-20 is in close proximity to the corrective and restorative process of 18:15-17, the later verses are not a part of the process. By virtue of transitional language ("Truly, I say to you") and a comprehensive shift in pronoun number (singular in 15-17, plural in 18-20) it is evident that the latter three verses have primary application only for the disciples Jesus was addressing. Of course, in all Scripture there are secondary applications which may be drawn by all believers, it is critical that there be proper distinction between primary and application. In short, not all believers engaging in the corrective and restorative process are endowed with the unique authority and power shared by the disciples.

Even still, that distinction does not weaken the process described in 18:15-17. Jesus prescribes it and it is the central Biblical passage for understanding how believers should interact with an offending brother. There is sufficient authority and power in following that process. If Jesus is both the Builder and the Rock upon which the church is built, we can trust Him to know how to best handle within that assembly sin, conflict resolution, and discipline: with obedience, consideration, discretion, privacy, patience, purity, and love.

28

Seven Informal and Formal Methods for Preaching and Teaching: (6) Formal Teaching – The Analytical Summary

Of the four methods for formal teaching, the analytical summary and the topical teaching are the most challenging methods. In the synthetic approach, one could conduct a reasonable overview of a book without a great deal of knowledge about many other books of the Bible. Likewise, in the exegetical journey itself, one is focused on handling a specific passage or number of passages, and thus the area of focus is necessarily narrow. Because the analytical summary considers theological concepts in a topical way, it requires a tremendous level of knowledge about the subject.

If, for example, we were going to teach on the topic of forgiveness, we would have to investigate every single Biblical passage related to forgiveness in order to make sure we can address the topic comprehensively and accurately. But the process would not end there. Additionally, we would have to investigate every single Biblical passage that we thought *was not* related to forgiveness – just to verify our suspicion, in order to ensure we aren't missing anything. The process of arriving at an informed topical study is actually rather burdensome. We simply can't speak comprehensively and accurately on the topic of forgiveness (or any other topic) without having investigated every passage of Scripture.

Imagine if we studied all of what the Bible says about spiritual gifts, but we missed just one chapter – 1 Corinthians 13; or if we investigated stewardship but left out 2 Corinthians 9; or if prophecy, and we omitted Revelation 20; or sanctification, and we neglected Romans 8; or creation, and we ignored Genesis 1. While doctrines of Scripture generally are not dependent upon one single passage, we certainly find that one single passage can indeed be pivotal for the doctrine.

The irony in the challenge posed by the analytical summary is that this approach is by far the most commonly employed of the three formal teaching approaches. Consequently, we might wonder how many topical handlings of Scripture are presented each week in churches that have not been exhaustively researched, but are instead the products of tiny sample size. In no way do I mean to discourage anyone from employing the analytical summary, on the contrary, it is a valuable piece of the formal teaching pie. I do, however, wish to underscore the danger inherent in the approach, and the deep responsibility shouldered by the one who would utilize the method. We cannot simply pick a topic, explore a few verses, write some complementary rhetoric, and think we have adequately prepared. Handling the Bible comprehensively and accurately requires much, much more than that.

Despite the ease with which the analytical method can be distorted, it is an important component of the formal teaching process. The analytical summary helps to put topics and doctrines into context, and helps us to consider how to appropriately respond to the Biblical text.

In order to communicate theology well, it is best, then, to (1) either limit the theological subject matter, or to (2) limit the sample size. If we choose to limit the theological subject matter, we are narrowing the topic to the point that we can comprehensively discuss an issue in a reasonable amount of time. For example, if we are considering the theology presented in the book of Romans, we would be dealing with roughly eleven major areas requiring extensive discussion, and which would not be practical for communicating in a single sitting. We are just dealing with too much information. (In the context of the corporate assembly of the church, dedicating a series to the issue might help to cover things more comprehensively, but elongated topical series' tend to remove the focus from the synthetic context-setting and the exegetical grounding in the text itself. So, we should be cautious about over emphasizing topical elements. In the estimation of this writer, it is far better to utilize other contexts [classes, Bible studies, etc.] for more exhaustive analytical summary.)

Perhaps it would be better in this case to limit the subject matter to a discussion of the theology of God in the book of Romans, investigating simply Paul's consideration of the Persons and work of God in Romans. This might be a bit more manageable for the learner, and would also provide a model that the learner can follow for investigating other areas of theological inquiry in Romans – or any other book. After all, it is not the job of pastors – or any other teachers – to ensure that they have taught every theological concept to their learners (that would take not just years, but lifetimes). But it is their job to teach their listeners how to investigate the concepts for themselves. The key here is to teach the content well, to model the method, and to encourage learners to engage in further study.

An alternative to limiting the subject matter is to limit the scope of investigation. Rather than considering the Biblical teaching of the Persons and work of God, it might be helpful to divide that study into manageable parts by considering, for example, the doctrine of the Persons and works of God *only in Paul's Epistle to the Romans*. Focusing more narrowly on book contexts for theological implications has traditionally been referred to as *Biblical theology*.[92] Engaging in this discipline might result in a Petrine eschatology, or a Johannine soteriology, or a Pauline ecclesiology, to name a few results. The investigations and outcomes are not as broad as those of systematic theology, but they are much more manageable, and provide a helpful starting point for theological inquiry and communication.

The case study below is a capstone analytical summary to a book study in Romans. The book study begins with the synthetic preview, finds its content with the exegetical journey, and is concluded with the analytical summary. In this case, to avoid the dangers of attempting to communicate too much information at one time, the subject matter is limited (to the doctrine of the Persons and work of God) and the scope is limited to Romans (in keeping with the conclusion of a book study).

Case Study: Theological Implications of the Doctrine of God in Romans

This analytical summary considers aspects of Theology Proper, Christology, and Pneumatology in Paul's Letter to the Romans. While it is fairly basic, the summary assumes that there is some thematic understanding already developed on the part of the learner, as there ideally has been substantial time allocated for the synthetic preview and the exegetical journey. The doctrines of God were chosen in order to (1) provide some basic content, so that listeners can walk away from the study with a deeper understanding of and appreciation for who God is and what He has revealed about Himself in this letter, and to (2) provide a model for the analytical summary, so that learners will develop the capability to handle other aspects of theology in the letter on their own.

---

[92] While I generally employ the term *Biblical theology* to connote a comprehensive or systematic theology that is Biblically derived, the more traditional understanding is that the term refers to systematic theology within narrow Biblical contexts.

SECTION III: OVERVIEW OF THE EXPOSITIONAL PROCESS   249

Slide #1

```
Romans
on
God
```

Rationale

The title slide is designed to be simple and unintimidating. In this case I have chosen to avoid technical terms to minimize complexity at the outset, so as not to de-motivate learners, though complexity increases as we walk through the analytical summary. Learners will be stretched, but not beyond their capacities for understanding.

In preparation for the analytical summary, the teacher must determine which area(s) of theology will be considered, because in this format, if we cover all eleven areas of theology, the analytical summary would require far too much time to maintain the rhythm of moving apace through Biblical books. Remember, our focus is to teach listeners how to handle the processes and content for themselves, so we bear no obligation to be exhaustive in the analytical summary, as the summary provides (1) some content and (2) models the process, setting the stage for the learners' individual and personal Bible study.

250 INTEGRATING EXEGESIS AND EXPOSITION

Slide #2

> # 3 Aspects of Bible Study
> - Synthesis – big picture
> - Exegesis – details
> - Analysis – categories/topics
> - All 3 aspects are exegetical, not eisegetical

Rationale

Here we remind learners of the three perspectives in Bible study – the synthetic, exegetical, and analytical. We want people to be clear regarding where we are in the process and from what vantage point we will be coming. The arrow provides a visual reminder of those things. Finally, we emphasize that even though only one of the three perspectives bears the term *exegesis*, technically, all three are exegetical at their core – meaning that each are engaged and their conclusions are derived by the exegetical method (drawing the meaning out of the text) rather than the eisegetical one (reading meaning into the text).

Slide #3

> # 11 Topics of Theology
> - Bibliology – study of the Bible
> - Theology Proper – study of God
> - Christology – study of Christ
> - Pneumatology – study of the Spirit
> - Angelology – study of angels
> - Anthropology – study of mankind

Rationale

To continue the context-setting, we identify eleven topics of theology, so that listeners can begin to categorize topics in their own minds, and so that they begin to develop an adequacy in theological study. The topics are organized according to a logical theological flow. Bibliology provides the authoritative basis for study of the categories to follow. Theology Proper considers the Person and work of God. Christology discusses the second Person of the Trinity, while Pneumatology considers the third. Angelology can be considered at any point in the process, but is generally considered after the doctrine of God and before the doctrine of man, primarily due to an assumed sequence of creation (with angels presumably present at the creation of the earth, Job 38:4-7). Next is introduced anthropology, the study of mankind. To this point we have moved from authority, to the consideration of God, to created spiritual beings (angels), to created natural beings (humanity).

Slide #4

> ## 11 Topics of Theology
> - Hamartialogy – study of sin
> - Soteriology – study of salvation
> - Israelology – study of Israel
> - Ecclesiology – study of the church
> - Eschatology – study of last things

Rationale

Next we consider hamartialogy, the doctrine of sin, immediately introducing the plight of humanity, and then the solution to that problem, in soteriology, the doctrine of salvation. Once we have mentioned individual sin and salvation, we move to more corporate elements, first considering Israelology, then ecclesiology, the study of the church. As is the case in the sequence of God's revealed plan, Israel precedes the church. Finally, we address in eschatology the doctrine of the last things, specifically focusing on as of yet unfulfilled prophecy.

This brief overview of theology is an important contextual exercise, helping the learner to understand the implications and significance of the analytical overview. Context, context, context.

Slide #5

> # Romans on God
>
> - God (Theology Proper)
> - 161 references
> - 11:33-12:1
>
> - Notice "of God" in ch.1:
>   - Gospel of God 1:1
>   - Son of God 1:4
>   - Beloved of God, Grace and peace of God 1:7
>   - Will of God 1:10
>   - Power of God 1:16
>   - Righteousness of God 1:17
>   - Wrath of God 1:18
>   - That which is known of God 1:19
>   - Glory of God 1:23
>   - Truth of God 1:25
>   - Ordinance of God 1:32

Rationale

Once we have provided a quick survey of the basic topics or categories in theology, now we hone in on Theology Proper. Notice the technical terms are somewhat de-emphasized. We are not trying to bury learners in technical data, nor do we want to dumb down what the Bible is teaching. But we need to acknowledge that many of the technical terms are artificial, and not necessarily prerequisite to the study at hand.

In this particular summary, we highlight the total number of references to God, simply to put things in perspective, and to be transparent that our examination of the *of God* phrases in chapter 1 is considering only a small sampling of what Romans provides on the topic. To sum up this category we note Paul's doxology and the expected response in 11:33-12:1. The purpose here is to recognize the Biblical connection between who God is, what He has done, and how He expects His people to respond to Him.

Slide #6

> ### Romans on Jesus Christ
> - Jesus (Christology) – 38 references
> - Who is He?
>   - 1:4, 5:15, 5:21 (Jn 20:28)
> - What does He do?
>   - Notice the use of "in/through"
>   - 2:16, 3:22, 3:24, 5:1, 5:17, 5:21, 6:11, 8:1, 8:39
>   - Bottom line: God's connection to man is exclusively through Christ (Jn 14:6, 1 Tim 2:5)

Rationale

Moving to the doctrine of Christ, we underscore the total number of references to Him, again, for broad perspective. In question form we consider the Person (who is He?) and the work (what does He do?) of Jesus Christ. We provide references in Romans and read those verses to discover the answers.

With reference to who He is, in 1:4 He is identified as the Son of God, Jesus Christ our Lord. In 5:15 He is referred to as the one Man. In 5:21 He is characterized again as Jesus Christ our Lord. To support the significance of this identification, we cite John 20:28, in which Thomas addresses Jesus as "My Lord and my God."

To answer the question of what He does, we consider the *in* and *through* prepositions, which show that Christ is the center of function and focus. God will judge through Jesus Christ (2:16). Righteousness comes through faith in Jesus Christ (3:22). Redemption is in Jesus Christ (3:24). Our peace with God is through our Lord Jesus Christ (5:1). Those who receive the abundance of grace and the gift of righteousness will reign in life through Jesus Christ (5:17). Eternal life is through Jesus Christ our Lord (5:21). We are to consider ourselves to be alive to God in Christ Jesus (6:11). Being in Christ guarantees no condemnation (8:1). The love of God is expressed to us in Christ Jesus our Lord (8:38). The conclusion we draw is that God connects with humanity in and through Christ. He is indeed the way, the truth, and the life, and no man comes to the Father but through Him (Jn 14:6). Further, He is the one mediator between God and man (1 Tim 2:5). This is a profoundly practical truth, as we seek to know Him better and approach Him as He prescribes.

Slide #7

> ## Romans on the Holy Spirit
>
> - The Holy Spirit (Pneumatology)
> - 34 references (to *pneuma*)
> - Who He is
>   - 8:9, 8:26 (Himself, the Spirit)
>   - Spirit of God, of Christ – (notice the Trinity)
> - What He does
>   - 5:5, 8:9, 8:11, 8:14, 8:16, 8:26

Rationale

Considering now Paul's teaching in Romans on the Holy Spirit, we note the number of references to the Spirit, and highlight the two major discussion points: who He is (the Person), and what He does (the work). Romans 8:9 identifies Him as the Spirit of Christ, and as necessary for the justification event (compare with Eph 1:13-14 and 1 Cor 12:13). While 8:26 adds critical information about His ministry to believers, the passage also includes an important personal pronoun (of which the Holy Spirit is the antecedent), making clear that the Holy Spirit is a person, and not a force or manifestation.

Some of the works of the Spirit mentioned in these passages include: He plays a role in mediating God's love to us (5:5), He indwells believers (8:9), He is the channel through Whom our mortal bodies will be raised (8:11), He leads those who are the sons of God (8:14), He confirms that we are children of God (8:16), and He helps us in our weakness and intercedes for us (8:26). In these passages we are confronted with the intimacy of God with us. He is reliably ever-present for us. What will our response be?

Slide #8

Implications for the Romans

- (primary application)
- Note the relationship of the "of God" references throughout Romans 1-11, to the "of God" reference of 12:1
- Note the 64 imperatives in Romans, 11 of which are directly connected to the identity and/or character of God

SECTION III: OVERVIEW OF THE EXPOSITIONAL PROCESS

Rationale

Deriving the primary application requires looking carefully back at the exegetical process. In this instance, we are looking at the work done in the grammatical/syntactical analysis, recognizing that there are sixty-four imperatives in the Greek text of Romans. They are translated and listed in context below, and the eleven that are directly connected to the identity and character of God are listed in bold.

3:4	May it never be! Rather, let God	be	found true, though every man be
6:11	**Even so**	**consider**	**yourselves to be dead to sin, but**
6:12	Therefore do not let sin	reign	in your mortal body so that you
6:13	and do not go on	presenting	the members of your body to sin as
6:13	**of unrighteousness; but**	**present**	**yourselves to God as those alive**
6:19	in *further* lawlessness, so now	present	your members as slaves to
9:33	just as it is written, "	BEHOLD	, I LAY IN ZION A STONE OF
11:9	And David says, "LET THEIR TABLE	BECOME	A SNARE AND A TRAP, AND a
11:10	"LET THEIR EYES BE	DARKENED	TO SEE NOT, AND BEND THEIR BACKS
11:10	eyes be darkened to see not, AND BEND		THEIR BACKS FOREVER."
11:18	do not	be	arrogant toward the branches; but
11:20	you stand by your faith. Do not	be	conceited, but fear;
11:20	faith. Do not be conceited, but	fear	;
11:22		**Behold**	**then the kindness and severity of**
12:2	**And do not be**	**conformed**	**to this world, but be transformed**
12:2	conformed to this world, but be	transformed	by the renewing of your mind, so
12:14		Bless	those who persecute you; bless and

12:14 Bless those who persecute you;	bless	and do not curse.
12:14 persecute you; bless and do not	curse	.
12:16 associate with the lowly. Do not	be	wise in your own estimation.
12:19 your own revenge, beloved, but	**leave**	**room for the wrath** *of God*, **for it**
12:20 "BUT IF YOUR ENEMY IS HUNGRY,	FEED	HIM, AND IF HE IS THIRSTY, give
12:20 , FEED HIM, AND IF HE IS THIRSTY,	GIVE	HIM A DRINK; FOR IN SO DOING YOU
12:21 Do not be	overcome	by evil, but overcome evil with
12:21 Do not be overcome by evil, but	overcome	evil with good.
13:1 Every person is to	be	*in subjection to the governing*
13:1 Every person is to	be	*in subjection to the governing*
13:3 to have no fear of authority?	Do	what is good and you will have
13:4 But if you do what is evil, be	afraid	; for it does not bear the sword
13:7	Render	to all what is due them: tax to
13:8	Owe	nothing to anyone except to love
13:14 But	put	on the Lord Jesus Christ, and make
13:14 put on the Lord Jesus Christ, and	**make**	**no provision for the flesh in**
14:1 Now	accept	the one who is weak in faith, *but*
14:3 The one who eats is not to	regard	with contempt the one who does not
14:3 one who does not eat is not to	judge	the one who eats, for God has
14:5 day *alike*. Each person must be	fully	convinced in his own mind.
14:13 one another anymore, but rather	determine	this—not to put an obstacle or a
14:15 walking according to love. Do not	**destroy**	**with your food him for whom Christ**
14:16 what is for you a good thing be	spoken	of as evil;
14:20 Do not	**tear**	**down the work of God for the sake**

SECTION III: OVERVIEW OF THE EXPOSITIONAL PROCESS 259

14:22 The faith which you have,	have	as your own conviction before God.
15:2 Each of us is to	please	his neighbor for his good, to his
15:7 Therefore,	accept	one another, just as Christ also
15:10 Again he says, "	REJOICE	, O GENTILES, WITH HIS PEOPLE."
15:11 And again, "	PRAISE	THE LORD ALL YOU GENTILES, And let
15:11 Gentiles, AND LET ALL THE PEOPLES	PRAISE	HIM."
16:3	Greet	Prisca and Aquila, my fellow
16:5 church that is in their house.	Greet	Epaenetus, my beloved, who is the
16:6	Greet	Mary, who has worked hard for you.
16:7	Greet	Andronicus and Junias, my kinsmen
16:8	Greet	Ampliatus, my beloved in the Lord.
16:9	Greet	Urbanus, our fellow worker in
16:10	Greet	Apelles, the approved in Christ.
16:10 Apelles, the approved in Christ.	Greet	those who are of the *household* of
16:11	Greet	Herodion, my kinsman. Greet those
16:11 Greet Herodion, my kinsman.	Greet	those of the *household* of
16:12	Greet	Tryphaena and Tryphosa, workers in
16:12 Tryphosa, workers in the Lord.	Greet	Persis the beloved, who has worked
16:13	Greet	Rufus, a choice man in the Lord,
16:14	Greet	Asyncritus, Phlegon, Hermes,
16:15	Greet	Philologus and Julia, Nereus and
16:16	Greet	one another with a holy kiss. All
16:17 teaching which you learned, and	turn	away from them.

These sixty-four occurrences provide specific primary applications for the believers at Rome. Some of these are broadly transferrable to the church as a whole (e.g., the calls to action in 12:2), while others are not able to be applied in the same way by the secondary audience (such as the personal greeting imperatives of chapter 16). It is very important for the sake of the listener's proper understanding of how to handle the text that we model clearly the distinction between primary and secondary application.

Slide #9

> ## Implications for the church as a whole
>
> - (secondary application)
> - Example:
>   - Rom 6:11 "**consider** yourselves dead to sin, but alive to God in Christ Jesus…"
>   - Because of who God is, believers are to recognize their relationship to Him, and its grounding in Christ

Rationale

While there is only one direct primary application of a given passage (based on the principle of single meaning and the existence of the initial audience), there can be many secondary applications. God can use a passage in the lives of believers in many different ways. The meaning doesn't change, but the circumstances in which the passage can be employed are as diverse as are the happenings of life. So, we don't need to focus too heavily on secondary applications, but it is helpful to provide a brief example to engage the listeners to consider how God can use the passage in their own life.

The example mentioned here is Romans 6:11, a passage that challenges believers to think in a specific way about their relationship to sin and to Christ. Christian practice is rooted in mindset (e.g., Col 3:1-4), and consequently Paul emphasizes the importance of how we should think.

Slide #10

**Food for Thought:
Romans 11:33–12:1**

- Oh, the depth of the riches both of the wisdom and knowledge of God! How unsearchable are His judgments and unfathomable His ways! For who has known the mind of the Lord, or who became His counselor? Or who has first given to Him that it might be paid back to him again? For from Him and through Him and to Him are all things. To Him *be the glory forever. Amen.* **Therefore I urge you, brethren, by the mercies of God...**

Rationale

As a closing thought, this slide returns our focus to the doxology that concludes the discussion of God's mercies, and draws our attention to the expected response. Because of who He is and what He has done, it is only reasonable that we should respond as Paul prescribes. This refocusing helps to contextualize the arguments of Paul in the letter, and helps the learner extract from the letter a major component of purpose in Paul's writing: he tells believers of God's mercy, so that they will (1) know Him, (2) honor Him as He deserves, and (3) respond to Him with worshipful obedience. This doxological passage is the pivot or transition point that connects the *is* with the *ought*, and undergirds the call to transformative submission.

29
Seven Informal and Formal Methods for Preaching and Teaching: (7) Formal Teaching – Topical Teaching

To this point, we have gone to great lengths in these pages to encourage Biblical communicators to think exegetically – to communicate the Bible, rather than to communicate *about* the Bible. In particular, the patterns provided here for formal teaching have been centered on teaching books of the Bible. And though verse-by-verse book studies should account for the majority of your formal Bible teaching (to ensure the focus remains textual), there are occasions when a topical study can certainly be edifying. Perhaps you are in the middle of a book study, and Mothers' Day is fast approaching, and you wish to pause the book study in order to honor and exhort mothers. Or perhaps you have been invited to speak on a contemporary issue. Or perhaps you see a specific need in your own church context that you are compelled to address. Or perhaps you have been asked to present the message at a funeral.

For years during my pastoral ministry, when a holiday would arrive, I would introduce my teaching with something like this: "Because today is [insert holiday or special occasion here], I thought we would have a special message. Please turn in your Bibles to…" And we would jump right into the next scheduled passage in our book study. The folks would chuckle, because they understood the point I was making: *every passage is relevant for contemporary times* (or maybe the chuckles were due to my being boringly predictable). Often the passages we were scheduled to handle fit the context of the occasion or holiday so well, it was as if the timing was carefully orchestrated (typically it wasn't, by me or the other pastors). The reason the regularly scheduled passage fit so well is simply because the Scriptures are God-breathed, and useful for the equipping of the believer, for every good work.

As an exercise in approaching a topic, randomly pick a holiday or a special circumstance. Then randomly pick a Scripture passage without any consideration for how the passage might relate to the scenario you have selected. Consider the meaning of the passage, then the primary application, then finally consider some secondary applications. Can you think of any secondary applications that might tie into the context of the special occasion? For example, for a Mothers' Day message, is there any passage that would *not* be appropriate? Is there any passage that isn't somehow useful for the equipping of mothers for good works? In short, there is no need to abandon the verse-by-verse handling of Scripture simply to accommodate a special occasion or pressing need. Further, sticking with a verse-by-verse expositional approach will help the teacher avoid some of the dangers associated with analytical and topical teaching, as we discussed in the introduction to the analytical summary. Of course, there are settings in which a purely topical approach is very helpful, *but in the context of the corporate gathering of the church there is no better way to model the exegetical handling of Scriptures than a verse-by-verse approach.*

The process doesn't need to change in approaching a topic: select a particular passage specifically for its content relating to the occasion or issue at hand, and handle that passage in a verse-by-verse manner. In maintaining a consistent approach, we accomplish several important purposes: (1) we stick to the text and the context, allowing the text to set the agenda for the topic at hand, (2) we model a dependence on God's word rather than on our own creative prowess (nothing wrong with creativity, but just remember, it is God words that are inspired, authoritative, and useful – not yours and not mine), (3) we provide a practical model for the listener to follow regarding how to address issues: by allowing God's word to have preeminence in our lives.

Recently, a Christian magazine published an article citing "top" sermons for the year.[93] The topics covered in those ten sermons included:

> Homosexuality
> Marks of a Renewed Church
> Meditation for a Fallen Police Officer
> A Psalm for Thanksgiving
> What to Do When Your Fig Tree Doesn't Blossom
> Finding God in the Dark
> God is Holy
> The 10 Financial Commandments
> The World's Best Love Story
> What Child is This?

Now, without any intended critique of the authors and presenters of these messages or the messages themselves, and simply as an exercise in the relevance of Scripture to everyday issues, think about these titles and consider whether or not there is a particular passage substantial enough to handle in a verse-by-verse fashion, which allows for a broad understanding of the topic at hand and which provides an exhortation or call to action. It is actually easier than one might think.

---

[93] "Top 10 sermons of 2013 from preachingtoday.com" in Christianity Today, January 2, 2014, viewed at http://www.christianitytoday.org/mediaroom/news/2014/top-10-sermons-of-2013-from-preaching-todaycom.html.

The following case studies are provided simply to provoke thought about how to handle individual topics as they arise in your context. Some of these examples are more verse-by-verse in their approach, while others move from passage to passage following the narrative of the passage. In either case, they are brief samples of how we might approach some special topical situations.

Case Study: New Years Resolutions for Every Day (A New Years' Walk Through Psalm 90)

Of the one hundred and fifty psalms that constitute the largest book in the Bible, Moses penned only one, so we approach Psalm 90 with particular interest. What was so significant about the prayer of this one who spoke face to face with God (Exodus 33:11), that his prayer would later be included in this important collection?

The psalm is introduced as "A prayer of Moses, the man of God," telling us the kind of literature this is and identifying its author. Verses 1-2 focus on the character and sovereignty of God. He is transcendent ("even from everlasting you are God"), He is the Creator of all ("…you gave birth to the earth and the world"), and at the same time He is intimately involved with His creation ("You have been our refuge" [Heb., *maon*]). Because of who He is identified to be in verses 1-2, it is inarguable that He has the right to deal with His creation as the next verses describe.

Verses 3-11 consider God's rightful judgment on mankind. God is active in the physical death of men (3), and in the coming and going of generations (5-6). Verse 7 accounts for His activity in the physical death of men. That death is judgment, and an aspect of being "consumed" by His anger and "dismayed" by His wrath. Why the judgment? God has set the iniquities of mankind in His presence (8) – they are ever before Him.

In short, none can hide from Him. Because of His judgment (9), days turn (Heb., *panah*) or decline, and years finish with a moaning (Heb., *hegeh*). Human life is fleeting, short, laborious, and sorrowful (10), as a result of God's judgment on the iniquities mentioned in verse 8. This is all just a glimpse of the power of His anger, and His fury is proportional to the fear that is due Him (11).

While this appears to be a very bleak situation, it is vital that we remember Moses' opening stanza: "Lord, you have been our refuge in all generations" (1). God is holy, sovereign, transcendent, and fearsome, but these traits do not contradict the reality of His graciousness, and Moses appeals to that graciousness in the concluding verses of the psalm. "Cause us to know (hiphil [causative] imperative, *hiyodah*) to count rightly our days, that we may cause ourselves (hiphil, [causative] *wenabia*), to come in to a heart of wisdom" (12).

Moses requests that God grant the proper perspective for His servants to consider the brevity of our days so they may use those days wisely. Moses appeals to God that He return and be sorry on behalf of His servants (13), and that He completely and utterly satisfy (piel [intensive] imperative, *shebe'anu*) His servants with His lovingkindness (14). Moses asks that God proportionally make His servants glad according to the afflictions of the years (15), and adds, "that it – your work – may be seen to your servants, and your glory to their children" (16).

Finally, Moses requests the favor of *Adonai Elohenu* (the Lord our God) be on His servants, and emphatically requests twice – in the imperative – that God "make firm" the work of their hands. In verses 12-17 Moses uses seven imperatives when talking to God: (1) cause us to know, (2) return, (3) be sorry, (4) satisfy us, (5) make us glad, (6) make firm, and (7) make firm. He is emphatically requesting action on God's part. But it is quite notable that Moses requests action on God's part to enable action on the part of His servants: Cause us to number our days – that we might cause ourselves to come into a heart of wisdom. Completely satisfy us in the morning – that we may sing for joy and be glad all our days.

Moses expected that God's grace would enable His servants

to respond with wisdom, joy, and worship. Moses asked the Lord for specific intervention, in order that God's servants would respond to God the right way. When we ask God to intervene in our lives and the lives of others, what is our ultimate desire? Is it so that we can simply enjoy more pleasures (as in James 4:3), or is it so that we can respond to Him in a more fitting way? As we embark on a new year – however much of it He allows to experience on this earth – perhaps we can be ever aware of the brevity of our days, so that we can respond properly to Him. If we are constantly and consciously aware of the reality of our situation, we have an opportunity to walk wisely, making the most of the opportunity He has given us.

Case Study: Coniah's Judgment: Did the Grinch Steal Christmas?

In order to fulfill Biblical prophecy, the Messiah had to come from the seed of David. He had to be of the tribe of Judah, in the line of Solomon, yet he could not be of the seed of Coniah, whom (because of a litany of evils) God essentially removed from the royal lineage in Jeremiah 22:30: "Thus says the Lord, 'Write this man down childless, a man who will not prosper in his days; for no man of his descendants will prosper sitting on the throne of David or ruling again in Judah.'"

Consequently the genealogies introducing Matthew's and Luke's Gospels are important, in that they demonstrate the lineage of Jesus as legitimately Messianic. Yet the genealogies are different. Why? Matthew presents in his Gospel the genealogy from Abraham to Joseph, the husband of Mary. Matthew lists fourteen generations from Abraham to David, fourteen from David to the Deportation, and fourteen from the Deportation to Jesus. Not every name in the lineage of Jesus is mentioned, as some were excluded (Ahaziah, Joash, Amaziah, Jehoiakim, and Eliakim, etc.). It is also significant that Matthew mentions women in his genealogy (highly unusual in

Hebrew genealogies), specifically Tamar, Rahab, Ruth, (Bathsheba is alluded to but not named), and of course, Mary. Also note that forty-two generations are mentioned, yet only forty-one names, as David is mentioned twice, perhaps for the sake of symmetry. Joseph, the legal father of Jesus, is identified as the son of Jacob. Luke presents a different genealogy, working from Adam.

As in Matthew's, there are gaps in Luke's genealogy of Christ. It was more important for the Hebrew genealogy to demonstrate legitimate descent rather than to present a comprehensive listing. Luke traces from Nathan the son of David rather than from Solomon (as Coniah was in the line of Solomon), and identifies Joseph as "of Eli," suggesting that Joseph was Eli's son in law, by virtue of his betrothal to Mary. Actually, then, it seems that Luke recounts the genealogy of Jesus through Mary. Matthew traces Jesus' legal lineage and right to the throne through Joseph, recognizing God's covenant promises regarding Solomon. Luke traces Jesus' physical lineage through Mary, showing, perhaps, how Jesus avoided the curse of Coniah.

So there is really no dilemma in Jesus' genealogies: He is qualified physically by virtue of His bloodline through Mary, and if that wasn't enough in the eyes of some, He was also qualified legally by His relationship to Joseph, though He was (importantly) not descended from Joseph's bloodline. This key distinction (that Jesus was not of Joseph's bloodline) not only helps us understand how Jesus was not subject to Coniah's judgment, but also how God's very first promise of deliverance would be literally fulfilled (Gen 3:15).

Because of who Jesus is we can have joy – not just during holiday seasons – but by believing in Him, we can have joy that lasts forever. "Do not be afraid; for behold, I bring you good news of great joy which will be for all the people; for today in the city of David there has been born for you a Savior, who is Christ the Lord" (Lk 2:10-11).

Case Study: Memorials Demand Action

For many of us, holidays like Memorial Day are little more than sanctioned excuses to get a little rest or perhaps spend some time with family – and those are wonderful things. But I am reminded (pun intended) that the Biblical writers had something else in mind when they discussed memorials.

In Deuteronomy 5-6, for example, Moses presents to Israel a reminder of all that God had done for Israel and all that He had commanded. The reason is given in 6:2, "so that you and your son and your grandson might fear the Lord your God, to keep all His statutes and His commandments which I command you, all the days of your life, and that your days may be prolonged." God had made a covenant with Israel (the Mosaic Covenant, or the Law), that if Israel obeyed God's law faithfully, He would allow them to be blessed in the land He gave to them. Those were the basic conditions of the covenant.

The book of Deuteronomy records the second giving of the Law – a reminder for the new generation of Israelites who would be entering the Promised Land after the forty years in the wilderness. In this case, the reminder was, for Israel, a call to obedience. Even though we today are not in this covenant relationship (since the Mosaic Covenant was made only with Israel [Ex 19:3]), it serves as a reminder to us of God's character: He is holy, and has the highest standards (Deut 7:6, 14:2, 23:14, 32:51). He judges with impartiality (Deut 1:17). He is gracious and merciful (Deut 13:17). The Law was never intended to provide righteousness or salvation (Rom 8:3; Heb 7:11, 10:1). Instead, it was designed to provide an example and reminder for all of how we must come to God – by grace through faith in Jesus Christ (Gal 3:24). While certainly not on par with Biblical reminders (either in authority or depth), contemporary holidays can be very valuable – and not just for rest and time with family. Memorial Day, for example, was inaugurated to commemorate those who died in military service to their country. It is a bittersweet day, as we rejoice in the gracious freedoms God has granted us through the ultimate sacrifice of so many, all while considering the awful price that was paid. As Jesus said, "Greater love has no man than this, that one lay down his life for his friends" (Jn 15:3). And this memorial, like any other reminder, is not without its own action points.

In the closing moments of Saving Private Ryan (spoiler alert: read no further if you haven't seen the movie), with his dying breath, U.S Army Ranger Captain, John H. Miller implores Private James Francis Ryan to "Earn this!"[94] Many men died so that Ryan could live. In the film, Ryan later seemed haunted by those words, as none could ever truly earn such a precious gift. Similarly, we could never earn the most precious gift of life given by grace through faith (Eph 2:8-9), nor could we ever earn the precious gift of freedom bought with the lives of so many. How can we respond when given such priceless gifts?

Paul reminds us in Ephesians 5:20 to be "always giving thanks for all things in the name of our Lord Jesus Christ to God, even the Father..." Do we continually express our gratitude to Him for who He is and all that He has done for us? If not, we need to change our habits. Further, Paul exemplifies how to give thanks to God, all the while "praying always for you" (Col 1:3). Specifically, in this context he prays that believers (in Colossae) will grow in their understanding, in order to "walk in a manner worthy of the Lord, to please Him in all respects, bearing fruit in every good work and increasing in the knowledge of God" (Col 1:10). Do we pray for others that way – for their spiritual growth and walk? Do we pray, for example, for the families of those left behind who have made supreme sacrifices on our behalf?

Finally, Paul reminds us to do more, in addition to prayer:

---

[94] Robert Rodat, *Saving Private Ryan*, theatrical release, directed by Steven Spielberg, Amblin Entertainment, 1998.

"Let us not lose heart in doing good, for in due time we will reap if we do not grow weary. So then, while we have opportunity, let us do good to all people, and especially to those who are of the household of faith" (Gal 6:9-10). This Memorial Day, let's make the most of the opportunity – with thankfulness, and with prayer, let's do some good. I thank the Lord for His great gift to us, and I thank those who have suffered and died so that you and I can have the freedoms we enjoy. I pray for the families who are left behind, and express deepest gratitude to them: Thank you, and thank you again. I could never earn what God has given me through you, and I am deeply saddened by the price you paid. But so help me God, I will use wisely that time afforded me in part by your loved one's – and your own – sacrifice. May God bless you this day, and every day to come. May you know the richness of His comfort, His love, and His mercy, "so that you may not grieve as those who have no hope" (1 Thes 4:13). May you have a blessed Memorial Day, and may we use it well.

Case Study: Comfort in the Midst of Tragedy

It surrounds us constantly. We can't escape it, though sometimes we brush up against it without realizing how near it really is. The imminence of tragedy and heartache is a cold and unwelcome reality for all of us, as we were reminded by the awful flooding in Colorado, and by the murders at the Navy Yard in Washington D.C. If those aren't reminder enough, we could look to Syria, where Al-Nusra Front jihadists' cruelties are epitomized by the beheading of a man for his unwillingness to deny Christ, and their subsequent mocking that his Jesus didn't save him; or we could mourn the loss of a child near New Orleans, who after playing with a water toy in the backyard was killed by the Naegleria fowleri amoeba.

While jarring to most of us, these kinds of events are the daily fare of people all over the world. And if not the result of human cruelty, then we witness the earth groaning beneath our feet as it sweeps away thousands in floods, earthquakes, tsunamis, and eruptions. There is simply no place to hide from the sorrows and dangers of human experience. Even if we take our own lives in nihilistic desperation, we look forward to being held to account for our wasted stewardship, and we look backward to see behind us the wake of heartache and brokenness that we have wrought in loved ones left behind. Thankfully, there is more to the story than the "nasty, brutish, and short" life of Hobbes' lamenting.[95] When one seeks comfort and strength in the pages of Scripture, they will not find the absence of tragedy as the near-term reprieve.

Peter, for example, doesn't advocate that believers shall always escape from trials. Rather he offers believers a proper and therapeutic response: "In this you greatly rejoice, even though now for a little while, if necessary, you have been distressed by various trials..." (1 Pet 1:6). Rejoice??? How can there be any joy in such darkness? Of course, the Bible is not advocating some kind of psychobabble denial of the harsh realities surrounding us. Instead, it advocates perspective. Peter is not suggesting that the trials faced by believers are joyful in themselves. Instead he is pointing believers to their eternal hope and the fact that God will use the temporal distresses to refine believers: "so that the proof of your faith, more precious than gold, which is perishable, even though tested by fire, may be found to result in praise and glory and honor at the revelation of Jesus Christ" (1 Pet 1:7).

The joy isn't found in the circumstances of the moment – those can be exceedingly dark and worthy of the weeping they inspire. Rather the joy is found in knowing that God has not left us to the agonies of life, but has provided us hope for the future – a hope which allows us to benefit in no small way from the refinements and shaping of today. I cannot imagine the pain of those families in Colorado, Washington D.C., or Syria, and other

---

[95] Thomas Hobbes, *The Leviathan* (Oxford: Oxford University Press, 2014), 325.

parts of the world, as they try to make sense of the mind-boggling loss of loved ones.

As Paul exhorted us in Romans 12:15, there is simply a time to weep with those who weep. Certainly hope for the future is not incompatible with compassion in the present. As followers of Christ we can put our arms around those who are heartbroken, walk silently with them, and encourage them in His future hope as we may be given opportunity. All the while we should consider Paul's reminder regarding the importance of knowing God's plan for the future. He says in 1 Thessalonians 4:13, "we do not want you to be uninformed, brethren, about those who are asleep, so that you will not grieve as do the rest who have no hope." Because of the certainty of our future in Him, believers need not grieve in anguish as if there is no hope.

Of course, we all grieve loss. Even though, for believers, loss of loved ones in Christ is temporary (in light of a heavenly reunion), it is still extremely painful for that duration. (Again – weep with those who weep, don't tell them to stop weeping.) But the hope Christ offers of a future in Him provides a lasting joy without which, as Paul put it, "we are of all men most to be pitied" (1 Cor 15:19b).

Life is hard. Pain and death make it harder. Yet in the midst of these realities there is comfort and strength offered to all and found in the One who conquered death (1 Cor 15:53-57) and paid for our hope with His own blood. There is also an exhortation to believers, that their time here is not wasted and the path they trod is not without purpose: "Therefore, my beloved brethren, be steadfast, immovable, always abounding in the work of the Lord, knowing that your toil is not in vain in the Lord" (1 Cor 15:58).

30
Three Styles for Preaching and Teaching: Extemporaneous, Note Aided, and Read Presentation

There are three distinct approaches to the mechanics of presenting material, and any of the three can be utilized in handling the text well. It is recommended that a developing Bible communicator experiment with each of the three approaches to determine what best fits the personality and tendencies of the communicator. Further, it is excellent to be capable in each of the three, as different contexts may call for different approaches.

First is extemporaneous teaching, where the teacher opens the Biblical text, and teaches from it with no external notes, allowing the text to be the topic (John Calvin, for example was noted for his extemporaneous handling of Scripture). Regardless of what one thinks of John Calvin's theological conclusions, there is no question that Calvin was an excellent communicator of the Bible. John Currid provides a brief and thoughtful discussion of John Calvin's method of communicating the Bible, describing how Calvin would open the Bible in the original languages and teach extemporaneously, in a verse-by-verse fashion, for thirty-five to forty minutes.[96] Calvin's dependence on the original languages and his commitment to teaching the text, rather than teaching about the text, were exemplary, and a model for any Bible communicator to follow.

As a point of application, I would encourage Bible communicators to *always* have the Hebrew Bible or the Greek New Testament open beside their preferred translation as they are teaching (even a parallel Hebrew/English or Greek/English is helpful). This will help develop a proper usage of those texts, will help avoid overstating things in English, and will help communicators and their listeners gain skill in handling the text in those languages.

Also worth noting is that Calvin wasn't the top Hebraist or Greek scholar in Europe – he wasn't the expert, yet he worked diligently. That's significant, and brings another point of application to us. We're not necessarily being asked to be the best in the world in handling the Biblical languages. It's not about becoming an expert, it's about being able to handle the text and work in these languages. Even if we have to rely on tools sometimes, that is a part of the process. But we need to be able to develop some skill in handling the languages, because if we are working exclusively in English, we are missing a great deal of the text itself, and we aren't actually doing exegesis.

The extemporaneous model is advantageous primarily for its textual focus, but there are other advantages – such as providing the flexibility to the teacher to respond to questions and allow for deeper investigation in various areas of the text. The other two more choreographed methods make this type of responsiveness to listeners a little more difficult. Along with the advantages of the extemporaneous approach, there are some challenges, mainly in that the teacher must know the text very well in order to present it

---

[96] John Currid, Calvin and the Biblical Languages (London: Mentor, 2006), 26.

SECTION III: OVERVIEW OF THE EXPOSITIONAL PROCESS

in such a way. Extensive preparation is necessary. As a Bible communicator gains knowledge through exegetical study and experience through personal application and exposition, the process becomes more comfortable.

A second approach is note aided teaching, where the teacher utilizes summary or highlight notes as an aid. In this approach the notes wouldn't be read audibly but they would serve to remind the teacher of points of emphasis, to assist where memory might otherwise fail, and to help the teacher stay on topic. Note aided communication is very common, and at first glance appears as if it might be the easiest to utilize. In that approach, essentially, the speaker has written main points and highlights to work through, but the Biblical text still sets the overall agenda. This is a helpful approach, however, it actually can be challenging. In one sense, reading the whole presentation is a bit simpler in delivery because there is one process the speaker has to focus on: reading the presentation in a conversational way. But with the note aided approach, the speaker is half speaking extemporaneously and half reading – so the speaker has to function concurrently using two processes.

The most common problem arising from this dual processing is evident the first time the speaker looks away from the notes to address the audience extemporaneously. At that moment, the brain has shifted gears, and it is a challenge to return to those notes and find the right place. Many times a speaker will look away from the notes, be unable to find where he is in the notes and then simply launch into an unplanned oratory. This happens often with inexperienced speakers, but it is easily avoidable by managing notes well. Simple details like using large fonts, numbered bullet points, and wide spacing help the speaker stay on target. Nobody wants to interrupt their message with a thirty second pause to find their place, and it is remarkable how uncomfortable such delays are for the listeners as well. Manage the notes well (i.e., make them easy to read), and you will avoid the potential pitfalls.

A third approach is to read verbatim a written presentation of the material to be covered. This presentation model allows for the highest degree of precision in communicating the message, and has the added benefit of allowing the teacher to develop a good personal commentary on the passages and books being taught. Despite the added benefits, the third approach is typically the most challenging for the actual delivery, as it takes developed skill to be able to read in such a way as to sound conversational. Many of those who are known as great Bible communicators would write out their messages and deliver them verbatim (Jonathan Edwards, for example, employed this method), so there is a rich tradition of communicating the Bible in this way.

Regardless of which of the three methods of communication you choose, the need for diligence in preparation is the same.

> ... if I should climb up into the pulpit without having deigned to look at a book and frivolously imagine 'Ah well! When I get there God will give me enough to talk about,' and I do not condescend to read, or to think about what I ought to declare, and I come here without carefully pondering how I must apply the Holy Scripture to the edification of the people – well, then I should be a cock-sure charlatan and God would put me to confusion in my audaciousness.[97]

---

[97] Ibid.

31
Biblical Rationale for Dynamics in Preaching and Teaching

Just as we seek to discover our hermeneutic method from the pages of Scripture, and just as we seek to apply those principles consistently, we also need to recognize that Scripture has much to say regarding how we should communicate God's word to others. These principles on this topic even go so far as to help us think through the appropriate dynamics of communication.

Keep Things as Simple as Possible

In John 16:29 the disciples acknowledged that Jesus was speaking plainly or boldly (*parresia*), rather than with figures of speech, and they responded, "Now we know..." They were not confused about His message, and understood what He was telling them. While certainly there are appropriate uses of figurative language and illustration, it is generally better to communicate simply and straightforwardly in order to ensure the point is not lost in translation through the use of too many rhetorical devices.

It is worth noting that Jesus didn't use parables for the sake of making things easier to understand – in fact, His stated purpose in some cases was just the opposite (Mt 13:13,34; Mk 4:33-34). Notice that even when He used figurative language with His disciples, they misunderstood (e.g., Jn 6:51-61, 11:12-14) He later acknowledges the superiority of plain speaking as opposed to figurative (Jn 16:25). This is not to say we should not utilize parables at times, but rather we should not misrepresent how Jesus used that particular rhetorical tool and for what purposes. Though Paul made use of occasional metaphors (e.g., Gal 4:24, 2 Tim 2:4-6), he later confirms the importance of clear and distinct speech if the intent is that what is said is to be understood (1 Cor 14:9).

Some practical implications:
- Speak with clarity.
- Avoid wordiness.
- Use figures of speech judiciously.
- Speak distinctly, so as to be understood.
- Remember that if you can't say something concisely, you don't know it.

Speak Boldly

Because of the glory of the message and the hope it provides, Paul was able to say, "we use great boldness (*parresia*) in speech" (2 Cor 3:12). He adds that he *ought* to speak boldly (Eph 6:20). He modeled this boldness when he proclaimed the gospel to the Thessalonians even amid much opposition (1 Thes 2:2). Paul encouraged that *these things* be spoken confidently (Tit 3:8). The confidence didn't derive from the speaker, but rather from the message itself, because *these things* were God's words.

Some practical implications:
- Don't hide from controversial issues. Attack them head on with the truth and clarity of Scripture.
- Enunciate.
- Speak at an appropriate volume.
- Avoid nervous ticks (both in speech and action: avoid

uhms, you knows, I means, rattling keys, etc.).
- Embrace silence, which can be a very effective tool, giving listeners time to consider.

Speak to Please God, Not Men

Paul modeled speaking to please God rather than men, recognizing that God examines hearts (Gal 1:10, Col 1:10, 1 Thes 2:4). He later warns Timothy of the coming danger of people who will not endure sound teaching but will want their ears tickled (2 Tim 4:3-4). These people will prefer myths to truth, and will demand teachers who accommodate that preference. When we encounter those preferences, we have an obligation to Biblical integrity, no matter the consequences.

Some practical implications:
- Avoid peer pressure.
- Avoid outcomes based thinking: speak the truth, regardless of consequences.

Speak Humbly

In Luke 7:13-16 is the account of Jesus raising a woman's only son from the dead. Upon Jesus' command "the dead man sat up and began to speak." God doesn't need you and He doesn't need me. He has gotten along just fine for many years without us, and while He chooses to use us, He can raise up dead people, or rocks, or even a donkey to speak for Him if He so chooses. Just as there is no room for boasting in our efforts as related to salvation because they have nothing to do with our salvation (Eph 2:8-10), there is no room for boasting in His use of us either. As Paul said, we should boast in Him.

In our speaking, let's not confuse humility for weakness. Christ demonstrated humility, but never weakness. He acknowledged that the one speaking from himself seeks his own glory (Jn 7:18), reminding His listeners that He was indeed speaking from the Father (Jn 7:16). The principle He cited is also true in our case. If we speak from ourselves it is our own glory we are seeking. To speak with the proper humility means to boast in Him, and never in ourselves. It means that we are speaking from Him, and not from ourselves. As Peter put it, believers who are speaking should be speaking as if the very words of God (1 Pet 4:10-11). In other words, what we say should be consistent with and representative of Him. And as Paul put it, when speaking His message, there is an obligation to faithfulness, and no cause for boasting (1 Cor 9:16).

> Some practical implications:
> - Avoid excessive use of first person pronouns (I, me, etc.).
> - Wherever possible, refer to *you* when commending and encouraging, *we* when exhorting and reproving, and *I* when providing self-deprecating examples.

Speak Impartially

The scribes and chief priests unsuccessfully attempted to find some inconsistency in Jesus, hoping that they could have Him condemned. In one of their attempts they acknowledged the relationship of correct teaching and impartiality, noting that Jesus was teaching correctly and was not partial, or that He was not showing favoritism (not receiving appearances or faces, *ou lambaneis prospon*). Likewise, while Paul had a particular method of seeking audiences in the synagogues, wherever he found pliable listeners he would invest himself, even challenging societal norms (e.g., Acts 16:13), just as Jesus had done before (e.g., Jn 4:9). James adds that in the body of Christ we are not to show favoritism (Jam 2:1-9).

Some practical implications:
- Avoid appealing only to certain demographics.
- Make eye contact with as many people (of all ages etc.) as possible.
- Be encouraging to all wherever possible.
- Avoid appeals to authority other than Scripture (be careful with quoting secondary sources), as this can reflect partiality.

Don't Put the Cookies on the Floor

The stated goal for believers in the sanctification process is that they will have a more accurate and intimate knowledge of Christ (e.g., Eph 1:15-23). He chastises the Corinthians for the immaturity and fleshliness (1 Cor 3:1-3), and for their lack of knowing God (1 Cor 15:34), and he challenges them to maturity in being of the same mind (1 Cor 1:10). Peter adds later that Paul's writings include difficult things to understand but are inspired by God and are of wisdom (2 Pet 3:15-16). All Scripture is authoritative and useful (2 Tim 3:16-17), even if not always easy to understand. The teacher need not feel the burden of trying to simplify that which is not simple. The student bears the responsibility of investigating and coming to a deeper knowledge of the truth – as the Bereans modeled (Acts 17:11).

Some practical implications:
- Don't dumb-down what the text says.
- Show your work. Model, don't hide your exegetical process.
- Try to speak at a level just slightly above your audience, challenging them to reach up just a bit.
- Remember that the goal is to teach your audience how to handle the word of God for themselves, so that they can study and grow on their own.

Maintain Priorities

Paul demonstrated a tremendous amount of humility in his preaching and teaching, acknowledging that Christ had not sent him to preach in cleverness of speech, but to proclaim the gospel (1 Cor 1:17, 2:1), so that the cross would not be emptied of its power (*kenoo*). What a vital lesson this is: our focus is to be the message itself in all its simplicity, because the power is in the message, not the messenger.

Paul acknowledged being unskilled in speech (2 Cor 11:6), and he humbled himself for the Corinthians' benefit (2 Cor 11:7), not demanding they support his ministry financially. He did not employ all the skills at his disposal, nor did he make demands of them related to his preaching/teaching ministry so that more important goals could be achieved. Paul was willing to stay out of the way so that God could work through His message. "For I will not presume to speak of anything except what Christ has accomplished through me…" (Rom 15:18).

> Some practical implications:
> - Stick to the text, don't wander or meander.
> - Don't say everything you can say, just what should be said.
> - Don't be the center of attention, let Him be that.
> - Remember the goal: preaching so that people can be introduced to Christ, teaching so that people can learn to handle the Bible for themselves, and grow to maturity.

Speak for Profit

One of the reasons for Paul's critique of the Corinthians' misuse of the gift of tongues was that it simply wasn't profitable for the listener (1 Cor 14:6, 19). He adds later that all of his speaking to the Corinthians was that they might be built up (2 Cor 12:19).

Some practical implications:
- What we say should be intended to edify.
- Some recognition of the need of the moment can be helpful.
- Some recognition of the maturity (or lack thereof) of listeners can be helpful.
- Remember that music also provides a means of teaching for profit. Ephesians 5:19 prescribes that believers be "speaking to one another in psalms and hymns and spiritual songs..." Don't neglect the didactic functions of song.

Speak With Purity

In Colossians 3:8 believers are told to put aside obscene speech (*aischrologion*). While there is no such thing as an inherently bad word, the speech of the believer is always to be seasoned as with grace (Col 3:6) to be able to meet the need of the moment

Some practical implications:
- Deliberately choose words for their impact, avoiding words that would detract or distract.
- Use questionable or culturally taboo terms only when necessary, especially if the text employs such terms (e.g., Zeph 1:17, Gal 1:8-9).

Speak the Truth in Love

Without love, we are just noise (1 Cor 13:1). Ephesians 4:15 reminds us that we are to be always speaking the truth in love. The interconnectedness and interdependence of truth and love is evident here. We can't demonstrate one without the other. Paul explains that the goal of the instruction is love (1 Tim 1:5). Consequently, if our teaching and learning is not resulting in love then we aren't doing it right.

Some practical implications:
- Speak considerately of anyone you discuss, whether present or not.
- If critiquing someone (e.g., perhaps for a disagreeable doctrinal stance) as a necessary part of the teaching, guard their dignity as if they are in the room listening. Don't distort the truth, and don't be unloving either.
- Training up listeners in the instruction of the Lord is loving. Creating dependence upon you as the teacher is not.

Don't Appeal to Vanity

The apostles' ministry did not include flattering speech (1 Thes 2:5). They did not appeal to pride or vanity. Those that do appeal to vanity and pride are described as being in error (2 Pet 2:18), and grumblers, following their own lusts, and seeking to gain advantage (Jude 16). Notice that when Paul referenced himself as a positive example (apart from what Christ specifically did in him), he was hesitant or sheepish, not wanting any to think he was self-promoting. In 2 Corinthians 11:1 he asks his readers to bear with him in a little foolishness as he recounts his ministry. In 11:21 he reiterates that he is engaging in foolishness. In 11:23, he acknowledges that he is speaking as if insane. Paul is just that intent on not making appeals to vanity.

Some practical implications:
- Avoid, if possible, illustrations that present the speaker as exemplary – outside of appeals to Christlikeness and what He has accomplished in us.
- Be cognizant of the importance of sincerity. False humility, pseudo compliments, and buttering up are all forms of appeal to vanity.

- Don't be manipulative. Don't work from false premises in order to motivate action on the part of the listener.

Speak Accurately

While the message may often be either contemptible (2 Cor 10:10) or convicting, our communication of it should always be accurate and exemplary (1 Tim 4:12). What we say must be true. Our speech should be sound, beyond reproach, in order that even those who oppose the message will be able to offer no other critique (Tit 2:8). "...laying aside falsehood, speak truth..." (Eph 4:25). Titus' ministry was to be characterized by his speaking the things which are fitting for sound teaching or doctrine (Tit 2:1). Peter adds that whoever is speaking should be speaking as if the very words of God (1 Pet 4:11).

> Some practical implications:
> - Be consistent with hermeneutic and exegetical usage. Avoid subtle inconsistencies that might simplify a message or make a teaching more palatable.
> - If you quote or reference information beyond Biblical data or common knowledge, always cite the source (not in full bibliographical form, of course, just in such a way as not to give the listener an inaccurate understanding that the speaker is the one deriving the information).
> - Cut straight. Handle the text well. Put in the time to understand, practice, and communicate God's word accurately.

Speak With Authority

Paul charges Titus to speak, exhort, and reprove with all authority (Tit 2:15), because if he was speaking *these things*, they were inherently authoritative, being from God. The authority didn't come from the one speaking, exhorting, and reproving (i.e., Titus), rather it derived from the Author of the word from which the speaking, the exhortations, and the reproving came. Recall that Jesus was teaching (not preaching in this case) in the synagogue, and his listeners were amazed that He was teaching them authoritatively (Mk 1:22). Luke describes one such instance in which Jesus was teaching in the synagogue, reading from Isaiah and declaring that a particular portion had been fulfilled in their midst (Lk 4:16-21).

> Some practical implications:
> - Remember that the word is authoritative, not us.
> - Remember that what we say will have value insofar as it corresponds with His word. Anything beyond that is mere speculation having no authority.

Don't Speak Ignorantly

In 2 Corinthians 12:4, Paul describes his being caught up to the third heaven and hearing things which man is not permitted to speak. Paul was limited in what he was allowed to discuss of these events. In this case, he was limited due to having particular knowledge. Admittedly, Paul was, along with the other apostles, a unique case, because of the special revelation he received. Still, earlier in the letter he reminded the Corinthians not to go beyond what is written (1 Cor 4:6), prescribing for the Corinthians a similar limitation, even if for different reasons. Paul's speech was limited due to knowledge.

The Corinthians' thought and speech was limited due to lack of knowledge. There are things that are not revealed in Scripture, and if we are to be communicating Scripture effectively, we need to be careful, like the Corinthians, not to exceed what is written lest we become arrogant in foolish speculations about things of which we have no knowledge (e.g., 2 Tim 2:16, 23).

Some practical implications:
- Study. Fulfill the steps necessary to handle the word well, so as to not think, act, or speak from ignorance.
- Don't speak dogmatically on what the text doesn't reveal. Become comfortable with the phrase, "I don't know," and the necessary silence that follows. We can have certainty regarding what is revealed through what is written, but anything beyond what is written is for us in the realm of the speculative. If the text doesn't reveal it, we can't be dogmatic about it.

Speak With Appropriate Detail

The author of Hebrews models speech that includes an appropriate level of detail for the task at hand and for the time allotted. The writer acknowledges in one context that he could not at that time speak *according to a part*, or in detail (Heb 9:5). Compare the content of Romans and Ephesians: the two letters are similar in that the first sections of both letters address the believers' position in Christ, while the latter sections of both discuss the believers' walk. In Romans Paul spends eleven chapters considering the positional aspects, while in Ephesians he accomplishes the same task in three. There is an obvious difference in the level of detail included.

Some practical implications:
- Know the schedule, stay on schedule. If you have thirty minutes to communicate, use an appropriate level of detail to wisely spend that time.
- If a speaker exceeds the allotted time, either there is a lack of consideration for the audience, a lack of discipline and purpose, or there is a failure to properly assess the level of detail appropriate for the task at hand.
- Consider for example the different levels of detail required for teaching a Bible survey in various settings.

Such a survey could be delivered in an hour, or in a series over the course of a few weeks, or in more elongated series over the course of a semester or a year. In each case, the level of detail required would be different.

Conclusion: Speak With Caution, as Accountable to God

2 Timothy 2:15 indicates that there is a testing and approval for workmen who are handling God's word. It should be handled accurately (or, literally, cut straight), because it is the word of truth. James cautions that believers be slow to speak (Jam 1:19), and adds that believers should speak and act as those who will be judged by the law of liberty (2:12). Because of the immensity of the responsibility, and the strict judgment associated with that responsibility, James cautions his readers not to become "many teachers" (Jam 3:1).

32
Technology and Biblical Communication

As has always been the case, technology has profound impact on communication and pedagogy. The Millennial generation (born between the 1980's and the early 2000's) has seen radical development in technology, as the digital revolution continues to bear the fruit of convenience and accessibility. In light of greatly increased accessibility afforded by advancement in technology, Millennials digest information differently than previous generations.

Roughly 70% of practicing Christian Millennials read the Bible on a cell phone or online with other devices.[98] Even now, I still hear pastors occasionally grumbling that people don't bring their Bibles to church with them anymore. In truth, it is now simply much easier for a person to carry their Bible with them – and that is a good thing. Of course, I prefer to be armed with both digital and print copies of the Bible, but the convenience of always having a Bible present (via cell phone or other device) is an advantage previous generations never even imagined. One implication is that it is now simpler for a person to integrate God's word into every

---

[98] Barna Group, "How Technology is Changing Millennial Faith," October, 15, 2013 at https://www.barna.org/barna-update/millennials/640-how-technology-is-changing-millennial-faith.

aspect of their life, being able with a push or a swipe to read what God has said. Now, certainly, there is far greater competition for thoughts and attentions than there has been in the past, but every advantage seemingly is accompanied by potential disadvantages as well. Admittedly, it still gives me great pleasure to hear the rustling of pages among a crowd of people when we turn in our print Bibles to a particular passage, but at the same time it is wonderful to know that just about anyone who can access a cell phone has the ability to read and study and utilize resources not generally accessible just a few years ago.

More than half of Christian Millennials (56%) are using online searches to investigate churches, and nearly the same percentage (54%) are watching online videos about faith or spirituality.[99] The implications of this are profound. If we are not communicating in the formats that people are digesting their information, then they are simply not hearing the message.

Further, 38% of Christian Millennials are fact-checking online what they are being told by pastors and other leaders.[100] This reflects that there is some critical thinking taking place (would be good if the percentage was higher), and indicates that there are some who are interested in discovering truth. Now is not the time to dumb-down Biblical teaching because "regular people just can't handle Biblical meat." Instead, facing increasingly thoughtful learners, we should be making the most of the opportunity to invest in them with real substance. In fact, a very high percentage (96%) of Christian Millennials believe the Bible contains everything a person needs to know to live a meaningful life, and that it is the word of God.[101] It is evident by these numbers that Christians who have the greatest access to technology (as do Millennials), also have a high

---

[99] Ibid.
[100] Ibid.
[101] Barna Group, "Millennials and the Bible: 3 Surprising Insights," October 23, 2014 at https://www.barna.org/barna-update/millennials/687-millennials-and-the-bible-3-surprising-insights.

view of Scripture. It would seem foolish to approach a demographic that is primed and interested in God's word with a dumbed-down pedagogy, talking about the Bible in simple platitudes rather than teaching it vigorously. Further, it is important to recognize that learners can go online and read commentaries, listen to teachers, preachers, messages and sermons, and even take classes at their leisure at any point as they are asking questions or thinking through issues. This highlights the need for training up people to develop their own capability in handling the Scriptures.

Technology advances and methods evolve. The message however, does not change. We have great freedom in methods of presentation and use of technology as long as those aspects do not alter the message. So, as we consider how to effectively study, practice, and share the word of God, we need to give attention to how we are engaging people who live in a digital world. Unfortunately, often we adjust the message in order to appeal to various cultures, when we should maintain the purity of the message, and present it with precision and with clarity to any culture where God grants opportunity. We need to be aware of technological advances and trends, and should capitalize on these things when profitable for achieving the goal. We must also keep in mind that our use of technology needs to complement the message, not cloud it.

33
What Are the Essentials?

Aristotle introduces his *Nicomachean Ethics* with these words: "Every skill and every inquiry, and similarly every action and rational choice, is thought to aim at some good; and so the good has been aptly described as that at which everything aims."[102] While Aristotle identifies different intermediary goods on his way to his ultimate good (happiness), he underscores the importance of the question, "Good for what?" In Aristotle's view, we can't really define good until we understand at what goal the good aims. While his conclusion is problematic, his line of questioning is insightful. Likewise, we can't answer the question "What are the essentials?" until we first answer the question, "Essential for what?"

One popular website asserts that, "The Bible itself reveals what is important and essential to the Christian faith. These essentials are the deity of Christ, salvation by God's grace and not by works." While this sounds like a helpful enough answer, I wonder upon what basis the writer identifies these doctrines over others as essential. Are these intermediary essentials or they ultimate essentials? To answer this Biblically we have to answer the

---

[102] Aristotle, *Nicomachean Ethics*, Roger Crisp, trans. (Cambridge, UK: Cambridge University Press, 2000), 3.

question of what is the central or single-most important issue in all of the Bible. The most common response to that query is the doctrine of salvation. But can we justify that Biblically?

In Ephesians 1 Paul discusses the role of Father, Son, and Spirit in the salvation of the believer. In 1:6 the Father's predestining and choosing is "to the praise of the glory of His grace." In 1:12, the redemptive work of the Son is "to the praise of His glory." In 1:14, the sealing work of the Holy Spirit is "to the praise of His glory." These passages give us insight into the reality that salvation is good, but it is an intermediary good rather than a final one. Salvation is not the end or the ultimate good, but rather salvation serves the purpose of contributing to His glory. We can examine the Biblical accounts of every revealed work of God, and each serves one purpose: His glory. It is worth noting at this point that if a person is seeking his or her own glory we would understand that person as narcissistic, but we have to remember two important ideas when we think about God's glory.

First, the word *doxa* has to do with quality or splendor, and can be understood much like the expressive sense in which an artist creates. We speak in terms of "expressing oneself," and I would suggest that is exactly what God is doing with His universe. He is expressing His character, and does it all for the ultimate purpose that His splendor (or character) will be clearly manifested to all creation at the time of His choosing. Second, God warns us against pride because it takes our eyes off of Him (e.g., 1 Jn 2:16-17), but He is not bound by the ethics He gives to us. Some accuse Him of hypocrisy at this point – being a bad parent or role model, illogical, unfair, etc., but these accusations (besides being problematic in themselves) miss the point that as the Creator He has certain sovereign rights and the perspective needed to make everything work for His intended purpose (to His glory).

As we understand Ephesians 1, we recognize that salvation is an intermediary rather than final good. So back to our original question: "What are the essentials?" If salvation is an intermediary good, then I cannot consider only those things necessary for salvation as essential. Ironically, to do so would be narcissistic, as I would be asserting that the only things that really matter are the things pertaining to my own salvation. What a self-centered view of reality this would be. And yet, so many of us understand essentials in this way. In light of this, I would suggest there are three layers of essentials we should consider: (1) essentials for God's glory, (2) essentials for salvation, and (3) essentials for knowledge and understanding.

Essentials for God's Glory

If God's glory is the ultimate good, and if we understand that all things are designed for that end, then everything is an essential. What business do we have in declaring something as of greater or lesser importance when we have no comprehension of how those things contribute to the greatest good that is God's glory? We have no tools for making such estimations (the Bible doesn't make such distinctions, but rather points us constantly and simply to God's glory). Paul tells Titus to "speak the things which are fitting for sound doctrine" (Tit 2:1). The focus is not on the importance of a teaching, but on its accuracy or correctness. Ours is not to create a hierarchy of doctrinal importance; ours is to handle doctrine (or teaching) accurately.

Essentials for Salvation

When we are considering salvation (or any other intermediary good, for that matter), we can justifiably look to the Bible for essentials pertaining to that good. With respect to salvation, we simply consider what are the necessary elements for one to be saved (that is not to say other aspects are unimportant, just that they are not central to salvation itself). In 1 Corinthians 15:1-4, Paul describes the Gospel as that "by which you are saved" upon receiving, and highlights the death, burial, and resurrection of Jesus.

John records Jesus words in John 3:16, "For God so loved the world that He gave His only begotten Son that the believing one in Him will not perish but has eternal life" (translation mine). Later John summarizes the purpose for the writing of his Gospel as "so that you may believe that Jesus is the Christ, the Son of God; and that believing you may have life in His name." Simply put, salvation comes by belief in the person and work of Jesus. Yes, there are nuances and interesting discussion points, but the Gospel itself is just that simple.

Essentials for Knowledge and Understanding

Whereas we understand that God's glory is the ultimate good and purpose for all things, and we understand that there are intermediate goods that contribute to that ultimate good (salvation, for example), we must consider another category of essentials – the essentials of how we know or understand. What is essential to our understanding of reality? God has revealed Himself in creation, the Bible, and His Son. Creation introduces us to God (Rom 1:18-20), the Son explains the Father (Jn 1:18), and the Bible communicates many details of God's character and plan. God communicated (in the Bible) using specific human languages (Hebrew, Aramaic, Greek).

To understand what He has said, His audience must follow sound hermeneutic principles – to handle the words according to the rules and usage of the languages at the time the Scriptures were written (this is often described as the literal grammatical-historical method). Hermeneutic method is foundational in the discussion of essentials, because it provides the vehicle for understanding what God has communicated. Hermeneutic method is grounded on several Biblical presuppositions: (1) the Biblical God exists (Gen 1:1), (2) He has revealed Himself (2 Tim 3:16-17, 2 Pet 1:20-21), (3) natural man is broken by sin and cannot properly assess God's word (Ps 14:1, Prov 1:7, 9:10, 1 Cor 2:6-16) and needs divine help (not for understanding the words, but for judging them rightly), and (4) interpreters must use a consistent, proper hermeneutic to handle the word accurately (e.g., 2 Tim 2:15, 2 Pet 1:20-21).

Presuppositions and hermeneutic method are critical, and most doctrinal disagreements can be directly traced to either or both. Paul tells the Corinthian believers to agree (or speak the same thing, 1 Cor 1:10), based on the straightforwardness of God's revealed word (the gospel, 1 Cor 1:17-18). If we differ in our presuppositions and hermeneutics, we will differ in our doctrinal conclusions, and we will certainly disagree regarding the nature of Biblical essentials. Rather than focus on our disagreements in the realm of conclusions, we can give attention to the basics – presuppositions and hermeneutics, and in so doing we can uncover the origins of some of our disagreements and begin to remedy them in a Biblical way.

34
"I Have Many More Things to Say to You, But You Cannot Bear Them Now"

The words of Jesus, recorded in John 16:12 as part of the Upper Room Discourse, resonate profoundly as we consider our part in discipleship and discipling others through Biblical preaching and teaching. Jesus' words here are significant for their prophetic value, of course. His acknowledgment of the disciples' limited capacity to receive the truth at the time is also a helpful example for us. The comment illustrates a sensitivity and a gentleness on Jesus' part. He knew these men. He knew their needs and limitations. He was patient with them, and did not give them more than they could handle. For roughly three years He walked with them, He ate and drank with them. He did life with them.

Jesus demonstrated a sensitivity to the disciples' learning curve. How many times do we read in the Gospel accounts of instances where the disciples should have understood the truth, but it just didn't seem to click with them (e.g., Mk 10:37, Jn 6:6-7, 11:12-14, Acts 1:6)? The best Discipler modeled discipleship as a process that takes time, and He was willing to invest that time in the men He was teaching. He recognized that even at the conclusion of His earthly ministry with them, they were still not yet mature enough to handle many of the things that they still needed to learn. In their limitation He exercised compassion and understanding, providing for their continued learning through the ministry of the Holy Spirit. We can learn much about the teaching process from Jesus' example. One vital lesson is that in the discipleship process, *love is indeed patient*. His model for us as disciplers and spiritual parents teaches us to be aware of the capacities and limitations possessed by us and those learning from us, and reminds us to be thoughtful about how to stimulate one another to love and good deeds (Heb 10:24).

Further, the teaching process demands a *learning* process. Transformative communication is not simply the spewing forth of data, but rather is a deliberate and measured process of modeling how to study, practice, and communicate God's word. It requires an integration of the exegetical and expositional processes, so as to be grounded and balanced in our own study, practice, and teaching. As Paul warned Timothy, "pay close attention to yourself and to your teaching" (1 Tim 4:16). We are not primarily teaching others, we are teaching ourselves. (We must be transformed by the renewing of our minds.) We are not simply teaching about the Bible, we must teach the Bible itself. We are not teaching simply to occupy a ministry space, instead we are teaching for transformation, for spiritual maturity, for spiritual growth and independence. Fellow servants, we must not simply hand out fish. Instead it is incumbent upon us to be skilled fishermen and to teach others how to fish well, as God provides opportunity.

SECTION III: OVERVIEW OF THE EXPOSITIONAL PROCESS

Bibliography

Aland, Barbara, Aland, Kurt, and Black, Matthew, et al. *The Greek New Testament*, 4th ed. Federal Republic of Germany: United Bible Societies, 1993.

Aristotle. *Nicomachean Ethics*. Roger Crisp, trans. Cambridge, UK: Cambridge University Press, 2000.

Austin, S.A., Franz, G.W. and Frost, E.G. "Amos's Earthquake: An extraordinary Middle East seismic event of 750 B.C." in International Geology Review: 42(7), 2000: 657-671.

Baker, Charles. *A Dispensational Theology*. Grand Rapids, MI: Grace Bible College, 1971.

Barna Group. "Most Twentysomethings Put Christianity on the Shelf following Spiritually Active Teen Years." Viewed at http://www.barna.org/teens-next-gen-articles/147-most-twentysomethings-put-christianity-on-the-shelf-following-spiritually-active-teen-years, published 9/11/2006.

———. "Millennials and the Bible: 3 Surprising Insights," October 23, 2014, Viewed at https://www.barna.org/barna-update/millennials/687-millennials-and-the-bible-3-surprising-insights.

Bauer, Walter, Arndt, William, and Gingrich, F. Wilbur. *A Greek English Lexicon of the New Testament and Other Early Christian Literature*. Chicago, IL: University of Chicago Press, 1957.Berkhof, Louis. *Systematic Theology*. Grand Rapids, MI: Eerdmans, 1949.

Berry, Wendell. *Home Economics*. New York: North Point Press, 1987.

Bock, Darrell, and Fanning, Buist. *Interpreting the New Testament Text: Introduction to the Art and Science of Exegesis*. Wheaton, IL: Crossway Books, 2006.

Brooks, James, and Winbery, Carlton. *Syntax of New Testament Greek*. Lanham, MD: University Press of America, 1979.

Brown, Francis, Driver, S.R. and Briggs, C.A. *Hebrew and English Lexicon of the Old Testament*. Oxford: Clarendon Press, 1851.

Bruce, A.B.. *The Training of the Twelve*. Grand Rapids, MI: Kregel, 1971.

Carson, D.A. *Exegetical Fallacies, 2nd Edition*. Grand Rapids, MI: Baker Academic, 1998.

Chafer, Lewis Sperry. *Systematic Theology*, Vols. 1-8. Grand Rapids, MI: Kregel, 1993.

Chisholm, Jr., Robert. From Exegesis to Exposition: A Practical Guide to Using Biblical Hebrew. Grand Rapids, MI: Baker Academic, 1996

Cho, Jaeyoung. "A Critical Examination of Jonathan Edwards's Theology of Preaching. Ph.D Diss., New Orleans Baptist Theological Seminary, 2012.

Christianity Today. "Top 10 sermons of 2013 from preachingtoday.com," January 2, 2014, Viewed at http://www.christianitytoday.org/mediaroom/news/2014/top-10-sermons-of-2013-from-preaching-todaycom.html

Cline, Austine. "Defining Science – How is Science Defined?" from http://atheism.about.com/od/philosophyofscience/a/DefineScience.htm.

Cone, Christopher. *Prolegomena on Biblical Hermeneutics and Method, 2nd Edition*. Fort Worth, TX: Tyndale Seminary Press, 2012.

_____. *A Concise Bible Survey: Tracing the Promises of God*. Fort Worth, TX: Exegetica Publishing, 2012.

_____. "Integrating Exegesis and Exposition: Preaching and

Teaching for Spiritual Independence" (paper presented to The Council on Dispensational Hermeneutics, College of Biblical Studies, Houston, Texas, October 3, 2012).

———. "Brothers We Are Not Chefs" (paper submitted to The Council on Dispensational Hermeneutics, October 7, 2012).

Couch, Mal. *An Introduction to Classical Evangelical Hermeneutics*. Grand Rapids, MI: Kregel, 2000.

Currid, John. *Calvin and the Biblical Languages*. London: Mentor, 2006.

Dana, H.E. and Mantey, Julius. *A Manual Grammar of the Greek New Testament*. New York, NY: Macmillan Publishing, 1955.

Dictionary.com. "Transformative." Viewed at http://dictionary.reference.com/browse/transformative.

Edlin, Richard. *The Cause of Christian Education, 2nd Edition*. Northport, AL: Vision Press, 1998.

Edwards, Jonathan. "Sinners in the Hand of an Angry God, " July 8, 1741, Enfeld, Connecticut, viewed at http://www.ccel.org/ccel/edwards/sermons.sinners.html

Elliger, Karl and Rudolph, Wilhelm. *Biblia Hebraica Stuttgartensia*. Stuttgart: German Bible Society, 1997.

Elliott, Ted and Rossio, Terry. *Pirates of the Caribbean: At World's End*, theatrical release, directed by Gore Verbinski, Disney, 2007.

Fee, Gordon. *New Testament Exegesis: A Handbook for Students and Pastors, 3rd Edition*. Louisville, KY: John Knox Press, 2002.

Fruchtenbaum, Arnold. *Israelology: The Missing Link In Systematic Theology*. Tustin, CA: Ariel Ministries Press, 1989.

Gesenius, H.W.F. *Gesenius' Hebrew and Chaldee Lexicon to the Old Testament*. Grand Rapids, MI: Baker Book, 1979.

Grassmick, John. *Principles and Practice of Greek Exegesis, 2nd Edition*. Dallas, TX: Dallas Theological Seminary, 1976.

Guthrie, W.K.C. *A History of Greek Philosophy, Volume I: The Earlier Presocratics and the Pythagoreans*. New York, NY: Cambridge University Press, 1962.

Harris, R. Laird, Archer, Gleason, and Waltke, Bruce. *Theological Wordbook of the Old Testament, Vols. 1 and 2*. Chicago, IL: Moody Press, 1980.

Hayes, John and Holladay, Carl. *Biblical Exegesis: A Beginners Handbook, Revised Edition*. Atlanta, GA: John Knox Press, 1987.

Hobbes, Thomas. *The Leviathan*. Oxford: Oxford University Press, 2014.

Hodges, Zane and Farstad, Arthur. *The Greek New Testament According to the Majority Text, 2nd Edition*. Nashville, TN: Thomas Nelson, 1985.

Institute for New Testament Textual Research. *Novum Testamentum Graece: Nestle–Aland*. Stuttgart: German Bible Society, 2012.

Johnson, Elliott. *Expository Hermeneutics: An Introduction*. Grand Rapids, MI: Zondervan, 1990.

Kantenwein, Lee. *Diagrammatical Analysis*. Winona Lake, IN: BMH Books, 1991.

Koehler, Ludwig and Baumgartner, W. *The Hebrew and Aramaic Lexicon of the Old Testament*, 2 Vols. Boston, MA: Brill, 2002.

Kuyper, Abraham. *Principles of Sacred Theology*. Grand Rapids, MI: Baker Book, 1980.

Lewis, Gordon, and Demarest, Bruce. *Integrative Theology*. Grand Rapids, MI: Zondervan, 1996.

Lerner, Robert. "apocalyptic language." Brittanica.com, viewed at http://www.britannica.com/EBchecked/topic/29733/apocalyptic-literature.

Licona, Michael. *The Resurrection of Jesus: A New Historiographical Approach*. Downers Grove, IL: IVP, 2010.

Louw, J.P. andA lbert Nida, Eugene. *Greek–English Lexicon of the New Testament: Based on Semantic Domains*, 2 Vols. Swinden, UK: United Bible Societies, 1999.

MacArthur, John. *Preaching: How to Preach Biblically*. Nashville, TN: Thomas Nelson, 2005.

Metzger, Bruce. *Lexical Aids for Students of New Testament Greek.*

Princeton, NJ: Bruce Metzger, 1983.

Mounce, William. *The Analytical Lexicon to the Greek New Testament.* Grand Rapids, MI: Zondervan, 1993.

Nietzsche, Friedrich. *Thus Spoke Zarathustra,* (Pennsylvania: Penn State University, 1999.

New American Standard Bible: 1995 Update. LaHabra, CA: The Lockman Foundation, 1995.

Pasquariello, Gino. "The Way In and the Way On: a Qualitative Study of the Catalysts and Outcomes of Transformative Learning." Ed.D Diss., Asuza Pacific University, 2009.

Pentecost, J. Dwight. *Designed to be Like Him: Fellowship, Conduct, Conflict, Maturity.* Chicago, IL: Moody Press 1979.

Ramm, Bernard. *Protestant Biblical Interpretation: A Textbook of Hermeneutics.* Grand Rapids, MI: Baker Books, 1970.

Rodat, Robert. *Saving Private Ryan,* theatrical release. Directed by Steven Spielberg, Amblin Entertainment, 1998.

Russell, Bertrand. "Why I Am Not a Christian," March 6, 1927. Viewed at http://www.users.drew.edu/~jlenz/whynot.html.

Ryrie, Charles. *Basic Theology.* Wheaton, IL: Victor Books, 1982.

———. *Biblical Theology of the New Testament.* Dubuque, IA: ECS Ministries, 2005.

———. *Balancing the Christian Life: Biblical Principles for Wholesome Living.* Chicago, IL: Moody Press, 1969.

Sagan, Carl. *The Cosmos.* New York: Ballantine, 1980.

Schreiner, Thomas. *Interpreting the Pauline Epistles.* Grand Rapids, MI: Baker Academic, 2011.

Scofield, C.I.. *Scofield Bible Correspondence Course, Volume I.* Chicago, IL: Moody Press, 1959.

Shedd, William G.T.. *Shedd's Dogmatic Theology, Vols. 1-3.* Nashville, TN: Thomas Nelson, 1980.

Spiritualmilk.com. "Theistic Cosmology" viewed at http://www.spiritualmilk.com/id27.html.

Stuart, Douglas. *Old Testament Exegesis: A Handbook for Students and*

Pastors, 3rd Edition. Louisville, KY: Westminster John Knox Press, 2001.

Strong, Augustus. *Systematic Theology*. Philadelphia, PA: Judson Press, 1947.

Swete, Henry Barclay. *The Apocalypse of John, Third Edition*. London: MacMillan and Co., 1911.

Swindoll, Chuck, and Zuck, Roy. *Understanding Christian Theology*. Nashville, TN: Thomas Nelson, 2003.

Tan, Paul Lee. *The Interpretation of Prophecy*. Dallas, TX: Bible Communications, 1974.

Terry, Milton. *Biblical Hermeneutics: A Treatise on the Interpretation of the Old and New Testaments*. Grand Rapids, MI: Zondervan, 1976.

Thiessen, Henry. *Lectures in Systematic Theology*. Grand Rapids, MI: Eerdmans, 1992.

Thomas, Robert. *Evangelical Hermeneutics: The New Versus the Old*. Grand Rapids, MI: Kregel, 2002.

Traina, Robert. *Methodical Bible Study: A New Approach to Hermeneutics*. Grand Rapids, MI: Francis Asbury Press, 1985.

Van Til, Cornelius. *An Introduction to Systematic Theology*. Phillipsburg, NJ: Presbyterian and Reformed, 1974.

_____. *Christian Apologetics, 2nd Edition*. Phillipsburg, NJ: Presbyterian and Reformed, 2003.

Virkler, Henry. *Hermeneutics: Principles and Processes of Biblical Interpretation*. Grand Rapids, MI: Baker Book, 1981.

Wallace, Daniel. *Greek Grammar Beyond the Basics: An Exegetical Syntax of the New Testament*. Grand Rapids, MI: Zondervan, 1996.

Waltke, Bruce and O'Connor, M. *An Introduction to Biblical Hebrew Syntax*. Warsaw, IN: Eisenbrauns, 1980.

Westcott, B.F. and Hort, F.J.A. *Westcott–Hort Greek New Testament With Dictionary*. Peabody, MA: Hendrickson, 2007.

Weingreen, J. *A Practical Grammar for Classical Hebrew, 2nd Edition*. New York, NY: Oxford University Press, 1959.

Williams, Ronald. *Hebrew Syntax: An Outline, 2nd Edition*. Toronto: Toronto University Press, 1988.

Zuck, Roy. *Basic Bible Interpretation*. Wheaton, IL: Victor Books, 1991.

Made in the USA
San Bernardino, CA
01 September 2015